W9-BUI-240

WITHDRAWN
No longer the property of the
Boston Public Library.
Sale of this material benefits the Library

OTTOMAN ODYSSEY

ALSO BY ALEV SCOTT

Turkish Awakening

OTTOMAN ODYSSEY

Travels Through a Lost Empire

ALEV SCOTT

PEGASUS BOOKS
NEW YORK LONDON

OTTOMAN ODYSSEY

Pegasus Books Ltd.
148 West 37th Street, 13th Floor
New York, NY 10018

Copyright © 2019 by Alev Scott

First Pegasus Books hardcover edition May 2019

All rights reserved. No part of this book may be reproduced
in whole or in part without written permission from the publisher,
except by reviewers who may quote brief excerpts in connection with a review
in a newspaper, magazine, or electronic publication; nor may any part of this
book be reproduced, stored in a retrieval system, or transmitted in any form or
by any means electronic, mechanical, photocopying, recording, or
other, without written permission from the publisher.

ISBN: 978-1-64313-075-0

10 9 8 7 6 5 4 3 2 1

Printed in the United States of America
Distributed by W. W. Norton & Company, Inc.

In memory of my Granny Şifa,
and other victims of nationalism.

Contents

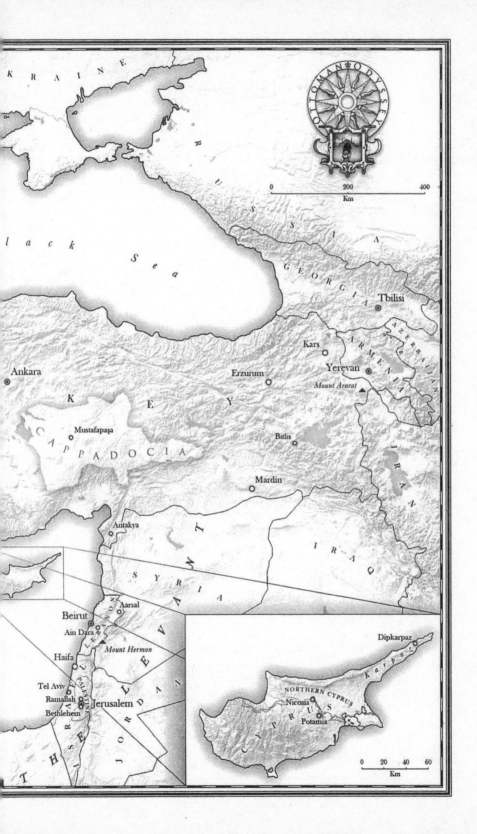

Introduction

Sultans Old and New

In the capital of Turkey, in a palace with a thousand rooms, a man sits on a gilt throne. Some of his soldiers are ornamental and armed with sabres, others fly F-16s and protect him from military coups. The year is 2018. The man is President Erdoğan. The fantasy is Ottoman.

The Republic of Turkey emerged in 1923 from the ashes of the Ottoman Empire, which at its zenith stretched from Mecca to Budapest, from Algiers to Tbilisi, from Baghdad to the Crimea, connecting millions of people of different religions and ethnicities. An Ottoman subject was an Eastern Orthodox Christian from Odessa or a Jew from Mosul, a Sunni Muslim from Jerusalem or a Catholic Syriac from Antakya. The sultan, who was also the caliph, leader of the Islamic world, allowed non-Muslims to organize their own law courts, schools and places of worship in return for paying 'infidel' taxes and accepting a role as second-class citizens: a system of exploitative tolerance that allowed diversity to flourish for centuries in the greatest empire of early modern history.

In recent years, a bizarre reinvention has been taking place in Turkey: its politicians are reclaiming the legacy of its Ottoman past, while the country remains as nationalistic as ever. In 2017, the country voted to grant unlimited powers to President Erdoğan, nearly a century after the abolition of the Ottoman Sultanate. For some, this was an unfathomable act of political suicide, an event that marked the end of democracy in Turkey. For others, it was a reharnessing of the strength the country needs to lead the Middle East by shining example and stand up to Europe: a return to the kind of power exemplified by the Ottoman Empire.

'The last century [the period of the Republic] was only a parenthesis for us. We will close that parenthesis. We will do so without going to war, or calling anyone an enemy, without being disrespectful to any border, we will again tie Sarajevo to Damascus, Benghazi to Erzurum to Batumi. This is the core of our power. These may look like different countries to you, but Yemen and Skopje were part of the same country a hundred and ten years ago, as were Erzurum and Benghazi.'

The words of Ahmet Davutoglu, Foreign Minister in 2013, sold Turkish voters a heady – if vague – pride in a long-fallen empire, and a belief that it could be effortlessly resurrected. In fact, the discrepancies between the Ottoman glory days and the reality of modern-day Turkey are stark, but Erdoğan and his Justice and Development Party have been adept at claiming the best of the empire and ignoring the worst of it. On 8 February 2018, the government launched a new website portal[1] which provided Turkish citizens with access to their family trees via digitalized census and tax records stored in the state archives of Istanbul. These archives stretch back to the 1830s, recording the births and deaths of Ottoman subjects scattered across the empire. Within hours, millions had rushed to the *e-devlet* ('e-government') portal in an orgy of self-discovery; the website promptly crashed.

Bulent Çetin was one of the lucky ones who managed to access the site to download his family tree in the first couple of hours. He found that most of his mother's side of the family were born outside the borders of modern Turkey, in what was previously Ottoman territory: his great-great-grandfather in Macedonia in 1869, his great-great-grandmother in the Caucasus in 1864. Somehow, they produced Bulent's great-grandfather in Sivas, in central Anatolia, in 1897, and subsequent generations remained within Turkey, resulting in the birth of Bulent himself in the Republic's capital of Ankara in 1986. Like many Turkish citizens, Bulent sees no contradiction in being a patriot who is also proud of his Ottoman ancestry, telling me he feels Turkish because 'we are all united under this flag, within this country, sharing the same destiny.'

When the website relaunched six days after its crash to a renewed wave of interest, there were unforeseen consequences: Turks who discovered ancestors from ex-Ottoman territories now in the European Union – Bulgaria and Greece, most commonly – started making applications for second citizenships[2] to these countries, reflecting the anxiety felt in Turkey over the past few years of political turmoil. As Bulent noted, all Turkish citizens are theoretically 'united', but not all want to share in a destiny that looks increasingly bleak; they would rather use their Ottoman heritage to escape the backward-looking Turkey of today.

While right-wing politicians in Europe, the US and Turkey have misleadingly evoked the glory of vanished empires to harness nationalist votes in recent years, the Left are also guilty of nostalgia, of looking through rose-tinted spectacles at a particular version of the past. In the case of the Ottoman Empire, the diversity of its subjects is sometimes presented as proof that everyone lived in a constant state of peaceful coexistence. This is not true; non-Muslims were second-class citizens, and at the turn of the 20th century there were horrific systematic abuses of these subjects as the empire began to eat itself. Yet the fact remains that its 600-year-old social diversity is almost impossible to imagine today in countries like Turkey, a country that suppresses difference even in thought.

Halfway through my research for this book I was barred from Turkey, which drastically changed both my life and the course of the book.

I had first decided to write about the social legacy of the Ottoman Empire while I was in south-east Turkey in 2014, near the Syrian and Iraqi borders. Unlike most of Turkey, where signs of its former wealth of peoples, cultures and religions have been systematically eroded over the past century, towns like Mardin and Antakya offered a glimpse of the Ottoman world I was trying to reimagine – at least, a Levantine corner of it. But by 2015, al-Qaeda and IS had crossed the Syrian border and established cells in these towns. The risk of kidnap for Western journalists was high; even veteran war reporters avoided the area, and suddenly the gentle historical field trips I'd planned seemed a little naïve. Still, I had most of Turkey open to me, and its neighbouring countries, to continue my research. Then, in 2017, while travelling in Greece, I failed to get permission to cross over the land border back into Turkey, and discovered I had an entry ban on my passport, placed by the Interior Ministry. The ministry staff offered no explanation for this, but I knew it was my political journalism, and my appeals were ignored.

That is how this book became an odyssey encompassing eleven countries of the former Empire. I found myself speaking Turkish with car mechanics in rural Kosovo and with the children of Armenian genocide survivors in Jerusalem; I discussed Ottoman religious diversity with Lebanese warlords and professors in Turkish universities in Sarajevo. My entry ban motivated me to go out and explore the ways in which the empire shaped the histories of people in the Balkans, the Caucasus and the Levant. I found myself asking questions about forced migration, genocide, exile, diaspora, collective memory and identity, not just about religious coexistence.

Many of the communities I interviewed were descendants of ancient minorities that were allowed to flourish in the empire, and then intimidated, ignored or expelled from modern Turkey. Others, living hundreds of miles from Turkey, believed themselves to be Ottoman in some vague but visceral sense, encouraged by the current Turkish government's attempts to resurrect regional influence. In the century that has passed since the death of the empire and the formation of the nation state in its former territories, much has changed – primarily how people live together, and their sense of belonging to a greater whole. All across the remains of the Ottoman Empire, new states have been 'stretching the short, tight skin of the nation over the gigantic body of the empire,'[3] to quote the historian

Benedict Anderson. But amidst this change, other things have come almost full circle, such as the paranoia and sweeping powers that come with one man rule – a phenomenon not restricted to Turkey in the year 2018.

Names and Pseudonyms

Zigzagging between the past and present in this book, I have generally referred to towns like Constantinople, Smyrna, Salonika and Antioch by their modern names (Istanbul, Izmir, Thessaloniki and Antakya) for simplicity. By the late 19th century, the Ottoman Empire was widely referred to in the West as 'Turkey' and Ottomans as 'Turks' (both of which had a negative connotation), even though the empire was still home to millions of non-Turkish Ottoman subjects; I have used 'Turkey' only to denote the Republic, in existence since 1923. I refer to most of my interviewees by their real names, but many of the people I interviewed in Turkey asked for pseudonyms. They feared reprisals for speaking about the discrimination faced by minorities, or they were wary about being quoted in a book written by a blacklisted journalist. To my surprise, however, a couple of my Turkish interviewees refused my offer of anonymity. They were proud to have their family stories immortalized in print, proving that people's attachment to their roots can outweigh the claims of a nation state – even one as ferociously possessive as Turkey.

I would like to thank everyone who, wittingly or unwittingly, named or unnamed, helped and inspired me to write this book.

A HISTORICAL NOTE

Classified Infidels

The cultural and economic wealth of the Ottoman Empire was a direct consequence of the system of taxation and governance that allowed non-Muslims to live in a caliphate. These non-Muslim 'people of the Book' (i.e. Christians and Jews) living under Islamic dominion were known as the *dhimmis* and were grouped within religious communities classed as *millet* or 'nation' groups, primarily the Greek and Russian Orthodox Churches, the Apostolic, Orthodox and Catholic Armenian Church, the Assyrians (Syrian Christians) and the Jews. Non-Sunni Muslims such as the Alawites were not allowed to form their own *millets* but were regarded simply as Muslims – that is to say, Sunni.

In principle, the lives of *dhimmis* were dictated by all kinds of Ottoman laws, but in practice, these were often ignored. The historian Philip Mansel[4] illustrates this in the case of religion-based, colour-coded dress laws, which were variously implemented and disregarded until the 19th century: 'Only Muslims could wear white or green turbans and yellow slippers. Greeks, Armenians and Jews were distinguished respectively by sky blue, dark blue (later red) and yellow hats, and by black, violet and blue slippers . . . [however] the rules were often flouted: the status of Muslims was so attractive that the minorities' desire to resemble them was irrepressible. Individuals could also buy exemption from dress regulations.'

The difference between the Ottoman mindset towards belonging and identity, and the modern Turkish one, is in some ways encapsulated in the meaning of the word *millet*, which comes from the Arabic *milla* (nation). In 19ᵗʰ-century Ottoman Turkish, its primary meaning was ethno-religious community; in modern Turkish, it simply means 'nation'. Community identity became state identity after the theoretically secular Republic formed in 1923. There was no room for the religious *millet*s – there was only one identity, one *millet*: Turkey, a home for Turks who were pre-identified by the state as Sunni Muslims. This attitude translated to an intolerance for anyone who resisted their new label of 'Turk', even when that amounted to little more than continuing to speak in Armenian, Greek or Kurdish. The Republic had zero tolerance for such deviations from the sanctioned norm, which explains the surface-level homogeneity of modern Turkish society – it is still ill-advised to be different.

The roots of the *millet* communities went beneath the Ottoman Empire to the Persian Sassanid Empire⁵, which existed in the region south-east of Turkey during the 4ᵗʰ century. The *millet*-based version of tolerance was fundamentally connected to Islam, which recognizes itself as the third of the religions 'of the Book', i.e. the monotheistic faiths, and acknowledges its connection to both its predecessors, Judaism and Christianity. As long as the *dhimmis* swore allegiance to the sultan and recognized Islam as the supreme religion of the empire in which they lived, they were broadly speaking left alone to govern themselves, run their own justice and education systems, and collect the requisite non-Muslim taxes, which included the *cizye* and the *ispençe*, historically presented as payment for the sultan's protection (the *dhimmis* were exempt from military service). Many of the *dhimmi* conversions to Islam stemmed from a desire to avoid these taxes, which were one of the main sources of income for imperial coffers.

Many *dhimmi* subjects achieved great wealth and prominence in a world where Muslims were encouraged to live modestly and spend their time reading the Koran; at the same time, they also took jobs which Muslims considered 'dirty'. The historian Bernard Lewis notes that, 'as well as the more obvious dirty jobs, the *dhimmi* professions included what was also, for a strict Muslim, something to be avoided – namely, dealing with unbelievers. This led at times to a rather high proportion of non-Muslims in such occupations as diplomacy, commerce, banking, brokerage, and espionage. Even the professions of worker and dealer in gold and silver, esteemed in many parts of the world, were regarded by strict Muslims as tainted and endangering the immortal souls of those engaged in them.'[6]

Some sultans embraced the *dhimmis* more enthusiastically than others, and some were guilty of hideous cruelty to non-Sunni Muslims, who were regarded with more hostility than Christians or Jews on the grounds that they were heretics practising a warped version of Islam. Selim the Grim, who murdered his own brothers and forced his own father to abdicate to secure the throne, drastically expanded the empire's territories in the east. He massacred 40,000 followers of Alevism (an offshoot of Shia Islam, not to be confused with the Alawites of Syria) on one march in 1514, when he defeated Shah Isma'il of Iran[7]. In 2016, President Erdoğan horrified Turkey's current 15 million Alevis – the country's largest minority – when he inaugurated the 'Sultan Selim the Grim Bridge' in Istanbul[8].

Although the *dhimmi* always came second to Muslims, they were also seen as sources of income, and non-Muslims within the empire were not targets of systematic violence until the 19th and early 20th centuries. By this point, the last few sultans were resorting to increasingly cruel methods to stem the tide of growing nationalism among their minority subjects as nation states began to spring up around the peripheries of the empire, while also introducing reforms to keep these same subjects happy – a bizarre carrot and stick approach. Before he died in 1839, Sultan Mahmud II set the wheels in motion for a series of reforms known as the Tanzimat, essentially an attempt to westernize the failing empire by accommodating its non-Muslim minorities more fairly. Midhat Pasha, a prominent backer of the Tanzimat and the instigator of the first constitution of the Ottoman Empire, the short-lived, liberal constitution of 1876, dreamed of an empire where 'there would be neither Muslim nor non-Muslim but only Ottomans'[9]. Less than a century later, there were no Ottomans at all.

Although the Tanzimat was intended to make the empire stronger, it in fact fostered nationalist movements by diminishing the importance of the Church, especially among Eastern and Greek Orthodox Christians. Suddenly, these Christians began to identify themselves along nationalist rather than religious lines – as Armenians, Russians,

Bulgarians or Greeks – as the empire's neighbouring states became the 'kin-states' of these minorities, and as sympathy began to grow for the Christians brutally punished by Ottoman forces for pursuing independence, like the Bulgarian nationalists killed in the 1876 Batak uprising. For the last few decades of the empire, the Tanzimat contributed to a cultural swansong as minority communities mixed more freely and openly in public life but it was too little, too late to keep the empire intact. Nationalism and, more dramatically, the First World War, destroyed any modern version of Ottoman multi-culturalism that might feasibly have emerged in the 20th century.

The legacy of a hugely diverse empire like the Ottoman Empire is that its heart – Turkey – has produced an ethnically complicated people. This has only been partially acknowledged, because of the pressure on both religious and ethnic minorities to assimilate after the creation of the Republic. Several of Turkey's political parties claim the ethnic superiority of the 'Turkic race'[10], of which modern Turks are the supposed heirs. The reality is that most people in this country have a great-grandfather from Macedonia or Albania, or a great-aunt from Syria or Greece, and can tell a seemingly fantastical family story of exile and survival.

Turkey: Heart of the Empire

'*Either I conquer Istanbul, or Istanbul will conquer me*'

Sultan Mehmet II, 1452

There is an absence in Turkey that is at first hard to identify. It lies in shadows and silence, in obsolete place names, faded inscriptions and a surplus of antiques. It is the ghostly presence of people who used to live here, for many more years than they've been absent.

Walk up the marble steps from Istanbul's Taksim Square to Gezi Park, and you are walking on tombstones taken from a demolished 16[11]th-century Armenian cemetery a few miles down the road[11]. Climb into the hills above the Mediterranean coastline and you find the abandoned homes of Greek Orthodox Christians and Jews. Float in a hot-air balloon above the fairy chimneys of Cappadocia in Central Anatolia and you pass over cave churches where locals congregated less than a hundred years ago.

The fates of the minority communities once living in Turkey were tied to the demise of the 600-year-old Ottoman Empire. By the early 20th century, the empire had grown so weak that it was known in the West as 'The Sick Man of Europe' and by the end of the First World War in 1918 it had collapsed in all but name, its territories lost to the Allies. British forces occupied Istanbul, the empire's capital for over 500 years, allowing the last puppet sultan, Mehmet IV, to cling on for another four years before he escaped to Malta.

In the face of total occupation, Mustafa Kemal Pasha – later Atatürk, 'Father of the Turks' – fought a fierce and ultimately victorious war of resistance to save at least Anatolia, the heartland of the empire. In 1923, he declared a Republic of Turkey with its capital in Ankara. This new state was to be for self-identifying Turks only; such a dramatic reordering of what remained of a once-vast empire was necessary for its survival, but the stiflingly nationalistic atmosphere of the new Republic forced many of the remaining minorities either to leave or to relinquish their real identities so as to pass as 'Turks'. Minorities become even more invisible as the decades passed, and their cultural impact dimmed; the families and congregations who remain have a proud but sad attachment to the past.

Istanbul

I met seventy-six-year-old Ivan in the pouring rain in Taksim Square in March 2014. His Russian credentials were immediately obvious: steely blue eyes, a yellow-tinged beard and a kind of dogged, cheerful pessimism. His spoken Turkish, however, was that of a native, and he holds only a Turkish passport. He was born in Kars, the old Russian garrison town on Turkey's border with Armenia, after his parents fled Moscow at the outbreak of the Second World War, and was brought up in Istanbul.

'I went to the Russian Embassy to ask for a passport,' Ivan told me, blowing cigarette smoke slowly through his beard, 'but they said no. "You have Turkish nationality. You cannot be Russian."'

Ivan fumed, literally, at the memory.

'I said, what about Gerard Depardieu? They said he was a special case. Pah!'

Ivan is resolutely Russian, whatever his passport says, and obsessed with the fast-disappearing Russian Orthodox community in Istanbul, though he himself is not religious. His allegiance to the Church is his way of expressing his true national identity, a very Ottoman mentality born of the empire's *millet*-ordered society. The nominally secular republic of Turkey has resisted such distinctions, because Turkish citizens are assumed to identify as a Sunni Muslim.

Ivan took me to see one of the last remaining Russian church services in the city, a strangely secretive evensong in St Panteleimon, a tiny chapel on the top floor of a dilapidated building in Karaköy, near the Golden Horn. St Panteleimon and the monastic dormitory below it have been in use since 1878 when the dormitory served as a pit-stop for Russian pilgrims en route to the monastery of Mount Athos in Greece. Now, services are attended mainly by Moldovan, Bulgarian and Georgian Christians, most of them women who work in the homes of rich Istanbul families, while St Andrei, the chapel just next door, is the preserve of the handful of White Russian families who remain in the city, relatives of the thousands who escaped here from the Bolshevik Revolution of 1917. Ivan hinted darkly that the two congregations do not get on, a tiny localized class war, but they are both reminders of the gamut of Russian, Balkan and Caucasian congregants of the Eastern Orthodox Church, rich and poor, that have lived here in varying numbers for centuries.

A wizened old lady led us into the chapel, which was crowded, the air heavy with the scent of melting wax. On every inch of wall and ceiling were carefully restored gilt icons of Christ and the Apostles. Facing the congregation was an altar thronged with candles, and on either side, two large Cyrillic letters, X and B (for Христос Воскресе – 'Christ has Risen!') garishly lit by flashing pink light bulbs. The whole effect was reminiscent of the kitsch ecclesiastical aesthetic of Baz Luhrmann's iconic film *Romeo + Juliet*. Hidden behind a screen, two ladies sang in Russian, their sopranos occasionally supplemented by an unseen, rich bass. Eventually, the embodiment of this bass made an entrance from behind a curtain: spectacularly huge and bearded, he waved his smoking pendulum of frankincense with unhurried majesty, a red-and-gold embroidered cassock draped around his shoulders. As he walked round the chapel, the congregation turned to face him like sunflowers, bowing as he intoned. I was led out at this point because I was wearing trousers – the old lady explained kindly that men wear men's clothes and ladies wear ladies' clothes. She found a floral gypsy skirt in a cardboard box, tied it round my waist, gave me an approving look and pushed me back inside the chapel.

Both the social and architectural legacies of Ottoman Istanbul are fading, and services like those at St Panteleimon have an almost furtive aspect to them. Old Greek and Armenian districts are full of once-splendid houses with crumbling neoclassical facades, flanked by purpose-built apartment blocks; furniture abandoned by their owners gathers dust in antique shops down the road. Place names have become redundant; Arnavutköy – 'Albanian Village' – is now a collection of expensive houses on the European waterfront, and Polonezköy, 'Polish Village' – once the 19th-century home of Polish émigrés – is a collection of kiosks in a park on the outskirts of the city, a Christian graveyard the single, fitting reminder of its previous existence. The banking quarter in Karaköy is still heavy with the grandeur of granite-columned exteriors but inside, in place of the tills and halls which were once thronged with Jewish bankers and Levantine merchants, laminated red letters spell out HSBC and an ATM flashes in the corner behind a glass pane. Down by the shore of the Golden Horn, the elegant grey-stoned Greek Orthodox patriarchate is almost unchanged. Its view, however, is no longer of the Genoese-built Galata Tower across the water. In front of that, a new bridge stretches to the opposite shore and every four minutes a high-speed train thunders across the water before disappearing into the ground.

The Empire had its seat here from 1453, when the twenty-one-year-old Sultan Mehmet II conquered the city, until 1922, when the last sultan, Mehmet VI, was exiled. 'Ottoman' (*Osmanlı* in Turkish) is an anglicisation of Osman, the Turk from central Asia who in 1299 planted the seeds of the empire in the Anatolian town of Söğüt, from which he waged war against the crumbling Byzantine Empire in the west. Osman's fledgling empire reached its height centuries after his death, in the early 17th century. By this point, Istanbul was the greatest capital in the world, a city of several hundred thousand people, so rich and bustling that authorities had begun to worry about its over-population[12]. Mosques, churches, synagogues, hospitals and schools enriched the nexus of a fast-growing empire, catering to an array of subjects who were perhaps at their most diverse under Suleiman the Magnificent, who ruled between 1520 and 1566. His favourite court architect, Mimar ('Architect') Sinan, was born into a Christian family – either Greek or Armenian – in Kayseri, central Anatolia, before joining the janissary corps and converting to Islam. He designed some of the most iconic mosques in the world, including Suleiman's eponymous Suleymaniye Mosque in Istanbul. His architectural achievements outside Turkey serve as landmarks of 16th-century Ottoman expansion: the Juma-Jami Mosque in Yevpatoria, Crimea (1564), the Tekkiye Mosque in Damascus, Syria (built for Suleiman's son, Selim I, in 1566) and the Banya Bashi Mosque in Sofia, Bulgaria (1576) among them. The Armenian Balyan family, famed architects of the 18th and 19th centuries, built the lavish Dolmabahçe Palace on the banks of the Bosphorus among other iconic buildings. Their legacy shows both how much the empire relied on its non-Muslim subjects, and how high these non-Muslim subjects could climb – Jews and Christians were typically the sultan's most trusted military commanders, doctors, architects and advisors.

Almost all the contemporary accounts we have of Ottoman life in Istanbul were written, unsurprisingly, by men. Evliya Çelebi, a court favourite of Sultan Murad IV in the mid-17th century thanks to his note-perfect, eight-hour recitations from the Koran, was also the Ottoman Herodotus, known for blending fact and fantasy in his collection of travel writing, the *Seyahatname*. A devout Muslim who wryly described sex as 'the greater jihad'[13], he was a strange mix of intrepid explorer and court sycophant. He commented extensively on the daily habits of the sultan in his chronicles of life in Topkapı Palace, and occasionally on the social life of the city. His account of a Greek goldsmith who worked in his father's workshop in Unkapanı, a western district of Istanbul, gives us an idea of the atmosphere of a city in which an 'infidel' would naturally exchange stories of the empire's glorious Christian past with a precocious Muslim child spouting Persian.

'One of the goldsmiths in our shop was an infidel named Simyon. He would read aloud from the history of Yanvan, and I would listen and record it in my memory. From childhood on I used to hang around with him, and being clever for my age, I learned fluent Greek and Latin. I instructed Simyon in the [Persian–Ottoman] dictionary of Şahidi, and he instructed me in the history of Alexander the Great, which included an account of the ancestors of the Roman emperors going all the way back to the Amalekites and to Shem the son of Noah.'[14]

Some of the more atmospheric descriptions of Ottoman life in the city were made by an English woman writing in the early 18th century, when the empire still retained much of the wealth and cultural diversity of its zenith in the previous century. In 1716, Lady Mary Wortley Montagu and her husband, the newly appointed British Ambassador to the Ottoman Empire, set off from London for Istanbul; between 1717 and 1718 they lived in a house in Pera, a cosmopolitan district just above Galata. It is obvious from Lady Mary's correspondence with friends in England that she would have made a far more successful diplomat than her husband, who was recalled to London after only a year (she was also something of a medical pioneer – having observed smallpox inoculation being used by Ottoman doctors, she introduced the method to English doctors who were at first sceptical before being convinced when Lady Mary demonstrated it successfully on her own daughter[15]). She made the most of her privilege as a woman to access the nuclei of Ottoman life, braving the steamy nudity of the *hamam* and learning Turkish by infiltrating the *haremlik* (women's quarters) of Topkapi Palace, where she befriended the women closest to Sultan Ahmet III and learned about political machinations hidden from her husband.

The district of Pera, where the Montagus lived, was full of a dizzying array of Ottoman subjects, visiting traders, diplomats and workers. The Montagu household itself was an immigrant hub: 'My grooms are Arabs, my footmen French, English, and Germans,' she wrote in one of her letters. 'My nurse an Armenian, my housemaids Russians; half a dozen other servants, Greeks: my steward an Italian; my janizaries [guards on loan from the sultan, like embassy guards provided by a host state] Turks; so that I live in the perpetual hearing of this medley of sounds, which produces a very extraordinary effect upon the people that are born here; for they learn all these languages at the same time, and without knowing any of them well enough to write or read in it. There are very few men, women, or even children here, that have not the same compass of words in five or six of them.'[16]

This proliferation of polyglots was not something unique to Istanbul; it existed throughout the major trading towns of the empire. For example, the historian Mark Mazower tells us that in Thessaloniki, 'as late as the First World War, Salonikan bootblacks commanded a working knowledge of six or seven languages'[17]. Smyrna was even more of a cosmopolis, composed of all the most eclectic groups of the empire, along with other major trading hubs of the Levant – Alexandria, Beirut and Tyre. In the 21st century, the tyranny of English as a global language means that – despite the many second, third or even fourth languages spoken in cities like New York and London – we are unlikely to experience that level of true linguistic diversity again.

Ziya

Ziya Gökmen is a dynamic, chatty man in his forties. He is fluent in several languages because he runs a tourist agency in Istanbul – a difficult endeavour in these times – and is more prone to dwelling fondly on the past than speculating on an uncertain future. One afternoon, he told me his family background over endless cups of tea in his office, occasionally picking up the phone to check a date or a name with his mother. He is fascinated by the Ottoman roots of his family – long before the Turkish government digitalized everyone's family trees, Ziya had his almost perfectly memorized.

'My grandmother Bedriye was born in 1912 in Macedonia, in a town called Ustrumca [modern Strumica], at the time of the watermelons. People at that time didn't record exact birthdays so they did it by the fruit season. So, when is watermelon – July, August? Let's say August.

'The First Balkan War started two months later, in October; it was fought between the Ottomans and the Balkan states who wanted to carve up the remaining European territories of the sultan. My great-grandfather Nazmi, who was a manager at Ziraat Bankası [a bank that still exists today in Turkey] got advance warning from Istanbul via the bank to leave ASAP and escape to Istanbul before the war really started; they had to go via boat from Selanik [Salonika, modern-day Thessaloniki]. So when Bedriye was still a tiny baby, they got on a horse and travelled a hundred and thirty-three kilometres to escape from the soldiers [who would have targeted the family as Muslim "Turks" – i.e. the enemy].'

At this point, Ziya rings his mother to check the 133km claim, and is reminded of some extra eyewitness testimony from his great-grandmother.

'Oh yes! My great-grandmother Hatice said they even left the chestnuts in the saucepan when they were leaving the house, they took whatever they could carry and left for Selanik. Most of the families in that area abandoned their babies. Hatice hid my two-month-old grandmother in the saddlebag – she had seen babies massacred by Bulgarian soldiers. She worried my grandmother would die of suffocation, but before they got to each check point, she checked the saddlebag to see if her baby was still alive.'

Ziya's absorption in his own story, in the every breath of his baby grandmother, is mesmeric.

'There were two boats in the dock at Selanik harbour – one going to New York, and one to Istanbul. They didn't let my great-grandpa get on the boat because only women and children were allowed, so he chose the Istanbul boat for his family because he knew the baby wouldn't survive the journey to New York. As my great-grandpa watched them board, he started chatting in Bulgarian with the soldier at the checkpoint, and gave him a cigarette. After a while of chatting together, they become friendly, and somehow the soldier helped him sneak through the checkpoint on to the boat to join his wife and baby.

'There is a saying in Turkish: *"Bir lisan bir insan"* – "Each language is one person" – you add a persona to yourself if you add a language. My grandmother's life was saved by her father knowing Bulgarian, and that's why it is so important in my family to learn new languages.'

Visibly moved, Ziya stands up and picks up an English dictionary from his bookshelf.

'Bedriye gave me this dictionary because she wanted me to learn English, she understood that a new language helps you to be harboured in a new country [Ziya studied in America]. I met her mother – my great-grandmother – in her nineties when I was a kid. She was speaking Turkish with a Macedonian dialect – *"yaporoz, edoroz"*, instead of *"yapıyoruz, ediyoruz"*.

'Because my great-grandfather was a civil servant working in a bank, he was given the advice to get back to Istanbul as soon as possible. That's why he survived – but others suffered much worse. Many left their babies with their neighbours, thinking they would die. Lots of Armenians did that in 1915. Many Turkish Muslim families today used to be Armenian or Greek before they assimilated, or they are the orphans of Armenians who died during the Armenian relocation.'

The term 'Armenian relocation' is a common euphemism for 'the Armenian genocide', which is never referred to in Turkey – in fact, the even more euphemistic 'events of 1915' is more often used to describe the massacres and forced marches of the majority of the

Armenian population of Ottoman Anatolia in the middle of the Great War. Ziya actually knows much more about this period of history than the average Turkish citizen, and is particularly interested in the overlap between Armenian survivors of the genocide and the Alevi community of Turkey, partly for personal reasons.

'People in Tunceli [a town in eastern Anatolia] who are Alevi used to be Armenian. In 1915, they decided to become Muslim rather than be deported but they thought Sunni Islam was too harsh, so they wanted instead to become Alevi. The grandmother of Derya [Ziya's wife] died a few weeks ago. Derya and her brother went to Çorum for the funeral and it took place in a *cemevi* (an Alevi house of worship] – they suddenly realized that their father's mother was Alevi but they never knew that. They asked their father, 'Dad, why did you never tell us?' He was a retired military colonel, and he told them, 'Kids, if my soldiers knew I was Alevi they would never listen to my orders.'

I often get asked by non-Turks whether my name has any connection to Alevism. 'Alev' means flame, and fire is used extensively in Alevi worship, but the more mainstream theory is that Alevism is a Turkish derivation of 'Alawite', i.e. a follower of Ali, the son-in-law of the Prophet Muhammad. Even without an etymological connection, however, I feel drawn to Alevis, because I like their extremely relaxed form of Islam. They drink alcohol, and women and men worship together, not in a mosque but in a modest, round room (the *cemevi*), which is often hard for outsiders to find. There is a typically unobtrusive, white-washed *cemevi* on Burgaz Ada, one of the islands off the coast of Istanbul which were home to many of the city's minorities during the Ottoman era, including Jewish and

Christian families. They were party islands for rich Muslim subjects too, and today they are full of Arab tourists from the Gulf delightedly eating ice cream while being driven around in horse-drawn carriages.

'Derya's mother's side of the family is blond and blue-eyed, and they are from the south-east of Turkey. There could be two explanations for this: that they are related to the crusaders and pilgrims who passed through en route to the Holy Land hundreds of years ago, or that they have Russian blood. In 1915, the Young Turks [revolutionaries who seized power from the sultan in 1908 and led the empire on to the losing side of the war] fought against the Russians at the battle of Sarıkamış in the mountains of Eastern Turkey near Armenia. They lost, and decided to relocate Armenians and Russian families in Eastern Turkey to Iraq and Syria. [Again, a circumspect reference to the Armenian genocide.] But some families – blue-eyed, blond-haired – remained.'

Blue-eyed Turks are one of my favourite subjects of conversation, and I tell Ziya so.

'Yes. We are all mixed up, you know. In Sagalassos [an ancient Greek site in modern south-west Turkey], Bulgarian archaeologists were carrying out excavation work and hired local Turks to work on the site. They found skeletons from the second century so they decided to compare the DNA of the skeletons with the local workers. It was a one hundred per cent match. They called the workers to explain the skeletons were their ancestors, and the workers were completely horrified. They went on strike, saying, "Are you trying to say we are Greeks?"'

The absurdity of this reminds me of the famous speech from the 1964 film *Zorba the Greek*, where the titular hero gives an angry speech about the perils of nationalism: 'I have done things for my country that would make your hair stand. I have killed, burned villages, raped women. And why? Because they were Turks or Bulgarians. That's the rotten damn fool I was. Now I look at a man, any man, and I say, "He is good. He is bad." What do I care if he's Greek or Turk?'

As I travelled across Turkey and to ex-Ottoman territories beyond its borders, I met for myself the people Ziya had told me about – the Armenians of the eastern empire, and the Balkans of the west – but first, I found an ancient minority community from the south-east of Turkey almost literally on my doorstep.

The Sacré Coeur

I used to live near Taksim Square in the district of Gümüşsuyu ('Silver Water'), on one of the highest points in Istanbul, with a panoramic view of the Bosphorus. About twenty metres from my door was the unassuming Sacré Coeur church, and at Easter, the usually tiny congregation would blossom – extended families would materialize in full regalia, grandmothers teetering in high heels, fussing over children with carefully combed hair. There was a sense of occasion, of celebration, and the collective body language of the congregation held an almost imperceptible defiance.

This was the Syriac Catholic community, which hails originally from Aleppo in northern Syria, and now has a base in the south-east of Turkey. The Syriac Catholic Church sprang from the more ancient Syriac Orthodox Church, established around

AD 500, after Jesuit missionaries sent to Syria from France in the 17th century began appointing their own patriarchs, causing a Catholic-Orthodox schism within the community. The sultan initially backed the Orthodox patriarchs, but after a protracted struggle both churches were accommodated. In the early 20th century, massacres of Syriacs along with Armenians were followed by state persecution after the founding of the Republic in 1923 (in 1925, shortly after the establishment of the Republic of Turkey, Atatürk expelled the Syriac Orthodox patriarchate from Turkey to Syria). Today, a very rough estimate of 10,000 Syriacs remain in Turkey (most of them Orthodox), many of whom no longer live in the south-east of the country but in Istanbul. Like most of the city's minorities, they are relatively wealthy and the younger generations have started to leave, part of Turkey's increasingly rapid brain drain, exacerbated by an increasing sense that local non-Muslims have become vulnerable in recent years.

On Easter Sunday in 2016, armed riot police stationed themselves outside the Sacré Coeur church, reinforcements waiting in vans parked up the narrow street, and civilian police in red security vests stood nearer the entrance as families arrived for the Easter service. This was a response to recent threats made by IS to the *kafir* (infidels); all churches and synagogues were on high alert throughout Istanbul. I joined the people streaming through the doors just in time for the 11 a.m. service. Inside, the church gave the impression of light and space despite being crowded, its high roof covered with a turquoise mosaic. Around 250 people had shown up, despite the police presence outside, and a sizeable, mixed choir was accompanied by an electric keyboard set to organ mode. At one point in the service, there was a muffled commotion in the choir; a girl stormed down the aisle in tears and a boy hurried behind her – a covert lovers' spat. Here was a community with inner relationships and gossip, all played out and dissected during the two-hour service and in the scrum outside the church afterwards, where chocolate eggs were handed out to the children. By the end of the service, so many people had arrived that there was barely standing room at the back; I felt guilty, a non-believer taking up a precious seat, but also too self-conscious to leave mid-service.

Many of the ancient minorities of Turkey have been forced from their ancestral homeland in the east of the country to the metropolis of Istanbul – or, in far greater numbers, further afield – to Europe and the United States. In Byzantine times, Anatolia was a Christian heartland, hosting some of the most important events and figures of Christian history. The Council of Nicea (modern-day Iznik) in AD 325 was the first ecumenical council of the Church, and resulted in the first articulation of uniform Christian doctrine, the Nicene Creed. The Council of Chalcedon in modern-day Kadıköy, Istanbul, was the third ecumenical council, at which almost everyone agreed that Jesus Christ was both perfectly divine and perfectly human. Smyrna – modern-day Izmir – was home to one of the seven churches addressed in the Book of Revelations, and Antioch – modern-day Antakya – is the seat of Eastern Christianity, where St Paul (born in Tarsus, south Turkey) set off on his missionary journeys. According to the Book of Genesis, Antioch is also the home of the first non-Gentile Christians (the first to actually be called 'Christian'). Much of the Christian history of Turkey is no longer evident, but the towns of

Antakya and Mardin are still home to both Christian and Jewish congregations.

I headed down there for the first time in 2012, just before the opposing factions of Syria's civil war began to spill across the border into Turkey; by the time I visited again in 2014, they had not only spilled over but established cells in these towns.

Antakya

A large signpost to HALEP (Aleppo) on the road from Hatay airport serves as a reminder of the proximity of Syria's devastation just twenty kilometres over the border. Antakya lies south of the port of Iskenderun on Turkey's Mediterranean coast; the surrounding province of Hatay used to be part of Syria, then existed as an independent state for one year in 1938 before finally being subsumed into the Turkish Republic in 1939, a sore subject for Syrians ever since. There are roughly half a million Syrian refugees in Hatay province, most of them Sunni Muslims fleeing the Alawite regime of Bashar al-Assad across the border, but also a number of Alawites fleeing the Sunni rebels in nearby villages – the divisions between the two groups means that more and more are leaving for the relative urban anonymity and safety of Istanbul. While many Antakyan residents I spoke to claimed that they are 'all brothers', this seems increasingly anachronistic: tensions have seeped into the town, and kidnaps and bomb threats are common. While I was there, a group of Sunni Muslim men wearing white marched down the central street, loudly protesting the arrival of more Alawites.

17

Those who live in Antakya like to compare it to pre-war Damascus and the town does have a very Middle Eastern feel, particularly the ancient warren of the *medina* (centre): baking sandstone houses, souks, narrow streets overhung by fig trees and vines, criss-crossed by the odd chicken or goat, and children darting through heavy wooden doors open to the hurly-burly of family life within. In shops and cafés, Arabic is liberally scattered through conversation, and Turkish has the harsh aspiration of the south-eastern accent and Arabic mother tongue. On my way to the pilgrim house where I would stay that night, a meandering walk led me via the smell of warm caramel to a tiny *atölye* (atelier) manufacturing stewed walnuts and pumpkin slices, bubbling away on little stoves in sugar water. Eventually, I found the pilgrim house, which is run by a sturdy German Catholic nun called Sister Barbara. A few hours after I arrived and dropped my bag, I had the awkward experience of encountering her in a bar on the outskirts of the *medina*; she sipped a beer, avoiding eye contact, so I followed her lead.

The town is still full of Orthodox, Protestant and Catholic churches and a single synagogue, which attracts only a handful of elderly worshippers. The old faithful attend their services doggedly and narrate the centuries-old histories of their communities with undimmed enthusiasm. When they speak of themselves, however, it is usually with a melancholic bent, conscious that they are literally dying out. One Jewish man showing me around the empty synagogue looked bowed down by sadness. At one point in the tour he stopped and turned to me: 'I sometimes worry that when I die there will be no one left to bury me.' The energy of the *medina* dissipated in this echoing testament to past faith.

Mardin, 500 kilometres to the north-east of Antakya, is a sprawling town of sandstone high on a hill, overlooking the plains of Mesopotamia. I visited in the early years of the Syrian war, arriving as dusk was falling and the call to prayer was ringing out from scattered minarets into the valley below, the amplified Arabic at odds with the quiet of the landscape. A minute later, a bell struck solemnly from the Syriac Orthodox church and as evening approached, the town came alive with light and sound, the tinkle of wine glasses and the swell of Kurdish, Arabic and Turkish conversation. The next day I attended a service at the church. Unlike the Catholic service in Gümüşsuyu, this was in Aramaic, and I spent some time after the service marvelling over the otherworldly script in a beautifully bound Bible I found near the altar.

I thought of the energy of the *medinas* of Mardin and Antakya when I read *Battle for Home*, an account by a Syrian architect, Marwa al-Sabouni, of her home city of Homs. She describes its pre-war transformation at the hands of inept 'urban planners' who, even before years of shelling wrought irreversible destruction, damaged a centuries-old communal spirit by replacing some of the ancient structure of the town with apartment blocks.

'It was common to hear the bells of Christian churches and the Muslim calls for prayer echoing through the streets at the same time.[18] [. . .] In Old Homs, neither Christians nor Muslims had to prove their social status through their religions; they belonged to the city, and the city embraced them through a common experience of the built environment, with their religions publicly honoured and placed at the core. In Old Homs, as in all old Syrian cities, alleys embraced houses, and mosques opened their front doors to the

facing doors of churches, and minarets and church towers raised
their praying hands in unity above the rooftops. This way of life
promoted cultivation and harmony.'[19]

In 2017, the Turkish government 're-appropriated' around fifty
properties belonging to the Syriac Orthodox Church, on the grounds
that their ownership deeds had lapsed after the reordering of municipal boundaries in 2012. Monasteries such as the 5th-century Mor
Gabriel became the official property of the Diyanet, Turkey's religious body which holds jurisdiction over mosques and Koranic
schools across the country, before an outcry reversed the decision[20]
As a leader who casts himself in the Ottoman mould, President
Erdoğan often makes grand gestures to accommodate minorities in
Turkey – for example, in the early years of the Syrian war he invited
the Syriac patriarchate back to Turkey, though nothing came of this
overture. In 2013, he also pledged to repatriate Syriac Orthodox
properties previously seized by the government, only some of which
have been returned. Social strictures on minorities introduced after
the formation of the Republic are still imposed – for example, Syriac
children must still take Turkish names as well as their family-given
Christian names.

The Greek Orthodox Patriarch Bartholomew claimed in 2012
that under the ruling Justice and Development Party (AKP) 'circumstances are better than the past for the Greeks and other minorities'.
It would not be difficult for any government to improve on the
record of the Republic, but the AKP's efforts are counterbalanced
by an overeagerness to identify with less politically correct examples
of Ottoman history, such as the decision to name Istanbul's third
bridge after an Alevi-massacring sultan.

Izmir and the Levantines

At the western end of the Anatolian trade route is Izmir – ancient Smyrna. Like Antakya, Smyrna has an ancient Christian history, but is defined by its even more ancient community of Greeks. Until the day it burned to the ground in September 1922 it had a majority of non-Muslim inhabitants (most of them Greek, and a significant number of Jews), which earned it the nickname *Gavur Izmir* ('Infidel Smyrna'). In Ottoman times, and indeed in Turkey today, members of the Greek Orthodox community are known as *Rum* – a reference to the Byzantine Christian Empire as the eastern division of the Roman Empire. *Rum* (literally "Rome") always refers to a Greek within Turkey, as opposed to *Yunan* – a Greek from *Yunanistan* (Greece).

In the latter centuries of Ottoman rule, a community of entre-preneurial Europeans from Italy, Britain, Spain and France based their highly profitable businesses in coastal towns like Izmir, not only a city of infidels but also 'the Pearl of the Aegean' and the most significant trading port in the Levant (literally the 'rising [sun]' or 'The East'). Essentially, the Levant is the Eastern Mediterranean, and in particular the major trade ports of Izmir, Mersin, Beirut and Alexandria, where Christian and Jewish merchants settled from Byzantine times, and in much greater numbers during the latter half of the Ottoman Empire. There are still around a thousand well-known Levantines in Turkey today, members of the grand old families: Jonathan Beard, for example, represents the sixth generation of the famous Beards of Alexandretta, or 'little Alexandria' (modern-day Iskenderun near Antakya, in the province of Hatay). The Beards moved there from England in 1846 to start a liquorice, cotton and tobacco business and, 170 years later, Jonathan Beard has a curious quasi-English accent in Turkish despite having grown up in Istanbul, and an occasional Turkish lilt in English. He states on the website of the Levantine Heritage Foundation that he indulges all his composite cultural parts 'without hesitation':

'As is dictated by our family rules I look forward to the day my eldest daughter Natalie takes over the business to become the 7th generation [of Beards]. I am proud to be referred to as a Levantine, I received my education in Arabic, Turkish, English and French and indulge in these cultures without hesitation. I look forward to returning to England one day but realize it shall not be permanent as the Levant and its beauty and intrigue is our natural home.'

In November 2014, the historian Philip Mansel told an audience at the British Consulate in Istanbul: 'We are all Levantines now.' The status of a Levantine has always been curiously exalted, even today – perhaps especially today, because the very use of the word recalls a bygone time where highly respected European families living on Turkey's coastline held a unique social status, boasting international connections that locals could not compete with and enjoying the support of local European consuls (the original Beards, for example, went into business with the British Consul in Iskenderun, Augustine Catoni, and subsequent generations kept up the partnership). Rich Levantines were the original Western ex-pats, several social levels above most economic migrants in the empire. They also had the oddly fierce attachment to their European roots that is typical of diasporic communities, artificially glamorized with distance and time.

The Lebanese writer Amin Maalouf is a Maronite Christian

from Beirut who now lives in Paris; his mother was an Egyptian Catholic of Turkish origin, and his father belonged to the Greek Melkite Church ('Melkite' comes from the Arabic for 'king' and was used pejoratively to describe those who backed the Byzantine emperor during the schism in Eastern Christianity after the Council of Chalcedon). In his novel *Balthasar's Odyssey*, Maalouf reimagines the life of a 17th-century Levantine book-dealer, Balthasar Embriaco, who runs a legendary bookshop in the Lebanese town of Gibelet, home of the Embriaci for centuries. One day, he decides to pursue a particularly valuable book across Anatolia to Istanbul and finally to Genoa, the lost home of his ancestors. In Maalouf's imagining, Balthasar's belatedly awoken love of Genoa has an element of sentimental hypocrisy: a wealthy ex-pat worshipping a city abandoned by long-dead relatives for the prospect of making money abroad. Maalouf presents Genoa as a Promised Land to the Embriaci, inviting a comparison to Jews who feel they can only be truly accepted and safe in Israel; at one point Balthasar declares that,

'My father always told me our mother country wasn't the Genoa of today but the Genoa of all time.'[21]

This seems to be the inverse of Mr Beard's attachment to Istanbul as his Levantine home and destiny combined. As a Lebanese native living in Paris, perhaps Maalouf attaches more importance to the self-identified exile than to the native in the split personality of Balthasar, who finally decides to remain in Genoa rather than return to Gibelet on the grounds that 'Genoa, where I'd never lived before, has recognized me, embraced me, taken me to its bosom like the Prodigal Son. I walk head held high along its narrow streets, say my Italian name aloud, smile at the women and am not afraid of the janissaries. One of the Embriaci's ancestors may have been accused of drinking too much, but they have a tower named after them too. Every family ought to have a tower named after them somewhere.'

The idea of an everlasting ancestral tower shows the human need for legacy. Oral history and family histories handed down through the generations are important, but deep down, people need something fixed to reassure themselves of their place in the world, their past, the presence of ancestors. Family heirlooms are not just valuable in worldly terms but in what they represent to living members of a past legacy. The irony of the Embriaci is that they were the most comfortably established family in Gibelet, enjoying local respect and wanting for nothing material – Genoa was a mental itch, an artificial longing that, when it materialized, was too powerful to resist.

'We are all Levantines now.' I took Mansel's words to mean that we are all part of a diaspora in some shape or form in the age of globalization. Yet, to paraphrase George Orwell, some diasporas are more equal than others. Mansel was addressing an audience of relatively wealthy Europeans and 'White Turks' – academics, diplomats and historical dilettantes, sure of our place in the world. We could perhaps claim the status of modern Levantines but most minorities in Turkey certainly cannot, not even in the old Levantine hub of Smyrna/Izmir.

In the excruciatingly hot June of 2016, a month before the infamous coup attempt, I flew with my friend, the photographer Bradley Secker, from Istanbul to Izmir, the most secular metropolis in Turkey – far more so than Istanbul, which has a high proportion of conservative rural migrants. Locals still consistently vote for the Republican People's Party (CHP), the party established by Atatürk himself on principles of secularism, despite its forty-year losing streak in general elections. During the 2013 anti-government protests in Gezi Park in Istanbul, crowds thronged the streets of Izmir in solidarity, calling for Erdoğan to resign.

Although the city has existed in various guises for 4,000 years, its current aesthetic is very much '20th-century sprawl', because at the end of Turkey's War of Independence in 1922 the city was burned to the ground – by incoming Turkish troops, according to the Greeks, and by retreating Greek troops, according to the Turks. Yet it retains something of the cosmopolitan vibrancy and fun it was once famous for, its streets full of tables spilling out of restaurants, crowded with people drinking beer and *rakı* (rather than *ayran*, or watered yoghurt, the recommended national drink of President Erdoğan), and international film and music festivals. Bradley and I arrived just before the Gay Pride march on 4 June 2016, which went ahead despite its cancellation by the governor the day before. A crowd composed mainly of teenagers marched and danced boldly down the corniche, swaddled in rainbow flags and yelling, 'We are here, darlings!' Meanwhile, riot police stationed themselves on street corners, as though for a terrorist attack (which was, incidentally, the excuse given for the cancellation of the march). In the same year, Pride was also cancelled in Istanbul, and police made sure no one marched by dispensing tear gas and rubber bullets into the gathering crowds.

But, like many places in Turkey, a relatively liberal attitude and thriving cultural scene does not mean that locals in Izmir are always tolerant, particularly towards people who look different. Bradley and I had come to Izmir to meet the self-described Afro Turks: black

Turks who are simultaneously the most noticeably different and the most overlooked of Ottoman minority descendants – in the words of the black Turkish Cypriot artist Serap Kanay, 'the most visible invisibles'.

The Afro Turks

Like all empires, the Ottoman Empire was built by slaves of varying legality. Many of them were taken as children from their families in Africa, Eastern Europe or the Caucasus, and their descendants grew up with no knowledge of their family's history bar a vague notion of geography. The huge demand for concubines meant that the Ottoman *noblesse* continued to buy female slaves long after the sultans of the late 19th century issued *firmans* (decrees) against the trade, in much the same way that illegal human trafficking is still alive and well in the 21st century. In fact, most of the sultans of the empire were the sons of Christian slave women who ended up in the *harem*. The most famous of these women was Roxelana (later Sultan Hürrem), an ethnic Ukrainian captured from the Kingdom of Poland at the age of fifteen at some point in the 1520s, and taken to the *haremlik* of Suleiman the Magnificent, where she became his favourite concubine, converted to Islam and contrived to make herself the first legal queen of the Ottoman Empire, spectacularly breaking the infidel glass ceiling.

Slavery was never banned in the empire, although in 1857 the British government managed to pressure the sultan into stopping the trade. Existing slaves were only freed in 1924 when the Republic's new constitution granted equal rights to all citizens. For centuries, Christian boys were taken from their families in Eastern Europe and the Balkans in a kind of 'blood tax' called the *devşirme*, converted to Islam and trained up to serve the state. Some of them ended up as *köçekler*, effeminate belly dancers who performed in social contexts where women were not allowed. Others received sizeable salaries as janissaries (*yeniçeri*, 'new troops', in Turkish), soldiers of the sultan. Since slaves were not technically allowed to serve in the Ottoman armed forces, in 1860 male Circassian slaves from the region just north of Georgia were bought from their owners by the Ottoman government and freed so that they could be recruited, a measure which was also partly designed to stop a nationalist-inspired slave revolt in the turbulent years of the late 19th century when Russia and Turkey were at war.

Until the late 19th century, around 16,000–18,000 African slaves were taken every year by Ottoman traders from Eritrea, Sudan and Egypt. They were put on to boats and often 'sorted' in the holding port of Alexandria on Egypt's northern coast before being shipped to Istanbul, Izmir, the Aegean islands and Cyprus. Black eunuchs wielded great power in the sultan's *haremlik*, especially from the 18th century onwards, and black slave children were occasionally presented as imperial gifts. The Russian writer Alexander Pushkin's great-grandfather, Abram Petrovich Gannibal, was kidnapped as a child from the shores of Lake Chad and taken to serve in the court of Sultan Ahmet III. In 1704, aged just six, he was sent to St Petersburg as a gift for Peter the Great, who brought him up as his godson and propelled him to great fame as a military engineer. The vast, anonymous majority of African slaves, however, had no such illustrious royal transfer or career. They worked menial tasks and have disappeared almost without trace from the history books.

In the 1880s, the Ottoman government chose the Aegean region near Izmir to relocate African slaves taken off ships in Istanbul in an effort to stop the slave trade; there were already many of them in the area because it was the nexus of multiple trade routes. The present-day Afro Turk community are the descendants of these slaves, and remain relatively unknown outside of the Aegean area. Even here, they are only accepted as part of the community in the villages where they live, but attract immediate attention in big cities, where they are mistaken for Eritrean or Somalian refugees trying to cross to Greece, or street hawkers. Many of them still struggle in the poorest bracket of society, working in tough agricultural jobs and subject to severe discrimination – One of my interviewees told me that in 2006, another young woman from the Afro Turk community in Muğla was refused a kindergarten teaching position because 'she might scare the children' (she later went to court, won her case, and qualified as a teacher).

My mother's great-grandfather was born in Egypt; we know very little about him, except that he was a black doctor brought over to Cyprus in the late 19th century to help with an outbreak of malaria. I have always harboured private doubts about whether it was possible for black men in Egypt to become doctors in the 19th century, although it is certainly the case that they could achieve prominence: for example, the historian Eve Troutt Powell describes the story of a certain Anbar Effendi in 19th-century Egypt, a freed slave who became a high-ranking commissioner. Either way, my mother's mysterious great-grandfather shaped her life. She was noticeably different from her friends – much darker, with Afro hair and a strikingly Egyptian profile, and she was bullied accordingly. When I met the Aegean Afro Turks and enthused that I, too, was part Afro Turk, they looked understandably sceptical until I showed them photos of my mother on my phone. Suddenly, there was a link, a reason to trust me, improbable though it seemed from my freckly face.

In the sleepy village of Naime, an hour's drive from Izmir, Bradley and I met an Afro Turk who claimed to be 106 years old. Dressed in baggy *shalvar* trousers, the ancient Hatice was huddled on a bench under the vine-covered veranda of her tiny house, her movements slow in the intense June heat. She squinted into the middle distance as she tried to remember the founding of the Turkish Republic: 'Yes, lots of drumming and trumpets,' she creaked, finally. Hatice's memories were understandably vague, but then something else occurred to her: 'Yes, Atatürk freed my father. He was a free man after the Republic, and after he was freed, he found himself some cows and a patch of land. Then he was murdered by bandits. We somehow survived.'

Hatice is the proud possessor of a Turkish ID card, but her parents were not. She knows very little about her family's roots, only that her ancestors were brought from the East African coast to the Ottoman Empire. Little knowledge of this African heritage remains; Hatice speaks only Turkish, and seemed irritated by my questions about her family history, most of which she could not answer. In common with many rural women of her generation, Hatice never went to school, married at sixteen and had nine children. Although free, her life has been particularly hard as a black woman in a country defined by fierce nationalism and a racism derived from the long-held belief that Turks are genetically superior to Arabs, and, by extension, anyone with dark skin.

Hatice's son, Esat, very smartly dressed in a slightly oversized but carefully pressed shirt, persuaded his initially reluctant mother to agree to Bradley taking her photograph, and was surprisingly cheerful when it came to the subject of the integration of Afro Turks in Turkish society. Under the shade of the veranda, he spread out a photo album filled with photographs of himself as a young man, carrying out his military service in Northern Cyprus, and working in a hotel on the Mediterranean coast. Esat was the only black man in these photos.

'I have many friends – yes, some call me "Arab", they joke about me, but not in a nasty way. Everyone can live in Turkey, variety is beautiful,' he insisted, perhaps sensing my scepticism. 'If a garden doesn't have lots of different flowers and trees, is it still beautiful? No! If people are racist, it just means they are ignorant. I don't take any notice. I am a Turk, that is all.'

Esat, anxious to belong, downplayed the prejudice I had heard about from other members of the Afro Turk community, including from his own brother, Orhan, who feels his family's difference keenly.

'It's a shame we have lost our African language, the language our great-grandparents spoke,' he told me, sitting outside the village's only café. 'Every minority in Turkey has its language – the Kurds, the Zaza, even the Laz [a Black Sea community]. But we have only Turkish, and we don't know anything about our ancestors. After years of suffering, you hide what makes you different. That is why our parents' parents did not teach us their [African] language.

They did not want to make us different, they wanted us to be only Turkish.'

As an assimilated ethnic minority without a minority religion to act as a unifying force, the Afro Turks have tried over the generations to integrate as much as possible, and intermarriage has meant that it is impossible to guess at their numbers. Recently, however, the self-identifying community of the Aegean region made an effort to reembrace their past, thanks in large part to the recently deceased Mustafa Olpak, a marble worker who in the late 1990s managed to trace his own heritage back to Kenya, via Ottoman Crete.

Olpak was inspired by his research to establish Izmir's Afro Turk Foundation in 2006, to connect the disparate community, and in the same year, he also reestablished the Calf Festival ('Dana Bayramı'), a spring tradition practised publicly in Ottoman times by the African slave community, and then in secret after Atatürk's ban on non-state-controlled religious institutions in 1925. The festival originally involved leading an elaborately decorated calf from village to village to collect money before sacrificing it to prevent droughts. In the 1960s the secret practice died out, only to be brought back by Olpak with a papier-mâché calf replacing the original sacrificial victim. Bradley and I met the sixty-one-year-old Olpak outside his shabby office in Izmir a couple of days before the festival – he was preoccupied and smoked incessantly, too busy buying plane tickets for far-flung members of the community to go to his chemotherapy session. Very sadly, he died from prostate cancer four months later, having at least lived to the see the ten-year anniversary of the Calf Festival he reintroduced.

On the morning of the festival, Izmir locals sat listlessly outside restaurants in the heat on the main boulevard. Waiters dozed, and all was quiet. Suddenly, the thump of drums broke the peace, and a troupe of straw-clad figures materialized at the end of the street. Bradly and I, and the astonished café patrons, watched as the troupe expanded into a procession of nearly a hundred people, some wearing elaborate Benin-style masks, others garlands and bright prints, while children formed the legs of the velveteen-covered calf decorated with ribbons and amulets, shuffling slowly along at the center of the action. Locals gaped as the crowd careered down the boulevard.

'Who are these people?' I overheard one elderly lady muttering to her neighbour.

'Africans, obviously,' the other replied.

'But I heard some of them speaking Turkish,' said a young man at the adjoining table.

'Black Turks? Certainly not.' The second elderly lady's tone was firm. 'These are Africans.'

Overhearing this conversation, my suspicions were confirmed: most locals have no idea of the existence of the community, even though there have been several prominent Afro Turks in the history of the Republic – Esmeray, for example, a singer and actress in 1970s Istanbul ('Dusky Moon'), the modern sculptor Kuzgan Acar or the pilot Ahmet Ali Çelikten, ('Arab Ahmet Ali'), who fought for the Ottomans in the First World War as one of the first black fighter pilots in the world. During Turkey's War of Independence, there were many Afro Turks in the rogue *zeybek* militias who fought the Greek invading forces in the mountains in the Aegean region before joining Atatürk's regular army. Yet, as a community, the Afro Turks are largely missing from the pages of Turkey's history.

Later, I noticed onlookers of the Dana Bayramı trying to speak to the participants in pidgin English; others mimicked the dances, laughing openly. Later, Bradley and I met the creator of the Benin-style masks: a cheerful local woman unconnected to the Afro community, but keen to help out, who told me she had copied the designs from the internet after googling 'African masks'. Once the parade had finished and costumes were removed, the straw-clad dancers were revealed to be African students at Izmir University, who had been invited to perform dances from their home countries of Burundi and Mali. No one was bothered by the fact that Burundian dances are only tangentially related to Afro Turk culture, which is what the historian Dr Michael Ferguson describes as 'a hybridized culture based on East and West African cultural practices' – essentially, a culture whose geographic roots are lost in the mists of time. This parade was a celebration not of specific roots but of a shared heritage largely lost in a history of oppression. It was a powerful statement of existence.

Ahmet Doğu, a retired worker in the former state-owned tobacco factory in Izmir and an enthusiastic founding member of the Afro Turk Foundation, is a large, straight-backed man. He looked younger than his sixty-five years, sporting a baseball cap and a white polo shirt tucked into chinos, not dissimilar to an American pensioner. Doğu's parents came to Turkey during the 1923 Greek–Turkish population exchange, when the two countries swapped their respective Muslim and Christian minorities to create homogenous nation states, taking a boat from Salonika to Samsun. As a child, Doğu remembers his father cursing in Greek when he was angry. Like most Afro Turks, when asked about his heritage he hazards a guess at Sudan, although in reality Sudan in this case was a generic Arabic term for Black Africa. Doğu did his military service in Izmir and stayed on. He was entirely frank about the discrimination he has faced as a black man in Turkey.

'Whether you like it or not, it does get to you,' he said soberly, sitting outside the Afro Turk Foundation's shabby one-roomed office. He told me about mothers on the street who mutter superstitious phrases as they pass him with their children. 'They pray that their children will not turn out so black,' he says, grimacing slightly. 'They touch wood and look away from me. But sometimes, they ask me to kiss their baby on the lips to stop it drooling, that is how the superstition goes.' More insidious, however, is the way Afro Turks are referred to in friendly social circles as 'Arab', a term which has been traditionally used in Turkey for anyone dark enough to be either Arab or African.

'We call ourselves Arab, too,' said Ahmet. 'It is better than "African", which has such bad connotations – when people think of Africans they think of cannibalism and backwardness. We do not want to be associated with that. These days, we also call ourselves Sudanese or Libyan or whatever, even though we don't know exactly where our families were from. Luckily, it is better these days. It was worse when people really had no idea about black people – at least now we are more on television, on the internet, because of American culture.'

Ahmet told me he had been married twice. 'My first wife was African like me, but the second one is like you – with red ears.' In answer to my quizzical look, he explained: 'We say that to mean white; if you get angry or hot your ears show red, ours don't. If we

34

ask about someone in the extended community, we say, *"Bizden mi kırmızı kulak mı?"* – "Are they like us, or red-eared?"'

In the village of Yeniçiftlik, close to Naime, Afro Turk children play in the street, still unaware of their relative enlightenment in the history of their community. Adil was a beautiful eight-year-old boy with green eyes from his white father; his grandmother, Fatma, told me that her grandparents were brought to work in the cotton fields under Sultan Abdul Hamid II in the first decade of the 20th century. The family has the second name 'Zenci', a pejorative Turkish word for 'black' (roughly – but not quite – equivalent to 'Negro'), which was given to her parents under Atatürk's Surname Law in 1934, when Turkish citizens were first allocated surnames.

The fact that the Zenci surname has endured indicates that the Afro Turk community is still subjected to crude stereotyping; yet skin colour is also a token by which they have felt united. One young woman I spoke to after the festival told me that her parents' generation has been plagued by competing desires: to become 'whiter', and to keep the community united by marrying within it.

'We are concerned that our blackness is dying out, we are becoming diluted as a community, but at the same time we often marry white people. Our parents say 'white is good'. They don't want their children to live through what they've lived through.'

In 1961, the American writer James Baldwin moved to Istanbul, famously declaring of his native land that 'To be a Negro in this country and to be relatively conscious is to be in a rage almost all the time.' Baldwin needed to work out his place as a black man in American society from a totally different cultural perspective. He lived on and off throughout the 1960s in Istanbul, in a house that

I discovered to my delighted surprise was 100 metres away from mine in Gümüşsuyu, just behind the German Consulate. In that house, he finished his novel *Another Country* as well as a collection of essays *No Name in the Street*; Baldwin's name in the streets of Gümüşsuyu was 'Arab Jimmy'. Thirty years earlier, the attitude of the Turkish diplomats to civil rights in America was considerably more progressive than domestic attitudes. The Turkish ambassador Münir Ertegün, appointed by President Atatürk, caused an outcry when he welcomed African Americans to jazz evenings at the embassy in Washington DC; when the State Department advised him to invite them in through the back door, he responded that they should enter 'through the front door as equals'. Both Baldwin's experience and Ertegün's actions show that perhaps it is only with distance that real perspective emerges regarding the place of minorities in society.

Baroness Hussein-Ece is a British Liberal Democrat working peer in the House of Lords; her cousin is the Turner Prize-winning artist Tracey Emin. Both are of Turkish Cypriot origin and share a great-grandfather who was kidnapped as a boy in Sudan and sold to a Cypriot trader in the late 19th century; eventually, he gained his freedom, married a local midwife and started a family near Larnaca. Shamelessly trading on my credentials as a fellow Turkish Cypriot of African descent, I went to meet the Baroness in the House of Lords to hear the full story.

We had tea in a high-ceilinged, wood-panelled room steeped in Ancient Power, humming with ancient English voices; it seemed strange to use Turkish phrases as we talked, describing our relatives to each other. 'Look,' said the baroness, passing me her phone, on which there were black-and-white photographs. 'Here's my uncle, they called him Kara Mustafa ['Black Mustafa']. As you can see, he's black, like my mother's first cousin, Enver – Tracey's father – that one there.' The baroness has striking green eyes and pale skin but she battles her Afro-prone hair with straighteners, as my mother does. She shows me a photo of her own mother. 'She was the keeper of our stories. I wish I'd asked her more about our family when she was alive.

'When I was preparing my maiden speech in 2010, I knew I was the first woman with a Turkish Cypriot background to enter the House of Lords. So I decided to talk about my background, about Abdullah [her Sudanese great-grandfather] and how my family came to the UK. We do not know much about Abdullah, other than a few family stories, and our physical features tell a story of course. Some of our relatives in Cyprus rang my mum up after I gave the speech, saying, "Why did Meral have to talk about this slave in our family?" But I'm proud of where I am today, and where I've come from. Why hide that?'

The Sudanese media had the opposite reaction to the disgruntled Turkish Cypriot relatives and exhaustively covered the baroness's speech and Abdullah's backstory. 'They loved the detail about Abdullah refusing to convert to Christianity, even though his Christian owner hung him from a tree by his ankles . . . You can imagine their reaction: "What a good Muslim!"' Soon the Sudanese ambassador had introduced himself to the baroness and come to tea in this wood-panelled room. In 2013, the University of Khartoum invited the baroness to a conference and she set off for Sudan on a kind of ancestral pilgrimage.

'We went to Friday prayers at the central mosque in Khartoum soon after we arrived, and the women came and embraced me after the prayers, it was really lovely. I kept looking round and thinking "You look like my uncle – you look like my cousin!" Suddenly our family aesthetic made sense.'

However, there were some dubious pretenders to the Hussein-Ece throne. 'Somehow, people found out where we were staying and we had people turning up at the hotel saying, "Oh, we think we're your cousins!" We weren't convinced, the look just wasn't right. Our hosts, including the Sudanese ambassador to London, took us on a trip up the Nile – they treated us so well, I have to say. I could imagine my great-grandfather playing by the banks of the Nile as a child, with his sister. It was such a moving experience.'

I asked the baroness whether there has historically been much racism against black members of the Turkish Cypriot community. 'Not really – most of my black male relatives married white women.' But perhaps it was worse for black women? 'Perhaps . . . Actually, now I think about it, there were some incidents. Tracey's uncle – my mother's cousin – was not allowed to marry a white girl he fell in love with. It drove him mad and he ended up in a mental asylum.'

We ended our strange, nostalgic tea party, set in the historic headquarters of a former empire also built by slaves, hoping that snobbery about African ancestry is on the wane. 'It's just so stupid, isn't it?' said the baroness. 'We're all mixed up. I did a DNA test and it showed I have twenty per cent African heritage, which makes sense, and thirty-five per cent Italian-Greek, which must be from the Venetian occupation of Cyprus. The rest is Anatolian – in common with most Greek Cypriots, by the way.'

I started this chapter by noting the absence of signs of Ottoman minorities in Turkey. Yet their legacy is present in the blood of Turks themselves, and in the family histories handed down through the generations. I learned from the Afro Turks that it is, in fact, a luxury to be able to trace your family tree, to retain the language and culture of your ancestors – even to know in which country your grandparents were born. When that knowledge is missing, people celebrate what little they do know to create a sense of identity, however vague. In the words of Balthasar Embriaco, 'Every family ought to have a tower named after them somewhere.' When that tower doesn't exist, we create it; once it exists, we can celebrate it.

Scattered Pomegranates

'*Here every man may dwell in peace under his own vine and fig tree.*'

The European Rabbi Yitzhak Sarfati,
Ottoman Edirne, 15th century

'*I am an Armenian of Turkey, and a good Turkish citizen. I believe in the republic, in fact I would like it to become stronger and more democratic.*'

The journalist Hrant Dink,
killed by an ultranationalist in Istanbul, 2007

Diaspora means 'scattered seeds' and it is striking that two of the major diasporas of the Ottoman Empire – the Armenians and the Jews – claim the pomegranate as their national symbol. The pomegranate represents fertility, abundance and prosperity; when applied to a diaspora, it suggests an ability to renew in adversity, far from home. This idea becomes even more powerful when the people in question has survived massacres, deportations and long-term persecution – such as the Armenians and the Jews. Like Persephone trapped in Hades, slowly eating pomegranate seeds from the world above, diasporas sustain themselves with memories of a lost home.

Sometimes a lost home persists more strongly in memory than in reality. Before I met minorities living in an empire-turned-nation state, I had not grasped what it might mean to be the last of an indigenous minority living in a 'homeland' when most of your community have gone. If home is where your people are, what is left for those who stay behind?

An Empire Enriched

In 2011, I lived in a flat in Galata, on a street of shops selling industrial light fixtures. In fact, I lived in a whole maze of light fixtures; in Istanbul, certain districts are traditionally devoted to selling one type of thing, so all the streets surrounding my flat were ablaze with 24/7 incandescence, broken only by the Neve Shalom Synagogue on Büyük Hendek Street. Built in 1951, the synagogue has no elaborate facade, just a calm art deco-style white front with a line of Stars of David etched above the doors. Sometimes, it was fenced off by police, particularly after a diplomatic dispute between the Turkish and Israeli governments or after a proclamation by the Islamic State, in the same way that police appeared outside the Syriac Church in Gümüşsuyu when I went for the Easter service.

The Neve Shalom is one of Turkey's few remaining synagogues in operation, hosting some of the 17,000 mainly Sephardic Jews that remain in the country, 95 per cent of whom live in Istanbul. The Sephardic community (*Sapharad* being Hebrew for Spain) has produced some of the greatest cultural and business icons of 20th-century Turkey, for example Vitali Hakko, who started the famous Vakko fashion company in the wake of Atatürk's 1925 Hat Revolution, which outlawed the fez and made the wearing of rimmed hats obligatory for all Turkish men. Hakko started a small shop called The Merry Hat, selling the Western-style hats which were suddenly, forcibly, in vogue, and today Vakko is one of the most successful companies in Turkey. Hakko's funeral was held in 2007 at the Neve Shalom Synagogue, only four years after it was struck by an al-Qaeda car bomb along with the Bet Israel Synagogue in the nearby district of Şişli.

My friend Dalya is a Turkish Jew in her early thirties, from Istanbul. She is no longer religious, and as a teenager started to distance herself from the socially isolated community she had grown up in. However, the synagogue attacks in 2003 affected her profoundly, as did the atmosphere of anti-Semitism that followed an incident in the same year, when Israeli forces attacked the Mavi Marmara, a Turkish aid flotilla attempting to reach Gaza, causing a diplomatic rift that has never quite healed.

'The Jewish community in Turkey get scared more easily these days. After the Mavi Marmara, we were basically being held responsible for whatever tactic Israel decided to take. Once I saw a swastika painted on a wall, around the time of the bombs. My parents had always told me that we were hated in our own country, and for me, that was a realization that they were right. I thought: "Yes, we are second-class citizens." It broke my heart. I had always said really proudly, "I am Turkish," but after that episode, I did not feel that way.'

At the time of the 2003 attack, the Jewish community in Turkey numbered around 30,000; in 1914, on the eve of the First World War, the number had been 200,000, partly bolstered by the influx of Sephardic Jews from Thessaloniki who moved to Istanbul as nationalist tensions rose in the Balkans at the turn of the 20th century. The community is disappearing at an exponential rate. Part of that is down to Turkey's decreasing prospects as an open and prosperous society, leading to a general exodus among middle-class Turks. However, there has been a revival of anti-Semitism in recent years that cannot be unconnected to a president who describes protesters as 'spawn of Israel' and tells his supporters that the anti-government Gezi Park protests were organized by the 'interest rate lobby', a mysterious group identified by his deputy prime minister as 'the Jewish diaspora'.

For hundreds of years, churches and synagogues were a natural part of the architectural and social landscape in Turkey, not targets for Islamist zealots, and their congregations did not have to hide their identity. Ottoman sultans were more accommodating of Jews than the previous Byzantine emperors. In the 19th century, the emergence of Arab nationalism began to create divisions between Muslims and Jews in the south-eastern reaches of the empire; at the same time, the empire also absorbed thousands of Jews fleeing pogroms in Russia.

When Osman I captured Bursa in 1326, making it the first Ottoman capital, the indigenous Greek-speaking Romaniote Jews were already living throughout what would become the Ottoman heartland: in Istanbul, Smyrna, Edirne, Asia Minor and Thrace. In the 14th and 15th centuries the Romaniots were joined by Ashkenazi Jews from Ukraine, who were so pleasantly surprised by life under the caliph that they invited others to join them from Europe. The major influx, however, came in 1492, when Sultan Bayezid II sent his navy to rescue the Muslims and Jews fleeing Spain during the Inquisition of Ferdinand II of Aragon. He insisted that the Jewish refugees should be welcomed throughout his lands, and was scathing of his critics: 'You venture to call Ferdinand a wise ruler – he who has impoverished his own country and enriched mine!'

This idea of enrichment is an important one; Ottoman rulers welcomed Jews and Christians not for humanitarian reasons but because they knew these subjects could make important contributions to the economic life of the empire. Jews were sometimes preferred over Christian subjects for certain positions of trust when the Ottoman authorities suspected that the latter might sympathize with the enemies of the empire, particularly in the 15th and 16th centuries as the empire expanded west into Christian lands. Some sultans were more pro-Jewish than others, but the trailblazing Bayezid II was proved right: within a year of arriving in 1492, two of his new Jewish subjects, David and Samuel ibn Nahmias, had established the first printing press of the Ottoman Empire and had started printing books in Hebrew (Bayezid II forbade the publishing of Arabic script on religious grounds), a crucial step in the intellectual enrichment of the empire. More than 500 years later, a parallel situation occurred in Atatürk's republic: in September 1933, Albert Einstein wrote to Ismet İnönü, Turkey's then prime minister, asking him to take in forty Jewish intellectuals who were being persecuted in Nazi Germany. Inönü agreed, inviting them to come and set up courses at Turkey's newly founded Western-style universities – it would be a symbiotic exchange, not an act of pure altruism.

Suleiman the Magnificent built on the legacy of his predecessor Bayezid II in trying to minimize anti-Semitism. In around 1554, he took the advice of his Jewish doctor, Moses Hamon, and formally denounced blood libels (accusations made by Christian subjects, particularly in Europe, that Jews kidnapped and murdered Christian children to use their blood at religious holidays). Moses Hamon also introduced Suleiman to Joseph Nasi (later known as 'the Great Jew'), whose family had been forced to convert to Christianity in Europe but had then escaped to Istanbul. He became hugely rich through Suleiman's support, and ended up settling Italian Jews in Galilee, where Suleiman granted him some properties.[22]

Jews fared much better throughout the empire than in Europe; in 1716, Lady Mary Wortley Montagu wrote a letter to a friend back in England from the town of Adrianople in Thrace, in which she expressed her surprise at their prominence in public life.

'I observed most of the rich tradesmen were Jews. That people are in incredible power in this country. They have many privileges above all the natural Turks themselves, and have formed a very considerable commonwealth here, being judged by their own laws. They have drawn the whole trade of the empire into their hands, partly by the firm union amongst themselves, and partly by the idle temper and want of industry in the Turks.

'Every bassa [pasha – lord and commander] has his Jew, who is his homme d'affaires; he is let into all his secrets, and does all his business. No bargain is made, no bribe received, no merchandise disposed of, but what passes through their hands. They are the physicians, the stewards, and the interpreters of all the great men. You may judge how advantageous this is to a people who never fail to make use of the smallest advantages. They have found the secret of making themselves so necessary, that they are certain of the protection of the court, whatever ministry is in power. Even the English, French, and Italian merchants, who are sensible of their artifices, are, however, forced to trust their affairs to their negotiation, nothing of trade being managed without them, and the meanest amongst them being too important to be disobliged, since the whole body take care of his interests, with as much vigour as they would those of the most considerable of their members. They are many of them vastly rich, but take care to make little public shew of it, though they live in their houses in the utmost luxury and magnificence.'[23]

Montagu, while broad-minded for her time, betrays the anti-Semitism of an early 18th-century English perspective: 'Even the English, French, and Italian merchants, who are sensible of their artifices, are, however, forced to trust their affairs to their negotiation'. Her attitude explains the letters of Rabbi Yitzhak Sarfati to the congregation he left behind in Germany in the first half of the 15th century, encouraging them to join him in Edirne, the capital of the empire at the time: 'Is it not better for you to live under Muslims than under Christians? Here every man may dwell in peace under his own vine and fig tree. Here you are allowed to wear the most precious garments. In Christendom, on the contrary, you dare not even venture to clothe your children in red or in blue, according to our taste, without exposing them to the insult of being beaten black and blue . . .'[24]

While Jews were allowed greater freedoms in the empire than in Europe, and could achieve much greater prosperity, they were still treated with a certain amount of distrust in some quarters. Ottoman Muslims like Evliya Çelebi, for example, were deeply suspicious of the Jewish practice of keeping Kosher and refusing to buy meat from Muslims. Writing about half a century before Lady Mary Montagu, Evliya declared in his travelogue *Seyahatname* that: 'The Jews never accept food and drink from other people. Indeed, they do not mingle with others – if they join your company, it is an artificial companionship. All their deeds are calculated to treachery and the killing of Muslims, especially anyone named Muhammad. Even wine they refuse to buy from other people.'[25]

His anti-Semitism suggests a kind of circle of mutual distrust between Muslims and Jews: the latter were distrusted and disliked because they kept to themselves, which bred a self-protective instinct to isolate themselves even more, which bred distrust, and so on. This was not universal, but it was not unusual, and is still evident today.

Thessaloniki

Greece, with its Romaniot history, has an especially rich Jewish legacy. The great Jewish centre of the Ottoman Empire for hundreds of years was Salonika, modern-day Thessaloniki, the second city of Greece. In March 2017, I drove there from Athens with my friend Mark, who was in the midst of writing his PhD thesis on the Greek historian Thucydides and welcomed the distraction. The five-hour journey was peppered with much excitement as we passed classical sites on our way: Aulis, Thermopylae and Mount Olympos, which almost caused an accident as Mark swerved at 85 km/h while taking in its majesty. It felt like we were rewinding the millennia as we approached Thessaloniki, a city which hosted a Jewish majority until 1912, when it was surrendered to Greek forces, who had outbid the Bulgarian nationalists for possession. Thessaloniki was one of the most prosperous harbours of the empire, in fact much more of a cosmopolitan trading centre than dusty old Athens. It was dominated by Jewish trade, commerce and real estate; when the Greeks entered the city, they found the lingua franca was Ladino (Sephardic Spanish), and in 1911, just before the Greek takeover, the Zionist David Ben-Gurion visited Salonika to study it as a model for the future state of Israel.

Today, it is – at first glance – a thoroughly modern city. Its history does not slap you in the face, as it does in Istanbul or Athens, and that is because in 1917 the old city was consumed in a nine-day fire, making a quarter of the population homeless, destroying mosques and synagogues and condemning the city to an uninspiring 20th-century architectural transformation, as was the case in Izmir.

The few relics that have survived, however, speak of a spectacularly diverse past – the Hagia Sophia Church is once again in full working order, less monumental than its namesake in Istanbul but painstakingly restored with the most dazzling gold-painted icons I have ever squinted at. The brick domes of the 16th-century, Ottoman-built 'Yahudi Hamam' (Jewish Bath), by contrast, are the only visible part of an edifice left to crumble – I peered through the dusty glass into rubble, the restoration clearly abandoned by a government with more pressing things on the agenda than 500-year-old minority bathing houses.

I found the Jewish community centre with difficulty; it is on the second floor of an anonymous, marble-floored office building near the *hamam*. Handing my ID to a guard, I was led in to a well-lit hive of quiet activity; I later found out that twenty people worked there, a fiftieth of the entire current Jewish population of Thessaloniki. The centre is a testament to how seriously the community take the archival management of its history, which is a troubled one; during the Nazi occupation of Thessaloniki during the 1940s, 54,000 Jews – 96 per cent of the city's entire Jewish community – were rounded up and taken to concentration camps in Germany and Poland, 45,000 of them to Auschwitz. There are only three synagogues left (thirty-two were destroyed in the fire of 1917) in the city; the main one, the Monastirioton Synagogue, was closed and guarded by police when I went to see it, much like the Neve Shalom in Istanbul. Inaugurated in 1927, it survived the Nazi occupation only because it was used as a warehouse by the Red Cross.

The woman who answered my questions in the community centre and did not want to be named was polite but cagey at first, glancing at my scruffy notebook before deciding I could be trusted. I asked her about the guards in front of Monastirioton Synagogue.

'They've always been there. We are very well integrated here but we do encounter anti-Semitism sometimes. There have been incidents in the past few years – for example, the Elie Wiesel Holocaust memorial in Athens was desecrated in 2014 by ultra-nationalist groups.' (This was followed by a second act of vandalism on the same memorial in December 2017.)

Two thousand Jews returned to Thessaloniki after the end of the Second World War, some of them survivors of the concentration camps, others returning from hiding places in the mountains. My interviewee had a dramatic but representative family story from the occupation: her grandmother met her husband-to-be in 1939 before they were separated by the war. She was sent to Bergen-Belsen concentration camp in Germany, while he joined the local resistance in Thessaloniki – 'that's how he survived the war'. On her return, they married. Many of those who survived the camps set out for South America rather than return to Greece, and many had already left before the occupation – for example Jack Sassoon, the father of world-famous hairdresser Vidal Sassoon, who relocated to Shepherd's Bush in West London along with several members of his community. My interviewee told me with regret that the centre had recently stopped organising Ladino lessons, although 'we try to keep the language alive'.

While their language ebbs in the 21st century, the suffering of Thessaloniki's Jews is finally being acknowledged after a long period of the previous century in which they were noticeably absent from Greek history books. In November 2017, the Yad Vashem Holocaust memorial centre in Jerusalem held a ceremony to thank a 106-year-old woman from Thessaloniki and her late husband for saving five members of a Jewish family from the Nazis by hiding them in their house. The mayor of Thessaloniki, Yiannis Boutaris, wore a Star of David during his re-election ceremony in 2014 in protest at the far-right Golden Dawn party's presence on the local council, and called the deportation of the Jews the city's 'darkest moment in history'.[26]

I reflected as I left Thessaloniki that there are subtler moments of darkness in the city's history that may never be acknowledged. How does one commemorate the confusion and heartbreak of the incoming refugees from Asia Minor in 1923 – the 'squirming, writhing mass of human misery' described by an American diplomat who watched 7,000 Greek Orthodox subjects of the former Ottoman Empire dock at Salonika port – or the suddenly pariah-like status of the ethnic Turks who stayed behind in Western Thrace? Today, Thessaloniki hosts a great number of refugees from the Middle East, the lucky ones who made it via Turkey to the Greek islands and to the mainland. Thessaloniki has always been a city of refugees, some more welcome than others.

Hidden Synagogues

Like Greece, Spain and Portugal are also trying to right previous wrongs – in their case, from half a millenium ago. In 2015, the two governments introduced a law to allow anyone in the world who could prove their Sephardic ancestry to be granted citizenship; it was a move designed to atone for the 'historic mistake' of 1492, when all the native Jews were expelled from the region by Ferdinand II of Aragon. Between 2012 and 2017, more than 4,500 Turkish Jews applied to take advantage of the offer. My friend Dalya is in the process of doing so, as is another Turkish friend, the photographer Yusuf Sayman, who didn't even know he had any connection to Judaism until he turned eighteen and was informed by a cousin that he belonged to a kabbalist sect.

I found out about Yusuf's mysterious roots when he casually mentioned that the mosque in the upmarket Istanbul neighbourhood of Teşvikye has a nickname: *gavur cami* or 'infidel mosque'. What does an infidel mosque even mean? I asked him.

'Have you ever noticed that no one cares if the women go in with their heads uncovered, and that women can also join in the funeral processions of the men?' Yusuf answered.

I had, but I had assumed it was because Teşvikye is a very secular, wealthy neighbourhood where no one bothered about these things.

'No' said Yusuf. 'It's because they're not really Muslim. They are dönme, and I know this because – surprise! – I am one too.'

The dönme are crypto-Jews who worshipped for hundreds of years in the empire, and later in Turkey, under the guise of Islam. Although they call themselves *Ma'aminim* ('believers' in Hebrew, *Mümin* in Turkish), they are known as 'dönme', which has a pejorative undertone – 'converted' or 'turncoat'. Their story was one of incredible subterfuge and persistence, and its hero was Sabbatai Sevi, a thirty-nine-year-old Jew from Smyrna who declared himself the Messiah and caused upheaval throughout the empire in the years preceding 1666 – what many believed would be 'The Year of the Beast', a kind of Satanic Judgement Day.

Sabbatai Sevi, who was worshipped across the empire from the distant Balkan towns of the west to Aleppo in the south-east, possessed all the peculiarities one would hope for in a self-proclaimed Messiah – a loud and persistent singing voice, bright red hair and amazingly progressive, if ambitious, ideas. He promised to cure women of 'the curse of Eve', advocated free love for both sexes and encouraged blasphemy. In the words of Simon Sebag Montefiore,

Sabbatai Sevi was 'clearly a manic depressive who swung between bouts of infectious self-belief, desperate melancholia and euphoric exaltation that led him to perform demonic, sometimes shamelessly erotic antics.'[27]

News of these antics – erotic or otherwise – reached Sultan Mehmet IV, who felt compelled first to imprison Sabbatai Sevi for a few months and then to order his execution: a figure declaring himself the Messiah was a gross contravention of the laws by which the caliph allowed other religions to exist under his rule. However, it was not to be. Sabbatai Sevi saved himself by ostentatiously converting to Islam on the advice of a sympathetic Ladino–Ottoman Turkish translator in the sultan's court, and promptly set sail for Salonika. Most of his flock abandoned him, disgusted by his conversion, but around 300 families followed him to the city, where he vacillated between preaching his newly proclaimed religion of Islam, and a kind of covert, Sufi-infused Judaism. Some of his followers did genuinely convert to Islam; others did not. Before he was banished to a remote Albanian port in 1672, where he soon died, he often travelled to Istanbul, where he advised the Grand Vizier on Judaism while receiving Islamic instruction in return.

What is interesting is the question of how Sabbatai Sevi got away with it, when it would have been easy for the sultan to go ahead with the execution and teach a lesson to other cult leaders. However, such was Sabbatai Sevi's influence that it is possible the sultan judged it best to avoid a potential insurrection, while taking care to publish the official story that a repentant sinner had converted to Islam. Either way, his legacy prevailed. At the turn of the century, the dönme community in Thessaloniki numbered about 15,000. In the 1923 population exchange between Greece and the new Republic of Turkey, they were counted as Muslims, rounded up and sent to Turkey, 400 years after the ancestors came over from Smyrna. There, in a Republic which, although officially secular, was far less accommodating of non-Sunni minorities, the dönme were regarded with suspicion and today, they are still targeted by a vague anti-Semitism, as well as something subtler: the disdain felt for people who have betrayed an ancestral faith in order to save themselves.

In Turkey, members of the dönme community typically do not find out their identity until they turn eighteen, as my friend Yusuf explained to me.

'Eighteen is traditionally the time when you're about to get married, so you're told to make sure you don't marry an outsider. But it has to be late because the whole thing is so secretive, you can't tell children because they might tell someone.'

Yusuf is unmarried, and actually found out by accident.

'It was weird, Alev. My parents were the least religious people in the world, both of them Marxists actually. I learned the word "Allah" at school, I had never heard it before. Then when I was eighteen this distant cousin from my mother's side of the family appeared, he must have been in his early thirties – he was crazily into this dönme thing. He started inviting me to Shabbat dinners. I had a year of Shabbat dinners, just him and me in his basement. He was on a mission to convert me – and he did, for a while.'

Yusuf proceeded to describe his 'dönme stage' like someone looking back with amusement at an adolescent punk or pothead stage.

'For the next couple of years, I was really into being dönme, it sounded super cool to be Jewish. I used to wear the Star of David on a necklace under my shirt, I even went on an exchange programme to Israel and desperately wanted to go to college in Tel Aviv. The funny thing was, all that time I had a photo of Yasser Arafat hanging in my bedroom. That crazy cousin went and lived in a kibbutz in Israel for three years, and he tried to get the rabbis to recognize the dönme but it didn't work. Then the other dönme got angry at him, and they made sure he couldn't work in Istanbul. Why? Because they want to stay secretive, not declared like the other Jews. And the Jews don't like the dönme because they are not 'proper' Jews.'

I asked him what his parents made of his rebellious dönme stage.

'My father didn't care. My mother really liked this cousin but she was very unhappy I was going to these Shabbat dinners. I think if he hadn't turned up she would never have told me. She wanted to be the last person to know about our dönme history, she wanted that knowledge to die with her. It wasn't an anti-Semitic thing, she wasn't ashamed – it was a Marxist thing. She was an atheist and I think she would have been annoyed if I turned out a practising Muslim, or a practising anything, actually.'

Then Yusuf stopped, half-remembering something.

'But I realized later that – unconsciously, I think – she would tell me stories about Jews when I was a child. For example, she told me that three people made the 20th century: Marx, Einstein and Freud. She was kind of telling me the Jewish story of history. She was mainly friends with non-Muslims too, I guess they had something in common – her best friend, she was properly Jewish, and her other best friend was Armenian.'

I asked Yusuf whether he felt any different when he found out about his family identity.

'I always felt different, when I was growing up. I thought maybe that was because my parents were leftists – there is a sense you're not the same as others. No one ever told me I was Muslim, it was obvious I was not Muslim. I remember having friends similar to me, but there was always some kind of connection to Islam in their families, some aunt who would go to the mosque, that we didn't have. Maybe I'm wrong, I am reconstructing memories right now – but all I know is I knew I was different as a child. When I learned that I was dönme, it made total sense.'

Ultimately, Yusuf is mainly interested in his dönme heritage for pragmatic reasons.

'You know Sephardic Jews are getting Spanish and Portuguese citizenship? I'm working on it, too, but it's a real pain in the ass – I am applying for Portuguese because the Portuguese government don't make you do a language test. It's harder for dönme to prove they're Jewish, although apparently, the Turkish government know exactly who the dönme are because in 1942 they put everyone's religious status on record for the *Varlık Vergisi*.'

The Varlık Vergisi was a property tax imposed in 1942 by the Turkish Republic after Atatürk's death on the country's non-Muslim minorities on the pretext of raising funds for a potential entry into the Second World War. In reality, it was nothing more than an ill-disguised method of transferring businesses and capital to the hands of the Muslim community, a grossly exaggerated version of the taxes imposed by the Ottoman sultans. Armenian Christians were the hardest hit, with assessments that often amounted to many times their net worth, followed by the Jews and Greek Christians who were treated only slightly more leniently (Muslims paid a comparitively negligible amount). Some of those who could not pay within the stipulated fifteen days committed suicide; others were sent to labour camps in eastern Anatolia, or fled the country, leaving most of their belongings behind (resulting in a great surplus of antiques in Istanbul, where most minorities lived). The result of the tax was that, as Yusuf pointed out, there was a record of the country's non-Muslim communities, soon much reduced. Even before the government introduced online access to the state archives, Yusuf had visited the *nüfus idaresi* [civil registry office] to access his.

'One of the ways you can prove that you qualify for Portuguese citizenship is that there are known Jewish or dönme institutions – for example, in Nişantaşı in Istanbul there is the Işık Lisesi [a high school founded in 1885 on the secular curriculum established by Atatürk's old dönme headmaster, Şemsi Efendi]. This is a known dönme establishment and my mum's dad was their lawyer, so that is proof. Also, certain parts of certain cemeteries are reserved for dönme, everyone knows that. And the Portuguese government accepts that.'

When I ask Yusuf why he is putting himself through all this paperwork, his answer is typically deadpan:

'It wouldn't hurt to have an EU passport.'

Another Turkish Jewish friend of mine, Sami, is in his sixties and received his Spanish citizenship in 2015, before the language test requirement was introduced. Over seventies are exempt, but Sami says he has plenty of friends struggling to pass. 'My friends are in their sixties, trying to learn Spanish, can you imagine?' Unusually, Sami comes from a mixed Jewish family – his father was an Ashkenazi

whose parents had come to Istanbul fleeing a pogrom in Ukraine in the late 1890s. His mother's Sephardic parents came from Salonika at the turn of the 20th century, along with thousands of other Sephardic Jews who left as nationalist tensions rose.

The Sephardic identity of Sami's mother is what got him his citizenship, when he submitted birth certificates provided by the Jewish Community of Istanbul. Sami had a secular upbringing but for his Ashkenazi father, 'one thing was a must: a bar mitzvah'. This required learning Hebrew for a year in preparation at the famous Ashkenazi synagogue in Yüksek Kaldırım in Galata, directly opposite a brothel. 'I used to look out the window of my Hebrew classroom and see the queues of men waiting outside . . .'

This brothel was one of many belonging to Madame Manukyan, an Armenian businesswoman who made so much money from her vast empire of real estate and government-registered brothels throughout the latter half of the 20th century that she was the top taxpayer in Turkey for several years in the 1990s, receiving an award for her services to the economy. With its synagogue and Armenian-owned brothel, Yüksek Kaldırım is a perfect example of the typically *'gayrimüslim'* or 'non-Muslim' areas of Karaköy and Galata, where Lady Mary Montagu observed the dizzying array of different Ottoman subjects in the 18th century.

Sami ended up marrying a Muslim. 'Our parents acted in an incredibly civilized way, and it was quite emotional. Of course, they would have preferred that we both married our own religion, but they did not interfere, and from the very beginning I was a much-loved son to her parents and Leyla was the most-loved daughter to mine.'

My friend Dalya had a much more isolated and religious upbringing than Sami, and has gradually grown to reject her Jewish community – but she is still taking advantage of the Spanish government's offer of applying for citizenship. Having grown up in a Ladino-speaking family, she found it easy to learn Spanish, and does not fear the language test.

'I think Ladino [Sephardic Spanish] died with our generation. It used to be the case that all generations lived together in one house, so you would have to speak Ladino to your parents as well as your grandparents; women in particular spoke it because they spent most of their time in the house. My father's grandmother never really spoke proper Turkish, and she was alive until 1984.

'But my parents' generation started living apart from their parents . . . We were not taught Ladino exactly but I've always had that Spanish sound ringing behind my ears. It was very easy for me to learn Spanish.'

Ladino is still clinging on in Turkey, but in a token way – Şalom, a weekly magazine published for the Jewish community of Turkey, still has one page written in Ladino. Like my friend Ziya, who had memorized the story of his grandmother's escape from Macedonia in 1912, Dalya relates the story of the hardships suffered by her grandparents with a fluency that suggests she has heard it many times:

'My anneanne [mother's mother] lived in Kuzguncuk [a famously diverse suburb on Istanbul's Asian coast]. It was 6 September 1955 when the Muslims decided to attack non-Muslim minorities [these were the infamous riots that caused tens of thousands of Greek Christians to leave Istanbul]. My grandmother told us that our family stockpiled food in their house, and huge barrels of oil on the

top floor. My grandfather came home and locked the women in a room. They started boiling the oil so they could pour it on anyone trying to get into the house. We were always told these stories as children . . . When I was young, I used to ask my parents: "Why do we stay here if we hate it so much?" They had no answer, but I guess we've all been born here, this is life as we know it. Also, people love complaining. They are happier living here and complaining, than having the courage to move.'

Dalya is acutely aware of what she perceives as the double-standards of her community, which have sprung up from deep-rooted insecurities.

'The Jewish word for a Muslim Turk is *vedre* which means "green" in Ladino. It has a very negative connotation. We were always told: "We Jews are not welcome here, we are second-class citizens, no one will help us, they're out to get us" but at the same time we were told "We are the chosen people" – it was very existentially confusing. We were all told the ideal was to move to Israel. In recent years, many Jews have moved out of Turkey, some have been scared about bringing up children under Erdoğan, others left for financial reasons. A few years ago, me and my sister applied for Spanish _citizenship but didn't get it [the decision to grant requests pre-2015 was discretionary, and candidates had to give up their existing citizenship] but since 2015 it is easier. My sister just did it, it's simple to prove. There is no marriage outside the Jewish community – if you're in, you're in, theoretically at least. The system is Orthodox, even though Jews in Turkey are not really Orthodox – so you just get the paperwork from the synagogue.'

I ask Dalya if her non-Jewish friends envy her.

'Oh yeah. I think anyone in Turkey would get another citizenship if they could. My Muslim friends were always telling me, "You're lucky because you can go to Israel," and now we have Spain too. On my *kimlik* [ID card, on which a Turkish citizen's religion is noted – 99 per cent of the time it says 'Muslim'] it says *musevi* not *yahudi*. There is an entire debate surrounding this. *Musevi* was a term created by Atatürk to denote Jewish Turks, that's how the story goes. Some Muslim people seem to think *yahudi* is rude, a bit like "Jew" can sound rude in English, I suppose. But Jews prefer it to *musevi*, I don't know why.'

I wonder if this is because Turkish Jews consider their Jewish identity as primary, not to be mitigated by having a nationalist stamp applied to it, as *musevi* does. Dalya confirms this.

'When I was a child, I had the extra identity of being Jewish that was much higher than being Turkish. I was a Jew who happened to live in Turkey. I've never heard any of my family members refer to themselves as Turkish. They say, "We live in Turkey," or "We are from Turkey."'

Dalya's observation made me think of Turkey-born Kurds who do not refer to themselves as Turkish, and certainly not as 'Turks'. In March 2013, a statue of Atatürk in the Kurdish-majority town of Batman was defaced in the night; the inscription on the base of the statue – '*Ne mutlu Türküm diyene*' ['How happy is the one who calls himself a Turk'] – was changed to '*Yurtta sulh cihanda sulh*' ['Peace at home, peace in the world']. The former phrase is more or less the national motto of Turkey, the second another famous quote from Atatürk. The presumably Kurdish vandal was making an important point about imposing on a varied people a national identity which assumes a racial identity: not everyone living in Turkey identifies as a Turk, unacceptable though that sounds to many ears.

'I became more conscious of being Turkish after I left Turkey,' Dalya continued. 'During the last few years of high school I had basically cut all ties with my Jewish community. In college in America, I had international friends but I became part of the Turkish community, half of us were Muslims, half were Jews. We got into the *gurbet* (diaspora) state of mind. That's when I felt really Turkish – I was nostalgic and homesick. We would listen to Ibrahim Tatlıses a lot [a hugely popular but somewhat passé Arabesque pop singer] – stuff we would never do here.'

I asked Dalya whether she thought her generation was less Jewish than that of her parents.

'I think the way we live is different. I often wondered as a teenager: why do I have Muslim friends and my mother doesn't? I think one factor is that our parents are a lot more relaxed than our grandparents, that had an influence on us. My parents were born in the late fifties, just after the riots in 1955. When they were growing up, things were much fresher in everyone's memory. But my generation, most Jewish families are well off, in good schools, and we feel less isolated, although recently the anti-Semitism has been scary.'

Dalya's story is double-sided. While the Jewish community she describes is undoubtedly self-protective and even exclusionary, one can see why. Jews suffer the same problem as Christians in Turkey – by identifying publicly as Jews, they face the generally unspoken but ever-present accusation: 'Why do you describe yourself as a Jew, rather than as a Turk?' There is no room for a dual identity; at least, that is how Dalya feels.

Talking to Dalya reinforced my belief that in the 21st century, in a nominally secular republic, the Jewish community is less integrated than it was in Ottoman times, when Jews were prominent subjects of an Islamic empire. On some level, they have become more secretive, more closed off, and this change in circumstances made me wonder about their relationship to the country they call home. Can a diaspora have a stronger sense of community than an indigenous people? The Jews of Antakya feel 'strongly' Jewish, but they don't feel secure in a town which is overrun by religious tensions, and no longer naturally heterogeneous in the way it once was. Their home can be an uncomfortable place to be, but it is still their home. The same is true of Armenians, for even more compelling, recent reasons.

1915

In Turkey, the weight of what is euphemistically called 'the events of 1915' by Turkish historians and politicians, and 'the Armenian genocide' by most of the world, lies heavily on the descendants of those who lived through it – or didn't. Some Turkish citizens are oblivious of their connection to the genocide; the orphaned or abandoned babies of victims of the massacres were often left with Muslim families who brought them up as their own, with Turkish names. The number of Armenians living in Turkey today is a matter of speculation, with estimates ranging from 20,000 to 60,000. These figures do not include those who will never know of their Armenian roots.

Mount Ararat in the extreme east of Turkey appears in posters on restaurant walls and in churches across the global Armenian diaspora. It is visible in the distance from Yerevan, the capital of the modern state of Armenia: snow-peaked and imposing, it is an ever-present reminder of a lost homeland just out of reach. While modern Armenia represents 'Eastern Armenia', the true heartland of Armenians across the world is still 'Western Armenia': the eastern region of modern Turkey. This area includes towns like Van, Diyarbakır, Kars, Bitlis and Erzurum, where Armenians and Kurds lived together for centuries. During the wars fought between Russia and the Ottoman Empire in the eastern reaches of the empire in 1828 and 1878, local Armenian militias joined the Russian side, which Sultan Abdul Hamid II interpreted as an attempt to establish an Armenian state, perhaps because a similar pattern was playing out west, in the Balkan territories.

In response, Abdul Hamid II encouraged local Kurdish warlords to attack their Armenian neighbours, and in 1915, it was Kurds who committed many of the massacres of Armenians, and who took over the homes they left behind when Ottoman soldiers forced them out of Anatolia on the infamous death marches. Today, Kurdish involvement in the massacres is slowly being recognized in the region, and while 'the G-word' is taboo among most politicians in Turkey, one of the few to have used it and encouraged a national recognition of the genocide is the Kurdish co-leader of the Peoples' Democratic Party (HDP), Selahattin Demirtaş, currently in jail on charges of terrorism (the HDP is accused of supporting the Kurdish PKK group engaged in a forty-year conflict with the Turkish army in the south-east of the country). In a twisted replaying of history, Kurds are now being forced out of their homes in former Armenian towns by the current Turkish government as its conflict with the PKK reignites again.

In 1914 there were, depending on whom you prefer to believe, between 1.3 million and 1.9 million Armenians in the Ottoman Empire, the first figure being the result of the official government census, and the latter one supplied by the Armenian patriarchate on the basis of various calculations. Both figures represented a much-depleted population after the massacres and attendant exodus during the last decades of the empire.

In the widespread panic of the First World War, a general belief among Muslims in the empire that the Orthodox Armenians were supporting the Russian side in a bid to establish an Armenian state within the empire (as indeed some were) tempered sympathy for the roughly 1.5 million Armenian civilians who were murdered or driven from their homes in 1915 (the Turkish government claims a much lower figure – around 800,000 – and denies that the killings were systematically ordered). However, some did try to protect their neighbours, and there were also a few high-profile voices raised in protest. One of them was Halide Edip, a feminist writer and administrator who spoke out against the bloodshed, warning that it would 'hurt those who indulge in it more than it hurt their victims'. (Later, she changed her tune – 'I did not know about the Armenian crimes, and I had not realized that in similar cases others could be a hundred times worse than the Turks' – and oversaw the enforced Turkification of Armenian orphans in special schools in Greater Syria). Another of the voices raised in protest belonged to Ali Kemal Bey, the great-grandfather of the British Tory politician Boris Johnson, whose career makes Johnson's look conservative with a small c, although there are intriguing parallels between the two men in the fields of both journalism and politics.

As a hearty supporter of the empire, Ali Kemal Bey worked as a spy for the sultan, as a deeply unpopular Interior Minister in the cabinet controlled by British occupying forces in 1919, as a manager of a bankrupt Egyptian farm, and as an outspoken columnist, editor and poet. He lived in exile in Europe and Egypt for much of his adult life, dodging arrest and assassination attempts on his sporadic return visits to Istanbul. At the age of fifty-four, he had accrued an English wife, a Turkish wife, three children, huge gambling debts, several prison spells and a dubious legacy of unfashionable political diatribes. He was reckless to a fault, but also incredibly brave.

In 1919, during his three-month stint as Interior Minister under the British occupation, Ali Kemal Bey issued a circular ordering officials to ignore the demands of Atatürk and his men. Previous to that, in 1915 he had repeatedly condemned in print the Armenian genocide, a position that earned him the displeasure of the public more generally. By the time he was snatched from a barber's shop by Atatürk's agents in Istanbul in 1922, he was a known and hated man, marked for death.

His support for the Armenians also played a gruesome part in how he was killed. Atatürk's men bundled him into a taxi, then on to a motorboat to Izmit, a town on the Asian coast south-east of Istanbul. There, after a rough and ready interrogation during which he was accused of being an infidel traitor, his unhinged captor, the general Nurettin Pasha, decided to take justice into his own hands rather than sending his prisoner on to stand trial in Ankara, the capital of the nationalist government. Having instructed an aide to gather a crowd of several hundred people and whip them into a state of frenzy, the mad *pasha* forced Ali Kemal out into the street. Within minutes the condemned man had been stabbed and his head bashed in with rocks, while enterprising members of the crowd made off with his gold watch and well-tailored trousers. His bloodied corpse was hung up by Izmit's railway bridge, with a sign hanging round its neck reading 'Artin Kemal' – an Armenian name mocking his sympathy for the victims of the 1915 genocide, and intended as a final insult to his memory.

Today, the Armenian diaspora numbers around 5 million and stretches east and west from Turkey; many live throughout France and Lebanon, while smaller numbers have settled in pockets of the UK like Ealing and South Kensington in London, and in Manchester. A community of Armenian Catholic monks have lived a life of seclusion since 1717 on the island of St Lazarus off the coast of Venice, formerly a leper colony. The original monks fled to Venice from Morea (the Peloponnesian Peninsula) along with many other refugees after it fell to the Ottomans in the Seventh Ottoman–Venetian war in 1714 (an event that Lady Mary Montagu mentions in one of her letters: 'Many thousands [of slaves] were taken in the Morea; but they have been, most of them, redeemed by the charitable contributions of the Christians, or ransomed by their own relations at Venice'[28]). Today, there are only a handful of monks left in the St Lazarus monastery, but they guard one of the most significant collections of Armenian manuscripts in the world; 200 years ago, their predecessors taught Lord Byron when he arrived for a crash course in Armenian in 1816.

The largest portion of the diaspora, however, at around 1.5 million, settled in America, most of them in California, which was rumoured to resemble the fertile landscape of western Armenia (modern-day eastern Turkey). William Saroyan was born here, an Armenian-American novelist whose Presbyterian minister father Armenak escaped the increasingly anti-Armenian atmosphere of eastern Anatolia for New York in 1905 and subsequently found himself a parish in California. However, according to William Saroyan's biographer Nona Balakian, Armenak's hopes of settling down in the parish were dashed when 'he discovered that he could not communicate with the Turkish-speaking Armenians there',[29] suggesting a significant difference in Armenak's eastern dialect, and perhaps a complete failure of Turkish as a lingua franca. The idea of Armenak Saroyan trying and failing to preach to an adopted flock composed of fellow Armenians in his native tongue is a tragic one; even more tragically, he died at thirty-seven of a ruptured appendix, something that haunted his son throughout his life.

William Saroyan wrote extensively about the experience of being first-generation Armenian-American, and of the defiance of the diaspora itself, as in this passage from *Inhale and Exhale,* a collection of short stories published in 1936[30]:

Go ahead, destroy this race. Let us say that it is again 1915. There is war in the world. Destroy Armenia. See if you can do it. Send them from their homes into the desert. Let them have neither bread nor water. Burn their houses and their churches. See if they will not live again. See if they will not laugh again. See if the race will not live again when two of them meet in a beer parlor, twenty years later, and laugh, and speak in their tongue. Go ahead, see if you can do anything about it. See if you can stop them from mocking the big ideas of the world, you sons of bitches, a couple of Armenians talking in the world, go ahead and try to destroy them.

Saroyan considers the Armenian legacy to be the continuation of its culture; he voices the tenacity of a scattered community that teaches its children Armenian a hundred years after their flight from the Ottoman Empire. Even those who do not speak the language are ideologically committed to the idea of their lost homeland and the injustice of those who fail to recognize the genocide.

One of the most famous of the latter group is Kim Kardashian, whose great-grandparents were among many who fled from the Ottoman Empire to California in the early 20th century. She flew with her husband Kanye West to Yerevan for the first time in April 2015, to meet the Armenian prime minister Hovik Abrahamyan a couple of weeks before the centenary of the genocide. As I was later to discover, the visit was greeted with a mixture of pride and bemusement by Yerevan residents, particularly when Kanye unexpectedly threw himself into a lake while giving a concert near the buildings of parliament.

In the wider diaspora, Armenians have generally been able to cherish their heritage without having to reconcile themselves to living under a government that fundamentally rejects their version of history, as Armenians have to do in Turkey. Around the time of the centenary in 2015, the issue of the Turkish government's continued denial of the genocide reached fever pitch. In May, shortly after the commemorations had taken place amid fierce spats between the Turkish and Armenian governments, I headed to Yerevan. I wanted to understand the Armenian version of Ottoman history not from the diaspora, but from those in an alternative homeland, one that most of the Armenians in the world have never visited.

Yerevan

My trip began in Tbilisi, Georgia, because diplomatic relations are so bad between Turkey and Armenia that at the time of my visit it was impossible to fly directly between them. As the trip progressed and I began to realize just how fresh and painful the genocide commemorations were, whenever anyone asked me: 'Where are you from?' I answered quickly: 'England' – though part of me was curious to see what reaction I'd get if I told the whole truth.

I set off for the Georgian-Armenian border with a young Armenian man called Gregor. As we left Tbilisi, we passed an explosive fight in the Meidani – real punches, men being kicked on the ground, not just macho shouting as I have often witnessed in Turkey. As we drove away, Gregor said with satisfied certainty: 'That would never happen in Armenia' – my first taste of the often jokey but ever-present rivalry between the two countries.

The drive into Armenia cuts through beautiful swathes of green mountains and forest dotted by medieval monasteries on distant hills. Just before the border we drove through a village in Georgia where most of the residents are Azeris, a Turkic ethnic group concentrated in neighbouring Azerbaijan. On the gates of some of the houses, red ribbons had been tied to denote the presence of unmarried girls, an advert for prospective grooms. The ancient custom of bride-knapping still happens within both Christian and Muslim communities, as well as in central Asian states like Kyrgyzstan; in short, a young man chooses a girl he wants, kidnaps her with the help of his friends (before the advent of cars, this was done on horseback) and takes her to his parents' house. If she is not rescued by her own family before the next day, she is considered sullied, and belongs to the groom's family. These days, thankfully, bride-knappings take place mostly 'for show', after the agreement of both families, so that a marginally more consensual form of arranged marriage has replaced brute force – hence the coy presence of red ribbon-flags.

Over the border into Armenia, the ever-greener landscape becomes dotted with copper mines constructed under Soviet administration, most of them long abandoned along with their attendant worker villages. The rolling hills were, however, largely untouched, and we often stopped to allow herds of fat-bottomed sheep to cross the road in front of us.

Armenia is extremely poor; in November 2017, its average monthly wage was £30, and when Syrian refugees of Armenian origin started arriving in the country in 2011, fleeing the war, they were envied by locals for their cars and cash. The government depends on Russia for subsidized electricity, supplying a population of around 3.5 million, most of whom live in Yerevan. Signs of the abrupt departure of the Russians in 1991 are dramatically obvious, for example in the skyscraper apartments half built on the outskirts of Yerevan in the shape of the Cyrillic letters spelling out the equivalent of 'USSR' – only the U, S and half the second S were finished, and still stand. At one point on our way to the city, we passed a village affected by the 1988 earthquake that had devastated the region: it was the ancestral home of Charles Aznavour, according to Gregor, who also told me with great emotion in his voice that the French-Armenian *chanteur* had donated generously to rebuilding it (in fact, Aznavour's mother's family was from Izmir and his father's from Georgia). Another village we passed through was inhabited primarily by Yazidis, a Kurdish speaking minority historically persecuted as "devil worshippers" because of their reverence for Melek Taus, the Peacock Angel. 'I don't know if they go to school,' Gregor said. 'I know the girls are married by fifteen. There is no discrimination against Yazidis in this country.' They were certainly safer here than in northern Iraq, where in 2014 Islamic State forced thousands of them to take refuge on Mount Sinjar and killed many of those who stayed behind. In January 2018, the Armenian parliament debated a draft bill to recognize the massacres of Yazidis by IS as a genocide – a political act of solidarity.

As we approached Yerevan, the playful and slightly self-mocking references to the rivalry between Armenia and Georgia continued, reminding me of Turkey's relationship with Greece. I recognize that combative pride because it is born of a feeling of persecution, of being badly treated by history but surviving against the odds – Turks feel it too. The resulting pride jealously guards all national achievements. When narrating the legend of the king who created the Armenian alphabet, and showing me a church slab on which both Georgian and Armenian was written, Gregor said: 'We say that he created not thirty-four but sixty-eight letters, but he gave the ugly letters to the Georgians.' Or: 'Some Georgians claim that this church was built by Georgians, Azeris also claim this but it is not true – Armenians built it.' Charles de Gaulle became the President of France 'because he was Armenian'. Armenia was the first country to get state Christianity (true – in AD 301, thirty-six years before Georgia). Its Orthodox Church is superior to both the Russian and Georgian Orthodox Church, Armenian *dolma* is better than Georgian, and of course there is only 'Armenian coffee' not 'Turkish coffee'.

During the Soviet occupation of Armenia, churchgoing was banned, but people still tried to find ways to pray. Outside the 12th-century monasteries in the startlingly green mountains there are black marks on the stone of the outer walls where people held candles, huddled outside the church in secret services. Although congregations can now gather inside again, some habits from Soviet times have remained, like the photographs of faces of the deceased painted on gravestones, a practice that started because crosses were not allowed under the Soviets. Despite, or perhaps because of the Soviet repression of religion, I was struck by how religious people are in both Georgia and Armenia today. It is perhaps more evident in the former, where everyone crosses themselves three times when passing churches, which is all the time in the city centre (and quite scary when being driven in a taxi). Pedestrians also stop to touch and kiss the icons of Jesus Christ outside the church.

One Sunday morning in Yerevan I found a huge congregation spilling out of the doors of the central Saint Sergei Church – old and young, all dressed in Sunday best. A thin man with dark stubble wore a bright pink 1970s-style paisley shirt; it was touchingly garish, clearly reserved for Sundays. Women covered their heads, however cursorily (one frail middle-aged woman had a gossamer-thin handkerchief perched on the top of her wispy bun with no attempt to tuck it in at all). A man went around with a box of spare scarves for women who had come without, a service also offered outside mosques in Turkey.

The service and the overwhelming sense of community reminded me of the St Panteleimon chapel in Istanbul: long, thin yellow candles were on sale by the door, and worshippers went into an antechamber to secure them in the water-filled trays before they prayed, almost in automaton fashion. Old women went around putting out the older ones with their fingers to make room for more, their hands covered in water and ash. One of them sold sachets of a light yellow, crystalline substance (perhaps a cheaper resin substitute for myrrh) – seeing that I did not have any, an old man gave me some of his. At some unannounced point in time, everyone turned towards the altar, which morphed into a stage when a young, good-looking priest with a short, dark beard appeared from behind the red curtain in his white cassock, intoning in a rich bass, accompanied by attendants with beautiful voices, arrayed in red. All the congregation knew when to cross themselves; sometimes they reached down to touch the floor in what seemed like a synchronized performance.

Long before the priest prepared to come down from his stage to parade around the church, everyone had formed into parallel lines, lining the route for his procession. A hushed struggle ensued as he approached, everyone surging forwards to touch or preferably kiss the banners held aloft by his team. Attendants had a bag ready for the mysterious crystallized substance to be dropped into, and the priest himself held an ornate metal cross, holding it out to people's lips at random. I hoped fervently that he didn't offer it to me, but, inadvertently, or perhaps perversely, I met his eye as he approached and before I knew it the metal was pressed against my mouth. As the banner emblazoned with Christ's head passed overhead, I felt churlish, motionless as everyone else's arms reached over me to brush against it. At the last moment, I gave it a cursory stroke. One man, taller than his neighbours, held it possessively, reaching up and kissing the edge before reluctantly letting go. As it moved on he kept his gaze fixed on it like a parent at the school gates, clearly wanting one last touch but restraining himself.

This was paganism in thin disguise, and I found it slightly unsettling, particularly as I had got swept up in it despite myself – I did feel vaguely privileged when the metal cross loomed towards me. I was also genuinely touched by one event: an old woman, back bent, white hair, all in black, came in and found an old man, obviously her friend. Perhaps they only meet on Sundays. He greeted her warmly, kissing her on both cheeks. I was struck by how impossible this scenario would be in a mosque – not only can men and women not touch, they cannot even look at each other, separated out of shame into separate sections in the house of God. Yet what could be more natural than what I just witnessed – a simple expression of affection between two human beings.

Something I could not fail to notice in Armenia was the ubiquitous purple forget-me-not, symbol of the genocide, that appeared on car windows, on the walls of shops and offices, formed out of public floral arrangements, and vast on banners on the highway, often accompanied by the words 'We Remember, We Respect, We Condemn' in both Armenian and English.

I had decided to visit Yerevan's Genocide Museum but some unconscious reluctance meant I left it until my last day. I arrived, finally, at the same time as a huge crowd of children, pouring out of a bus that had brought them from a school in the countryside. I walked with them to the Tsitsernakaberd memorial, a high, pointed stele made of twelve shards of metal representing the districts taken from Armenians in modern-day Eastern Turkey. Below it is a circular indent fringed with carnations laid by visitors who stay to watch the ever-burning flame in the centre of the ring, dedicated to the victims of the genocide. The walk from the memorial to the museum is through a park lined with fir trees, each with a plaque from a nation state announcing its commemoration of the genocide. Having lived in Turkey for years (and before that in the UK, a country which still does not officially recognize the genocide) I was struck by the sheer range of Armenia's supporters. The museum is underground, room after room of precise documentation of atrocities committed against Armenians in the Ottoman Empire from the mid-19th century to 1918 and beyond. There are around fifty exhibits in all – photos, text, film footage, posters and newspaper front pages from the early 20th century.

Just before I went into the museum, I finally started to turn over in my mind what I thought about the genocide, with a sense of having felt obscurely vilified over the last few days, as a Turk in a country where, historically, Turks have been the enemy. I realized with shame that I had never looked properly into this period of history. Growing up with a Turkish mother, and living for years in Istanbul, I had absorbed a certain suspicion that the West had used the genocide unfairly as a stick with which to beat Turkey for the crimes of their Ottoman predecessors, a theory that has always been popular among Turks hypersensitive to the idea that Western powers blindly support Christians over Muslims. Now, at the door of the museum, I faced up to my doubts, asking myself rhetorical questions that, as I write them now, seem absurd and ugly in equal measure:

'There must not be conclusive proof that a genocide was ordered, otherwise how could there be any debate? How could Turkey deny it? And what about the fact that some Armenians did remain in Turkey, like the community in Istanbul?'

The museum visit was harrowing and transformative; I was emotionally exhausted when I emerged. There was so much proof, too much proof, that a genocide had taken place, and there was one exhibit in particular that stood out for me amid the horrible photographs and accounts of murders, rapes and torture: a telegram from Talat Pasha, one of the three infamous Pashas who led Turkey into the disastrous war on Germany's side, after the Young Turk revolution of 1908. It was addressed to the governor of Aleppo and described the intention of the Young Turks to eliminate 'all Armenians'. Later, when I described it to a Turkish friend, he claimed it was a forgery, also the view of historians such as Bernard Lewis. One of the saddest legacies of the Armenian Genocide is the air of scandal it attracts. Finally, I began to understand the Armenians' frustration with Turkey's century-long denial, but also the gulf between the two nations' understanding of events, and the ugly battleground between historians and nationalists.

I wondered what would happen if all Turks were forced to see these exhibits, to visit this museum. I am sure they would not accept it at first, such is the weight of denial in Turkey, particularly in Turkish schools on impressionable young minds. The glorious sacrifice of Turkish soldiers at Gallipoli and in the 1922 War of Independence dominates the curriculum in Turkish schools, so that the popular conception of military force is overrepresented as the idea of martyrdom. Turks feel they owe their very existence to the soldiers of the First World War, and indeed those stationed on Turkey's borders today; it would be impossible for them to accept that their forefathers had committed acts of genocide. It is the one thing that almost all Turks, regardless of religion, background or political alliance, agree on: the genocide is a myth. Because of their education, which is dictated by the ongoing attitude of the government, Turks do not have the same tools as the rest of the world to discuss what happened.

Before my trip to the museum, I had asked Gregor whether Armenians resent Turks. 'Some do of course,' he answered. 'They cannot forgive. Others realize that we cannot be angry with Turks themselves, they probably are not taught what happened.' At the time, I felt patronized – 'not taught your version, you mean'. After seeing the exhibits in the museum, I acknowledged the truth of his words. Amid my shock and disgust at what I had learned, however, I also noticed the skewed language of the text accompanying the exhibits, particularly those describing the Armenians outshining the 'backward' people of the Ottoman Empire, i.e. the Muslims. The members of the Armenian Assassin group that murdered Turkish diplomats after the fall of the empire are referred to as 'revengers', and their Turkish victims were 'liquidated' not 'murdered' as Armenian victims were. There is no mention of Turks who helped their Armenian neighbours, as there is of the Germans who helped Jews in the Holocaust museum in Berlin, for example. For extremely understandable reasons, the museum is black and white in its portrayal of the villains and victims of 1915 – but that makes the process of reconciliation hard.

The relationship between Armenia and Turkey has parallels with the relationship between Israel and Palestine that criss-cross between the four countries – historical claims to land, displaced people, religious partisanship, genocide recognition and beleaguered diplomacy. There is a sense in both Turkey and Palestine that the West sides with their non-Muslim adversary (Armenia/Israel); there is fury in both Palestine and Armenia that land has been taken from them by a greater military force, and that fury is one of the uniting points of their diasporas, while, most obviously, both Israel and Armenia are consumed with the injustice of those who deny their respective genocides. Israel's claim to Jerusalem as its religious and historical capital mirrors Armenia's claim to Mount Ararat as the centre of the Armenian people.

The gulf between the story told in the museum in Yerevan and the Turkish version of the events of 1915 raised questions for me about how countries come to terms with their pasts, and the role of acknowledgement to ensure nothing similar happens again as the 21st century becomes increasingly dystopian. South Africa had its Truth and Reconciliation Commission to address the country's legacy of slavery and apartheid. Germany has fully acknowledged and documented the Holocaust with museums, television programmes and school books and, crucially, has honoured the gentile Germans who took huge risks to help their Jewish friends – something that the Armenians have generally failed to do, and which is perhaps fundamental to allowing Turks to feel anything other than universally villainized by the Armenian version of events. Perhaps, like Spain and Portugal offering citizenship to Sephardic Jews to atone for the Inquisition, Turkey should offer citizenship to Armenians to atone for the genocide – a considerably less attractive offer, but a symbolically important one.

Recognition of the Armenian genocide by Turkey would be of monumental importance – it seems to be the ultimate goal for Armenians, yet, as the centenary has come and gone, it seems increasingly unlikely to happen. I also wonder how Armenians would feel without this constant goal needling them, like the desire of a murder victim's family for a guilty verdict. Would an apology really help? Will the Armenians ever really forgive the Turks, or feel at peace? The genocide is so engrained in the Armenian psyche that it almost defines both the country and the diaspora, although many members of the younger generations are trying to move beyond this lasting burden, sometimes with tragic consequences.

Western Armenia

Hrant Dink was a figurehead for Armenian-Turkish reconciliation and was assassinated in Istanbul in 2007; 100,000 people marched at his funeral. An inquest four years after his murder revealed that police intelligence had 'deliberately not prevented' the murder, which happened in front of the offices of Agos, a newspaper he launched in 1996 in both Turkish and Armenian as a gesture of compromise that angered some in the Armenian community. Before he launched Agos, Dink had run an Armenian children's camp in Tuzla, near Istanbul, that had been seized by a court in 1979 and partially demolished in 2015. Now, an award in his name honours human rights activists across the world.

I returned to Istanbul with a new appreciation for how hard it must be for the Armenian community in Turkey to honour their history in a country that denies its very existence. I discovered that, while the Armenian diaspora at large have the relative luxury (also a burden) of cherishing a story that has been preserved with distance, it is easier for many Turkish-Armenians to simply step away from the claims of both countries on their identity.

Cenk Zakarian is an architect-turned-project manager at the Istanbul branch of a global consulting company. His Armenian father is a jeweller, a traditional profession for Armenians in Turkey, and his mother is Turkish. His father was the first of his family to marry a non-Armenian, and Cenk's paternal grandparents still have not accepted his mother – 'They do not spend time together' – but his mother's family is more open-minded about having an Armenian son-in-law.

'The Armenian community is defined by their church,' he told me when we meet for coffee near his company's office in Istanbul's commercial district. 'My extended family of Istanbul-based Armenians do not think of Armenia as our "homeland" – Turkey is our homeland. We Armenians keep community together via intermarriage and church attendance, and to a lesser extent, language.'

Cenk did not speak Armenian until last year, when he started taking classes. I ask him why.

'Because the language is disappearing. The western Armenian dialect is very different from the eastern dialect by the way, we have trouble understanding each other.'

One of Cenk's two brothers changed his name to Zakar because he encountered racial abuse from a Turkish colleague at work in a big multinational office in Istanbul (the patronymic 'ian' or 'yan' ending on Armenian surnames is distinctive). His other brother is a jeweller and lives abroad. Although his brothers were never baptized, Cenk was and occasionally goes to church 'out of curiosity, to observe people' at Easter and Christmas. He's only been to a mosque once – the famous Süleymaniye mosque in Istanbul – to look at the architecture of the famous 16th-century imperial architect Mimar Sinan, originally a janissary of (probable) Armenian origin. Now, Cenk realizes his decision to become an architect was perhaps based on a sense of a traditional Armenian métier.

Cenk does not think racism against minorities is getting any better in Turkey today. 'The nationalist roots are still there,' he tells me. 'I keep a low profile – I do not usually hand out my business cards or tell people my last name when I first meet them, particularly in Anatolian towns. I could expect a similar attack to my brother any day.

'The worst time for me was when I did my twenty-day military service in Antalya. It was the short service for people who live abroad [Cenk has lived in Africa, the US, Russia, and the Balkans] so the army shook off their nationalist dust on us – it was twenty days of opportunity for propaganda, making sure Turkish workers living in Germany and Holland got a good dose of nationalism. I formed a little group with other minorities – some Kurds and Alevis – for solidarity.'

Cenk prefers being abroad; he says he feels more at home. But he has come to terms with his identity as a *melez* ('mongrel') – he says he is 'indifferent' to the efforts of both Turks and Armenians to claim him. I ask him whether he is genuinely happy with his dual identity or whether he has merely decided to ignore it. He answers that he is content, and in fact grateful because 'without this dual identity I would have no question marks, I would not have been pushed to go beyond the claims of Turkish or Armenian identity, to explore my identity.'

When I ask him how he defines himself, his answer is 'a hundred per cent millennial'.

'I define myself by my achievements. They are who I am.'

Cenk is convinced that the Armenian community in Turkey is becoming diluted as religion loses its importance. 'People are getting more secular and open-minded, like my father marrying a non-Armenian. He never felt the need to attend church or marry another Armenian in a church. The Armenian community define themselves by the church so that [loss] is having a big impact.'

If Cenk is right, perhaps recognition of the genocide has become more important than either language or religion as a rallying call to keep the Armenian community together. As I thought of both the Jewish and the Armenian diasporas mourning and honouring their historic wounds as symbols of identity, I also found myself thinking of more joyful symbols: the pomegranate seeds scattered by Armenian brides at their weddings to symbolize future children and happiness, and William Saroyan's celebration of Armenian language and laughter:

And the Armenian gestures, meaning so much. The slapping of the knee and roaring with laughter. The cursing. The subtle mockery of the world and its big ideas. The word in Armenian, the glance, the gesture, the smile, and through those things the swift rebirth of the race, timeless and again strong, though years have passed, though cities have been destroyed, fathers and brothers and sons killed, places forgotten, dreams violated, living hearts blackened with hate.[31]

Ghosts of Troy

'Nowhere in this region can be fully understood or appreciated except in the context of a perpetually shifting symbiosis between Greeks and Turks'

Bruce Clark, *Twice a Stranger*

'I fear the Greeks, even when they bear gifts'

Laocöon of Troy (in modern Turkey), *Aeneid*

Cyprus

As a child, I spent my summers in Northern Cyprus, where my mother grew up. I remember an apolitical holiday atmosphere – humid heat, the smell of jasmine flowers and the sea, adoring relatives in cool, marble apartments who fed me enormous quantities of baklava – but I also remember a sense of unease. In those days, the border was closed and patrolled by soldiers, and I never met any Greek Cypriots, who lived in the south: the mysterious 'Greek side' sounded menacing to my child's ears. I absorbed the excitement and pride of my mother when the Turkish soldiers marched out of the army base near the medieval village of Bellapais where we often stayed. Over time, I realized we had to fly from London to Ercan airport via Istanbul, because Turkey is the only country in the world that recognizes the existence of Northern Cyprus as a republic, rather than as occupied land. There are no direct flights from anywhere else, and my elder sister and I joke that the only reason we know for sure Northern Cyprus exists is because we've been there.

Shakespeare's *Othello* has immortalized the Venetians' and Ottomans' struggle over Cyprus in the 16th century; the castle named after the Moor still stands in the northern harbour of Famagusta (incidentally where, aged six, I rode 'the only camel in Northern Cyprus'). The castle failed to do its job in 1570, when the Ottomans seized the island, divided the inhabitants into *millet* groups and taxed them accordingly. The Linobambaki are a relic of the Ottoman takeover: rumoured crypto-Catholics who, like the dönme, pretended to convert to Islam after the Ottomans took over, partly for self-preservation (they were treated more harshly than the resident Greek Orthodox population because the Ottomans feared their allegiance to the recently defeated Venetians), but also to avoid the non-Muslim taxes. Allegedly, they remained secretly Catholic for hundreds of years. My mother's memory of them, however, is that they were 'more Turkish than the Turkish', fighting so fiercely in the 1974 civil war that they retained their area which encroached into the Greek side of the island. When I suggested to my mother that, while excellent fighters, they may not have actually been practising Muslims, she disagreed with some force.

Like the Linobambaki, the Maronites (Eastern Catholics, named after St Maron of Syria) of Cyprus are a relic of a more pluralistic past. Only one Maronite village remains in the north of the island: Koruçam, or Kormakitis, near the western Mediterranean Forest. It is a strange pocket of Arabic-speakers; the residents are descendants of those who escaped here during the Islamic conquests of modern-day Lebanon and Syria starting from the end of the 7th century. Every weekend, ever since the border was partially opened in 2003, hundreds of Maronites who live in the south of the island cross over to attend Sunday service in the church in Koruçam, a pilgrimage that treats the Turkish-Greek political quagmire as incidental to a much older religious ritual.

In 1878, Sultan Abdul Hamid II signed a secret deal with the British to allow them control of Cyprus in exchange for their support for the empire (and fabled 'bags of gold' that were in fact simply taxes taken unfairly from the co-owned Cypriots), an agreement that was terminated with the outbreak of the First World War. However, British interference has lingered, and there are around 3,500 British soldiers in military bases on the island today; refugees from the Middle East and North Africa occasionally land on the beaches of these bases, choosing to claim asylum on British rather than Cypriot soil.

The 20th century forced the Muslims and Christians of Cyprus into 'Turkish' and 'Greek' contingents as Turkey and Greece fought bitterly over the island like a divorced couple over a child. Nationalist outbursts in both countries in the 1950s stoked tensions between their respective Cypriot communities, in particular fuelling the Greek political movement of *enosis*, which holds that Cyprus should be part of Greece, and is masterminded by the Greek and Cypriot Orthodox Churches. The island achieved a troubled independence in 1960, on the condition that Britain be allowed to maintain military bases. Archbishop Makarios III became the first president, leading a mixed parliament of Greek and Turkish Cypriots; shortly afterwards, a wave of violent attacks by Greek Cypriots led to the displacement of tens of thousands of Turkish Cypriots and the destruction of scores of villages. In 1963, Turkish Cypriot MPs withdrew from parliament in protest at the violence, the capital city of Nicosia was divided between north and south, and in 1974 there was a short but full-blown war. As I got older my mother began to tell me stories about this war that she had lived through as a young woman – horrible, violent stories of mutual hatred, the loss of loved ones and family homes, land severed by conflict and a botched political 'resolution' in the form of a dividing line across the frying-pan-shaped island.

On 15 July 1974, the Greek military staged a coup d'état, enacting the political movement of *enosis*. Turkish troops landed five days later and the bloody war that followed was ended by a ceasefire on 16 August 1974, after thousands were killed and hundreds went missing on both sides. A 'Green Line' fixed by the UN divided the island in two, confining Turks to the north of the island and Greeks to the south, so that people were cut off from their homes if they were unlucky enough to be Turks living in the south, or Greeks in the north. Today, land disputes still rumble on. In 2004, there was a UN-organized referendum on the unification of the island which failed when the south rejected the proposed 'bi-communal' state.

My mother's own house was targeted by Greek soldiers in 1974, and she volunteered for the local Red Cross and UNHCR units helping Turkish victims in the aftermath of the war; one of her saddest memories is writing letters on behalf of illiterate mothers to their missing sons, who were almost certainly dead. I sensed from her that Greeks could never be our friends; this border was final, the only solution to terminal hatred.

But something didn't quite fit in these narratives. I spent a lot of time as a child with my mother's mother, and I remember her chatting happily in a strange language – Greek, I later discovered – to an old lady she had befriended at our local park in London. Granny Şifa was born in 1918 in Korakou, a village south of the modern border in the Troodos mountains, when both Turkish and Greek Cypriots lived there, and when the third-last sultan, Murad V, was still on the throne in Istanbul. She had lived in Cyprus for fifty years before the partition, and had many Greek Cypriot friends; when she moved to England with my mother after the 1974 war, she was lonely and homesick. Unable to speak a word of English, she made friends where she could – anyone who would speak Turkish or Greek with her. According to my mother, she got on much better with Greek-speaking Cypriots than she did with Turks from the mainland. Her best friend was a depressed Greek Cypriot woman called Maria, who would summon my grandmother to her home in Muswell Hill to cheer her up when she felt low.

Granny Şifa was a sporadically religious woman – in truth, her interpretation of Islam was a kind of pragmatic superstition. Back in Cyprus, whenever she had been moved to pray for something, she would ask her Greek Cypriot friends to go and light candles for her in the church for the Virgin Mary (she would pray herself in the mosque too, of course, to double her chances). But when my grandmother was angry with the Greeks, she would curse them freely, and with no sense of hypocrisy. Indeed, she had a legitimate grudge – when she was a child, she had been stoned by a gang of Greek Cypriot boys and received a wound in her head that left a bald patch for the rest of her life. My mother was also routinely bullied by Greek Cypriot boys as a child, particularly by two brothers who used to try to feed her ham sandwiches knowing she could not eat them, and impersonate the muezzin calling her to prayer. Bizarrely, their father Spiros and my grandmother were great friends.

My grandmother was the living epitome of people's natural desire to live together, profit from each other and pursue friendships, and also of people's mistrust of 'the other' – when they remember to look through the lens of otherness. I sometimes wonder if my grandmother noticed this paradox in herself, the moments when her personal and national identities collided. As a child, I wasn't quite sure whether my grandmother was being a traitor when she chatted to that Greek lady in the park, or whether she was above the rules.

Foreign Soil

Two decades after those days in the park, on a hot September day, I visited Kayaköy, the ruined 'rock village' near Fethiye on the south-west coast of Turkey which was the inspiration for Louis de Bernières' novel *Birds Without Wings*. This book tells the story of an ordinary Anatolian community of Muslims and Christians, set in the fictional village of Eskibahçe in the last years of the Ottoman Empire. In those years, most Ottoman citizens could not foresee the impending national identities about to be foisted on them; they identified simply as Muslims and Christians, all subjects of the sultan. Though they were taught by their priests and imams to regard each other as infidels, they were still colleagues, friends – even spouses, sometimes. One passage in the book in particular made me think of my grandmother in Cyprus, just a few decades later – a scene in which a Muslim woman, Ayse, asks her Christian friend, Polyxeni, to pray to the Virgin Mary for her.

'Polyxeni went into the church and crossed herself. She kissed the icon, placed Ayse's coins in the box, and collected a wax taper, which she lit from another before she pressed it into the sand-filled silver bowl [. . .] "Sweet Mother," she began, "intercede for Ayse in her troubles, even though she's an infidel, but she's a good one, and she trusts in you, so that's not bad, is it?"[32]

This proxy praying was two-way. Polyxeni asks Ayse to return the favour by tying a rag to the *tekke* (religious lodge) of a Muslim saint in the village, and praying for her in turn.

"You can tie a rag yourself," said Ayse. "Everybody does. I even saw one of the Jews doing it [. . .] It might even be a Christian saint for all that anybody knows."[33]

My visit to modern-day Kayaköy was something of a shock. Once a prosperous village, bustling with merchants, artisans and farmers, it is now a ghostly sprawl of tumbled-down stone houses overrun by fig trees and lizards. The Muslims and Christians who lived there have all gone, the Orthodox Greek Christians in 1923, and then the remaining Muslims, reclassified as 'Turks' at the dawn of the Republic of Turkey, in dribs and drabs over the next few decades as the village crumbled into oblivion. The Christian families were the craftsmen and teachers, and when they left it began to suffer economically. Encouraged by rabidly religious imams, the remaining Turkish residents pulled the valuable wooden roofs from empty houses, desecrated the icons in the churches, and slowly the village began to collapse. An earthquake in 1957 finished it off. Now, there are few signs of its former, diverse community – some patchy frescoes in the gutted churches, and a Greek inscription above an old marble fountain.

Kayaköy is a reminder of both the physical and social destruction wrought by the population exchange of 1923, during which Greece and the newly formed Republic of Turkey swapped their respective minority populations of Muslims and Orthodox Christians to create homogenous nation states. In total, 1.2 million Christians were 'exchanged' for 400,000 Muslims – almost the totality of each minority population residing in each country, with the exception of the inhabitants of Istanbul, the two islands of Bozcada and Gökçeada, and the Thracian area of Greece, who were allowed to remain where they were. Ruined villages like Kayaköy are proof that a multi-layered community stripped of its foundations struggles to survive. Worse, the population exchange created a legacy of heartbreak – after the initial, brutal uprooting and forced exile of these minorities, they suffered years of social ostracism in their adoptive countries. In Greece today, the exchange is referred to simply as 'The Catastrophe'.

Orthodox Greek Christians were shipped off to mainland Greece and islands in the Aegean and Mediterranean, and Greece-born

Muslims were brought in to take their places in the new Republic of Turkey. Both struggled to start new lives among strangers – in most cases, the outgoing 'Greeks' could speak only Turkish and the incoming 'Turks' only Greek, and were treated not as long-lost returning kinsmen but as strangers (the Greek name for the incoming refugees was *Mikrasiates* – 'the Asia Minors').

The community of Sinasos in Cappadocia, in central Anatolia (modern-day Mustafapaşa) was a rare example of what happened when residents had time to plan their departure; while the convention on the population exchange was signed at Lausanne on 3 July 1923, the Greek Orthodox community of Sinasos did not leave until 2 October 1924. They used the time to gather support, both logistical and financial, from members of their community who had moved to Pera to set up a successful caviar business (and were thus exempt from the exchange, as residents of Istanbul), as well as support from relatives who had already moved to Greece. A special committee of elders arranged the journey to the port of Piraeus in Athens; before they left, they even managed to commission a couple of photographers to capture the most beloved parts of the town – including the churches and people's individual homes – for a photo album that was shipped out to the community once they had settled in Nea Sinasos ('New Sinasos'), on the island of Euboea, near Attica. The album – utterly useless in practical terms, but of great sentimental value – took its place among the heirlooms that the community had painstakingly transported with them.

De Bernières imagines a much more representative, shambolic departure for the Christians of Eskibahçe. Given a few hours' notice, they hurriedly collect their transportable belongings and the bones of their ancestors from the church ossuary in a mad, tragicomic scramble. Later, when they reach their departure port of Telemessos (modern day Fethiye), 'some Christians took a leaf or a flower or even an insect or a feather or a handful of earth because they wanted something from their native land'.

I always think of this line when I pass the sign in Athens international airport warning against bringing 'foreign soil and plants' into Greece because of the possibility of contamination – in 1923, the feared contamination from victims of the exchange was social. Anything 'Turkish' about the incoming refugees to Greece was rejected, and vice versa – hence the title of *Twice a Stranger*, Bruce Clark's book on the exchange, which describes the ostracism experienced by refugees who were supposed to be coming 'home'.

Both sets of refugees were – ironically – associated with the enemy in the wake of the bitter war of independence won by Turkey in the aftermath of the First World War. The Muslims coming from Greece to Turkey brought with them the Greek language and, in the case of the many Cretans, a kind of dance called the *pentozali*. Christian refugees coming from Turkey to Greece brought with them a culture that was regarded as equally alien – the Turkish language, and typically Anatolian food – hence *dolmades* (dolma – stuffed vine leaves), *boreki* (börek – savoury pastries) and *kourabiedes* (kurabiye – biscuits), which are staples in Greek cuisine today. There was even a new music genre – *rebetiko* – created in the 1920s and 1930s by the refugees who settled in shanty towns in the Piraeus, a kind of sombre oriental blues. Many of the original 'Pireotiko' songs were about drugs and underground life, while the more sentimental 'Smyrneiko' songs (from Smyrna, their melodies and instruments more closely resembling those from Asia Minor) were generally about a longing for home.

Rebetiko is still performed today in the traditional mournful manner; I heard it performed by young Greeks in tavernas in Lesbos, and got the sense it is very much a living part of Greek culture, not a dusty relic from a hundred years ago. Likewise, 'Karagiozis and Hadjiavatis' is the Greek version of the Ottoman shadow theatre show 'Karagöz ['Black Eye'] and Hacivat', which was performed throughout the Ottoman Empire during the holy month of Ramadan, with a supporting cast of Jewish, Arab, Iranian and Greek characters and universal storylines like wife-beating and other forms of exaggerated violence. 'Karagiozis and Hadjiavatis' is still performed in Greece today with live music; the stories are localized, so that supporting actors include the character of Vlachos, from Northern Greece, or from the Ionian islands. In 1876, the French writer Pierre Loti predicted the enduring popularity of Karagöz and Hacivat performances in his adopted home of Istanbul: 'The adventures and misdemeanours of His Lordship Karagueuz have entertained countless generations of Turks and there is nothing to indicate the popularity of this individual is nearing its end [. . .].'

A particular pitch of animosity has been kept alive over the centuries by governments in both Turkey and Greece, preying on old nationalist tensions, and sporadically fanned by outbreaks of xenophobic violence. In 1955, a rumour spread in Turkey that a Greek had tried to bomb Atatürk's childhood home in Thessaloniki, and this provoked a wave of attacks on resident Greeks in Istanbul and the destruction of their property, prompting nearly 15,000 to leave the city in the next few years – other minorities were also caught up in the mania, particularly Armenians and Jews. After the war in Cyprus in 1974, mutual hatred escalated again in both Turkey and Greece, and there is an evergreen political animosity that has been fanned most recently by the refugee crisis.

Ayvalık

In March 2016, Turkey signed a deal with the European Union – known as the 'common declaration' – to take back Syrian refugees who had fled from Turkey to Greece, in exchange for money and negotiation talks. I was living in Istanbul at the time and headed down to Dikili, near Ayvalık on Turkey's coastline, to cover the story for *Politico Europe*. It struck me that history was in some way repeating itself with this new shipment of unwanted people across the waters of the Aegean. Yet again, this misleadingly tranquil coastline, dotted with olive groves and fishing villages, was witnessing politicized human traffic on the borders of Europe.

Ayvalık – 'The Place of Quinces' – lies just ten nautical miles east of Lesbos, on which thousands of refugees are still held in two detention camps. It is a sleepy harbour town of vague nostalgia and faded beauty, of crumbling villas converted into cheap hotels, and abandoned churches converted into mosques or automobile museums – the adjacent island of Cunda, accessible via a bridge from Ayvalık, is given over to tourism, and several high-profile industrialists have built discreet holiday homes on its shores.

Until 1922, Ayvalık was an entirely Greek Orthodox town in the heterogeneous hotchpotch of the Ottoman Empire; a hive of trade and commerce, bustling with merchants, olive farmers and black-robed priests. All the Christians who once lived there were either killed in the last years of Turkey's War of Independence (1918–1922) or shipped off to mainland Greece in 1923, to be replaced by Muslim Ottomans, many of them from nearby Lesbos. The elder generations among the imported Muslims sit playing backgammon under slowly turning fans in seafront cafés today: weather-beaten but upright, dignified men chatting quietly in a mixture of Turkish and a Greek dialect learned from their parents, who were brought here from the Greek island of Crete (Turkish 'Girit') in 1923. The dialect is Cretan, or 'Giritli' as the Turks call it – a rougher version of standard Greek, which marks its speakers as non-natives in Turkey.

At 5pm every Friday and Sunday, to mark the beginning and end of the weekend, the Ayvalık Municipality plays the Turkish national anthem on loudspeakers in the town square. As the first few bars of the Istiklal Marşı (Independence March) ring out, everyone stops what they are doing and stands in complete silence for the duration of the recording. Most of the fishermen living here today are ultra-loyal followers of the Turkish Republic's secularist founder, Mustafa Kemal Atatürk, despite (indeed, because of) their Greek roots: they are steeped in the uniquely fierce nationalism of an adopted state, a nationalism which grows only stronger as the generations pass and the memories of displacement fade.

Ayvalık's current locals may be patriotic, but they are not religious; the call to prayer from Cunda's single mosque is inaudible, and the only covered women are day-tripping tourists from the mainland. A striking number of men sport Atatürk's distinctive signature as a tattoo, generally on the inner forearm. The newspapers in the seafront cafés are all copies of *Hurriyet* or *Sözcü*, Turkey's traditionally liberal dailies (although less outspoken by the day), and the blue eyes of the old men who read them signal an obviously different ethnic make-up to Turks from further east in Anatolia – indeed, it is debatable how clear the difference is between 'Greeks' and 'Turks' on either side of the Aegean, both from a cultural and genetic point of view. The inhabitants of Ayvalık are not unaware of this vague interweaving themselves, particularly the younger generations, who can look back at their family history with more detachment than those who remember traumatic details of the exchange, or heard it directly from their parents.

Murat is a tour operator in his forties who ferries Turkish tourists to the Greek islands in the summer season on a little boat. He speaks good Greek, not because his family still speak it but because he needs it for work. His pale blue eyes squint against the sun in a face wreathed in premature wrinkles.

'Look into my eyes and tell me – am I a Turk?' he demands rhetorically. 'No way.'

Murat's parents' generation would not dream of uttering such a statement – the incoming Muslims in 1923, who had lived in Greece for generations, were told that they were Turks now, coming 'home' to live among their brothers. Their status as refugees – people who had left their homes, most of their possessions, neighbours and friends, and arrived in a strange place where they had difficulty speaking the language – was officially swept aside as a matter of mere practicality, and socially, they were not particularly welcome. These Greek-born Muslim Ottomans were Turks now, expected to be unquestioningly proud of their identity and new home.

The terms of their 'return' had been fiercely negotiated in Lausanne between Allied representatives and envoys of Atatürk – including his right-hand man Ismet Pasha, who exaggerated his slight deafness whenever convenient. The Treaty was signed on 30 January 1923, formalising, extending and making compulsory an exodus that had already started – hundreds of thousands of Christians, primarily Orthodox Greeks, had already fled Anatolia since autumn 1922. In 1914, the number of Christians in the Ottoman Empire was around 6 million, or 23 per cent of the population. By 1924, after forced marches, massacres, voluntary exodus and the compulsory exchange, as well as the loss of vast swathes of the empire's territories, the Christian population was reduced to 700,000. Not everyone involved in the creation of the Republic of Turkey was in favour of this drastic reduction in the numbers of valued Christian members of society. The feminist writer Halide Edip, who collaborated with the Young Turks during the First World War by running 'Turkification schools' for Armenian orphans, and who was later accused of treason by Atatürk's government and fled from Turkey to Europe in 1926, wrote in her memoirs of her regret about the population exchange:

'A great number of the Christian minority, mostly Greek and some Armenian, spoke only Turkish and looked very Turkish. It was a mistake, I believe, and not good policy to let them enter into the exchange in the Lausanne Conference. If a Turkish church had been recognized independently of the Greek and Armenian churches, there were enough conscious Christian Turks, and a very valuable element too, who would have stayed in Turkey.'

'Christian Turks' would have sounded bizarre at the time, but in fact, there *was* a self-styled Turkish Orthodox Church, which has never been recognized, and has a tiny congregation (Sunday services today in Istanbul are often attended only by the priest and his mother). It was founded in 1922 in Kayseri, central Anatolia, by Papa Eftim (grandfather of the current priest, Papa Eftim IV), a Turkish-speaking Orthodox Christian who indignantly rejected the conflation of Christian identity and Greekness. His church went on to become one of the most aggressively nationalist institutions in the Republic; his granddaughter was sentenced to life imprisonment in 2013 for her involvement in the infamous Ergenekon movement allegedly directed by secularist Turkish army generals in the 1990s and early 2000s. Papa Eftim was so incensed by the continued presence of the Greek Orthodox Christians in Istanbul in the 1920s that he twice besieged the Greek Orthodox patriarchate with a mob of supporters, almost leading to the emergency removal of that patriarchate from its 1,500-year-old seat in Istanbul to Mount Athos when the patriarch himself was injured. Eftim considered himself the model Turkish citizen, oddly blind to the incompatibility of Turkish Republicanism and Christianity; crucially, he and his maverick church had the full backing of Atatürk, who was happy to take all the Turkish nationalist volunteers he could get.

Atatürk himself certainly believed that the population exchange was ideologically important on the grounds that his new Republic must be rid of 'un-Turkish' elements. The 1923 Lausanne negotiation came after four years of war, during which his soldiers managed to fight off Allied forces – primarily Greek – and save at least the Anatolian heartland of the previously vast Ottoman Empire to form the officially secularist Republic of Turkey, populated overwhelmingly by Muslims. In this barely there but proud new nation state, there was no room for the foreignness that refugees inevitably brought with them, only state-branded Turkishness. The new motto of this country was a kind of compulsory pride in a freshly minted identity, best exemplified by the famous slogan: *Ne Mutlu Türküm Diyene* – 'How happy is the one who calls himself a Turk' – the words written on the statue of Atatürk that was vandalized by a Kurd in the town of Batman in 2013.

While brutal, the 1923 Turkey–Greece exchange had both rhyme and reason, at least according to the logic of the time. In the early 20th century, newly formed nations were intended to be religiously uniform and ethnically uncomplicated, united and strong. The motley remnants of the polyethnic Ottoman Empire in 1923 were anything but that. The apparently obvious solution seemed to be to cleanse these new states of 'unsuitable' minorities, resulting in a Turkey purged of the Christians who had lived there for centuries, and a Greece purged of the Muslims who had lived there almost as long. However misguided or wrong we may consider such a ruthless uprooting today, the infamous population exchange of 1923 was at least partly conducted in a constructive spirit, unlike the deportations of 2016.

Ayvalık is one of the harbours from which tens of thousands of Syrian, Iraqi and Afghan refugees have departed under cover of night since the war in Syria broke out in 2011, hoping to reach Greece undetected – and alive. It is also near the harbour where these same refugees have been brought back under the terms of the EU–Turkey deal; in return for receiving these 'irregular' migrants, Turkey negotiated for billions of euros of aid, visa-free travel in the Schengen area and renewed EU negotiations. A month after the deal was signed, Pope Francis visited Lesbos and took twelve Syrians away with him on his papal plane in a symbolic gesture of rebuke to European governments who have failed to welcome refugees through their borders (disappointingly, these Syrians do not live in the Vatican but in refuge centres in Rome).

What of the local reaction? Some Greeks who had seen their livelihoods drop dramatically with the corresponding demise of tourism might have been forgiven for resenting the incoming refugees. But I witnessed great kindness from the residents of Lesbos, who have helped to feed and clothe the refugees and said they were inspired to act by the knowledge they are of refugee stock themselves – around 60 per cent of the 90,000 current residents of Lesbos are descended from Christians deported from Turkey in 1923. Near the eastern shore of Lesbos, I visited a small and ramshackle village called Nees Kidonies – 'New Place of the Quinces' (*kidonies* or *ayva* is the Greek for quince) or 'New Ayvalık'. High up on a hill, its view is of the original Ayvalık clearly visible across the bay.

Today, the Cunda community of Cunda island in Ayvalık is peaceful and close-knit. Its members talk of the past when prompted, but do not spontaneously offer their family histories – some wounds are still too fresh, and Turkish nationalism allows only so much deviation from a central story of unity and cohesion. Many of the older generations congregate every day in Taş Kahve (Stone Café), an old high-ceilinged café on the seafront. An ancient stove sits in the middle of the café and swallows nest all around the eaves, producing a shrill cacophony. Elderly men with knitted waistcoats and carefully parted strands of grey hair sit playing *Yanık* ('Burnt'), their favourite card game, or backgammon all day long, drinking *çay* and coffee. Occasionally they exchange a few words in Cretan Greek, before lapsing back into Turkish.

Hüsnü Bey, a retired state accountant in his early eighties, used to have a special green passport for state employees which granted him visa-free travel to Greece. He made a habit of popping over to Lesbos, and twelve years ago he visited Crete to find the birthplace of his parents. He explains with gentle regret that now he's retired, he's lost the right to a green passport. He speaks in the Cretan dialect with his friends, all children of Muslim Ottomans who arrived in 1923 from Crete and spoke it to their children in turn. One of the men sitting playing cards with Hüsnü Bey does not feel comfortable speaking Turkish – he can understand it, but prefers to speak in Greek. Another is the opposite – Hüsnü speaks to him in Greek, and he answers in Turkish. Bilgin Bey, the owner of the café next to Taş Kahve, is a second-generation Cunda resident, one generation younger than the old *Yanık*-playing men and yet he tells me he spoke Greek with his Cretan-born grandparents; on his first day in school, when the teacher pointed to a picture of bread, he automatically said its Greek name.

A hundred years ago, the zeitgeist feeling in this part of the world – and much of the West, too – was for nationalism and monolithic identity. As the decades passed, it became increasingly fashionable, at least within self-professed 'progressive' nations in Europe, to promote multiculturalism and the inclusion of minority identities within the nation state. Today, in the wake of the refugee crisis, Brexit and exclusionary politics, we seem to have seen a swing back

to nationalism. Now more than ever we have to deal with fundamental questions: who gets to decide where people belong? What
have we learned from the political lessons of the past, and how do
we achieve consensus on the responsibilities of dealing with 'other'
people? With great difficulty, it would seem.

The cynical deal between the EU and Turkey in 2016 betrayed a
fear of outsiders, and an acceptance of political blackmail as a means
of indulging that fear. The forced exchanges of 1923 – contrived
and crazy though we now consider them – were in many ways more
humane, and logical, than the deportations of today. The historian
David Feldman has said that 'History can explain to us why we are in
the situation we are in today, [but] it cannot make choices for us.'[34]
We leave those choices to our leaders, who tend to favour instant
political gratification.

There was one happy postscript to my trip to Ayvalık. In 2012,
a team of Greek and Turkish founding editors opened a publishing
house called Istos in Istanbul, dedicated to publishing Turkish and
Greek books in their respective translations in support of the small
Greek Orthodox Christian community still remaining in the city. I
went to the Istos offices in Karaköy four years later, and picked up a
copy of *Ayvali*, a graphic novel published in both Turkish and Greek,
about a young man's attempt to track down the Greek family who
lived in his parents' house in Ayvalık before the population exchange.
The book, and the publishing house that produced it, are the literary
embodiments of a shared attempt to understand the traumatic legacy
of the exchange.

Thrace

A year after my trip to Ayvalık I went to Greece to meet the Turks still living in Western Thrace, the older generations of whom are the children of the Ottoman Muslims who were exempt from the population exchange of 1923 and allowed to stay in towns a few miles west of the Turkish border (in other words, the same generation as the cards-playing old men in Ayvalık). The most significant city in Thrace is of course Thessaloniki, which the writer Giorgos Ioannou called 'the capital of refugees', and which once held a Jewish majority. The historian Mark Mazower makes the case that the incoming Christian refugees in 1923, who arrived daily in their thousands between 1922 and 1923, were 'the means by which the New Lands [territories in the north of Greece, until recently Ottoman] and their capital, Salonica, finally became Greek'.[35]

Like the neglected Jewish *hamam* that I described in the previous chapter, many signs of the city's previous Muslim presence do not announce themselves. The Hamza Bey mosque is locked, barred and dusty, its single minaret removed after the 1923 exchange – the city's Muslim minority is negligible, and even if it weren't, there are ugly political reasons why the Greek government would not bother to restore and open it, although technically, after a period of being used as a cinema and shopping mall, it is now the responsibility of the Greek Ministry of Culture.

In 2014, there seemed to be an improvement – rhetorically, at least – in Thessalonikan Greek–Turkish relations when the maverick, tattoo-sporting seventy-two-year-old Yiannis Boutaris was re-elected as mayor and declared that 'Turks are our brothers'. However, for decades, the Turkish and Greek governments have pursued a stubbornly reciprocal policy concerning the churches and mosques in their respective jurisdictions. The Turks refuse to allow the restoration of churches and monasteries on the traditionally Christian islands off the coast of Istanbul, for example, until a mosque is built for the Muslim population in Athens. While the Greek government has legislated to build the mosque, it remains mired in bureaucratic delay. The mighty Parthenon, originally built for the goddess Athena in 438 BC, was converted into a mosque by the Ottomans at the end of the 15th century, shortly after they conquered Athens. They added a minaret to the tower already built by the Roman Catholics who had previously occupied the city, but by 1687, the temple was being used as a gunpowder storeroom, and the invading Venetians blew up the interior with a direct hit during their siege of the Acropolis, almost destroying the dreams of the 17th-century Ottoman travel writer, Evliya Çelebi, who had prayed only twenty years earlier that 'a work less of human hands than of Heaven itself, should remain standing for all time'. Today, it is difficult to imagine the various incarnations – temple, church, mosque, armoury – of an incomparably majestic edifice now sadly riddled with scaffolding, cranes and tourists.

The all-important pilgrimage destination for every Turk that visits Thessaloniki is the childhood home of Mustafa Kemal Atatürk, which lies in the grounds of the Turkish Consulate, a short walk uphill from the harbour. If I had not visited it, there is a real chance I might have been excommunicated from the family. Turkey's founding father was born in 1881, in what was then Salonika. His home was a modest two-up two-down which today draws committed patriots to take exhaustive photographs of the four rooms, filled not with trinkets from his youth (these are lost to history, since the child Mustafa was yet to shoot to superstardom as the *pasha* who led Turks to victory and independence) but with odds and ends from his adult life, mainly pilfered from the museum of Dolmabahçe Palace in Istanbul, where he died in 1938. One glass cabinet contains his evening wear, another his collection of wooden spoons and egg cups; in the corner of one room is a spooky waxwork of his mother, clothed all in black, while Atatürk himself in both child and adult guise sits gravely in the other rooms: a Madame Tussauds solo exhibition, in situ. His school certificates adorn the walls (annoyingly for him, he was always second or occasionally third or even fourth to a boy named Ahmet Tevfik, who must have been truly brilliant). It is a monument to patriotism, to the worship of a founding father treated as a secular god.

After walking through the house, and experiencing the frisson of devotional pride which almost every Turk feels for Atatürk – even anti-nationalist, mongrel Turks like me – I popped next door to the consulate to get the stamp I needed to cross the land border into Turkey the following week. I had already tried to get one online and had been refused, but was fairly confident it was a system error that could be corrected in person. Not so: I was told by the bored civil servant in a tiny office that I was 'not eligible' for a visa, after years of living in Istanbul and taking my access for granted. If I wanted to appeal the decision, I would have to return to London and take it up with the Turkish Consulate there.

This information was devastating but not a complete surprise, given what I had been writing about the government in recent years as a journalist. However, the news transformed an experience which should have been a straightforward research trip into a kind of odyssey of lament. As I wandered through the Turkish neighbourhoods of Xanthi and Komotini in Western Thrace in the coming days, talking Turkish with local shopkeepers and eating Turkish food, it felt as though I was in a consolation prize-version of Turkey, just a few miles away.

Xanthi lies just south of the Rhodop mountain range that borders Greece and Bulgaria; a river, bordered by plane trees, winds through the quiet town, and picnicking families sit on its banks. Around 25,000 people in the town – about a third of the population – refer to themselves as 'Turks', speak Turkish and attend a school staffed by Turkish teachers, but the Greek government refer to them only as the 'Muslim minority'. They have been here for generations, because Xanthi, in common with the rest of Western Thrace, was exempt from the 1923 population exchange. Shop signs in Xanthi are in Greek, but some also have Turkish translations underneath, in Latin script. Sometimes, Turkish words are transliterated into Greek script, an odd deciphering experience for a Turkish speaker like me with a hazy memory of ancient Greek – μπακλαβά for baklava, for instance, or even weirder, Turkish names awkwardly converted into Greek characters which cannot adequately replicate the original sounds. I spent a few minutes puzzling over the names next to the buzzers at a block of flats before finally figuring out the Greek rendition of Sabriye Delioğlu. When she opened the door, she reminded me immediately of my grandmother – a brisk, cheerful woman in her early seventies with carefully combed hair, large square dark glasses and sensible shoes. She had a twinkle in her eye, and looked me up and down before giving me a bosomy hug. 'Little Alev! Well, here you are. Let me show you our neighbourhood.'

I was put in touch with Sabriye by an elderly Turkish gentleman, Emre, who now lives in Istanbul, where he has been since the late 1970s, when he left his home town of Xanthi, his family's home for many generations. I had met Emre in a café on the third floor of Metrocity, a vast mall in Istanbul, before I left; he was incongruous among the shoppers, immaculately dressed in a brown three-piece suit, and with a purple rinse in his white hair – a kind of Quentin Crisp figure, even down to his cut-glass British accent, which he acquired while working for the British Council as a younger man. As we drank our coffee, sometimes struggling to make ourselves heard above the tinny boom of the mall's sound system, he told me that in the aftermath of the 1974 war in Cyprus, nationalist tensions were exacerbated in both Greece and Turkey, and the Greek authorities stepped up their existing programme of persecution against the resident Turks in Thrace. By 1978, Emre had had enough and left the beautiful Ottoman house in which he had grown up and moved to Istanbul, where he became effectively stateless. Stripped of his Greek passport once he left the country, he lived without an official nationality for a decade, before the Turkish authorities decided to grant him a passport.

'Would you care to meet another Thracian exile?' he asked me, leading the way in stately fashion down the escalator to an optician's shop on the second floor. Here, I was introduced to the optician Adnan, who left Xanthi about a decade after Emre. Although Turkish like Emre, he is much more comfortable speaking Greek. The two men are at least twenty years apart in age and very different, but their shared sense of exile had made them friends. Emre, a man of leisure, often came to visit Adnan in Metrocity mall, walking serenely past the neon signs and mannequins in his smart suit and brogues to chat about the good old days.

So before I arrived in Thrace, Emre had given me some insight into the indigenous Turkish minority of the region, who are a stubborn bunch, discriminated against for decades in a low level but relentless fashion by the Greek government, who have always been wary of Turkish nationalism on Greek soil, and particularly since the 1974 Cypriot war. Turks in Greece are classed as 'Muslim' regardless of whether they are actually religious, to avoid recognizing that these people are Greek citizens who identify culturally, and indeed ethnically, as Turks – an impossible paradox for many.

In 1987, Emre's friend Sabriye worked as a teacher at the minority school and tried to set up the Turkish Teachers' Association of Xanthi, only to have it struck down by the Supreme Court in Athens on account of the word 'Turkish', a word which is banned when applied to official groups in Greece. All attempts at forming explicitly Turkish associations are banned to this day. In 2008, Sabriye and her fellow teachers took their appeal to the ECHR and won, only to have the ECHR's decision rejected by the Greek government. She complained to me of other, everyday injustices – for example, until the 1990s, when a report by Helsinki Watch embarrassed the Greek government by making the situation internationally known, Turks had been denied permission to repair their houses, and encountered problems trying to set up phone lines or buy cars, forcing people like Emre to give up in disgust and move to Turkey.

Sabriye is made of sterner, or at least more stubborn, stuff and took it upon herself to give me a tour of Xanthi, starting with her old haunt the local minority school, where Roma and Pomak children learn alongside the Turkish children, ostensibly because they are all Muslim, but actually because they are miscellaneous misfits (some of the Roma are Christian, for example, and Pomaks are Slavic Muslims from the Balkan region who are usually at pains *not* to associate as Turks, although many people think they are). The school has a sign in the national Greek colours of blue and white, emblazoned with the Greek flag and proclaiming its minority status in Greek characters – it could not be more nationalist-stamped. Next, we walked through some historically Turkish streets in search of Emre's house, which we eventually found: a large white building, now converted into apartments. Sabriye, her husband, Necme – a stooping, humorous man who ignored the incessant but affectionate scolding of his wife and told himself jokes when no one was listening – and Esref Bey, an old friend of Emre's who proudly owns the only Turkish coffee shop in town, posed in front of the house while I took a photo to send to Emre ('What a change!' was his uncharacteristically brief, and rather sad, response). Later, I discovered a much older, tumble-down house higher up in the town. When I stepped inside, climbing up a curved marble staircase with missing steps, and startling a cat, I discovered that the interior boasted cracked but still-beautiful stained-glass windows, a brass chandelier dramatically lying where it had fallen decades ago, judging from the dust, and even a bed frame in the corner of one of the rooms. A mysterious tableau of loss, typical of the area.

I noticed that the elderly Turkish entourage I had acquired spoke rather halting Greek in shops, despite the fact they had lived here all their lives. There was certainly no mention of Greek friends.

At one point, we piled into a car and drove off to a nearby village where a middle-aged Turkish couple, Nuri and Ayse, received us in a bucolic wooden farm house with many cups of tea and tales of school days – Ayse had been Necme's pupil in biology class, about forty years ago. Her husband Nuri showed me photos of the protests they staged in 1981 against the seizure of their land by the Xanthian municipality, appealing for support from the central Greek government. 'We stayed there fifteen days, but we didn't succeed,' said Nuri. 'The government told us to leave because of Easter, and then they didn't help us.'

The trip to Xanthi showed me that a diaspora community can be both entirely at home and entirely at odds with a host country, often simultaneously. By chance, I happened to be there on 25 March, Greek Independence Day, and watched headscarf-wearing Turkish mothers cheering as their miniskirt-wearing teenage daughters marched in a parade celebrating the beginning of the Greek War of Independence from Ottoman rule in 1821. The irony of the situation was not important, or perhaps apparent, to them; these mothers cared much more that their daughters had been selected for an important role in the celebrations, and were cheering as proud parents, not as Turks. The children, claimed both by the Greek state and by Turkish families, marched on, their sense of allegiance still malleable.

Politicians in both Turkey and Greece know the younger generations are there to be wooed, and the older generations to be kept sweet. In December 2017, President Erdoğan arrived with great pomp and majesty in Athens, the first visit by a Turkish president for sixty-five years, and possibly the last for another sixty-five. The

Greek prime minister, Alexis Tsipras, winced visibly throughout the visit, particularly when Erdoğan referred to the borders of Greece and Turkey drawn up in the Treaty of Lausanne as a 'mistake' (this was uniformly reported in Turkish pro-government papers as 'Erdoğan teaching a lesson to Tsipras'). He was soon off to the town of Komotini, a few miles east of Xanthi, which has a 50 per cent Turkish population. Here, he was finally given the rapturous welcome he craved – 'Reis [Leader] we would die for you!' his supporters cried, as he handed out toy dolls to the children crowding round him.

When I arrived in Komotini on a Saturday evening, the first building I passed after I parked the car was the ruin of an Ottoman synagogue built into the old city wall. A hundred yards away was a mosque. I walked on towards a noisy bar with its doors flung open, playing Turkish music – I could hear lilting, arabesque melodies from some kind of clarinet, hands tapping a drum, indistinct singing. 'Amazing!' I thought. 'This could be Istanbul.' Walking into the bar and hearing the Greek lyrics, I realized my mistake in prematurely "claiming" the music, which the waiter informed me was actually "Thracian". *Dolma* or *dolmades*? *Cacık* or *tzatziki*? *Oud* or *bozouki*? Music, like food, cannot be boxed into a nationality but type 'Thracian music' into YouTube and read the comments under any of the videos to discover the astonishing vitriol of people – Turkish, Greek, Macedonian, Bulgarian – who claim the genre as theirs, and theirs alone.

People are also willing to box themselves in, conceptually and geographically. I had been informed there was a specific 'Turkish quarter' in Komotini for the town's 50 per cent Turkish population and had been trying, without success, to find it as night drew in.

When the call to prayer rung out, I followed the nearest-sounding muezzin to a small mosque, which proved to hold just two elderly men praying under strip neon lighting. Across the street was a small cemetery with tombstones topped by the Bektashi fez rather than the usual Greek Orthodox cross. I was definitely in Turkish territory, and trudged confidently up the road in search of some kind of neighbourhood hub – a backgammon café, or a central square. Soon the houses thinned out. It was hard to see in the gloom, but I became gradually aware of a rural landscape around me; the air was heavy with wood smoke, dogs bayed in the distance, mud squelched underfoot.

Soon I was walking past shacks made of corrugated iron. Little campfires broke up the darkness; huddled around them on the ground were people speaking a strange language, neither Greek nor Turkish nor Pomak: it was Romani. Clothes were hung on ramshackle fences, bedding piled up by the doors of the shacks. A refugee camp calcified into permanence. A dog rushed up to me, barking – I crooned at it, over-friendly, and it sniffed me before trotting off. Soon people were staring at my European face and city shoes; I marched blithely along, determined to invite as little interest as possible with the aid of some swagger.

The rows of shacks became denser, the tracks between them busier, the looks more intent. Too late to turn back. I was walking aimlessly, with an increasingly false posture of confidence. Suddenly, around a corner: three women and three men sitting on plastic chairs by a fire, scribbling on pieces of paper on their laps – an adult literacy class perhaps, or a covert political society? The scene had a medieval aspect, all flickering firelight and secrecy.

They looked up in astonishment as I passed. '*Yassou,*' said one of the men, who was wearing a smart beige waistcoat entirely at odds with his surroundings. '*Merhaba.*' I returned his greeting in Turkish, embarrassed by my inadequate Greek. The looks of astonishment deepened.

'What are you doing here?' asked one of the women, continuing my Turkish.

'Oh, just . . . walking,' I replied lamely. 'I think I may be lost.'

'You're definitely lost,' said the man who'd first spoken. I noticed he had a dapper, square moustache. 'You are in the most dangerous ghetto of Komotini.'

We were equally and mutually intrigued, the mysterious scribes and I. They talked together in Romani, throwing the occasional glance in my direction, as I tried to see what they were writing. One of the women, who had a grubby child clinging to her knee, noticed me looking.

'We are writing to President Putin,' she said. 'We are asking him please to allow our brothers into Russia.'

'Your brothers?'

'We are the witnesses of Jehovah.'

This was so unexpected, particularly in Turkish phrasing, that I assumed I had misheard.

'There are only ten of us here but we are eight million brothers across the world, and we are all writing to President Putin today.'

'Good idea,' I said, feeling like Alice. 'I hope he listens.'

'Drugs, knives, there are very bad people here,' interjected the dapper man, gesturing at the nearby shacks. 'You cannot continue alone. You know who sent you to us?' He pointed a grave finger to the sky before allowing a beatific smile to spread across his face.

'God. He knew we would help you.'

As the male members of the group assembled to form my escort out of the ghetto, one of the women handed me some leaflets in Turkish. I gave them a polite glance before putting them in my bag – the usual colourful pictures of ecstatic-looking families under quasi-philosophical titles: 'In Hard Times, What Gives Us Comfort?' I looked back at the beaming faces watching me in the flickering light of the fire. This was too surreal.

'There are only ten of us here,' the lady repeated, proudly. 'But we are strong. God sent you, there is no doubt.'

The men took me through a passageway which opened into a makeshift shop selling everything from lentils to fizzy drinks. We were greeted by the owner ('my uncle', said the dapper man), who waved us through the front with the air of a speakeasy proprietor seeing off trusted customers. We emerged into the thick of the ghetto on the other side, and soon children were following us through the muddy tracks, as though I were the Pied Piper.

My hosts patiently answered my questions as we walked – they spoke Turkish because they had attended the local minority school, where it was taught; they also picked up some English from satellite TV. Now their children attended the same minority school but the quality of education was poor, and the Roma parents had higher ambitions: the Greek public school, where their children would be treated 'as the lowest' but would receive a better education. No, they were not persecuted by the other Roma, even the Muslims. There were about a hundred Jehovah's Witnesses in the whole of Komotini,

Greeks and Roma combined. They supported the Panathenaic foot-ball club, based in Athens. They wished me very well.

As we parted near the centre of town, the adults and then the children solemnly shook my hand, one by one.

'Remember, God sent you,' said the dapper man. 'Don't forget us.'

Not likely. The irony of this conversation was only really relevant to an outsider: these men self-identified primarily as Jehovah's Wit-nesses, then as Roma, but their most enthusiastic, tribal instinct was for an Athenian football team they had only ever seen on a television screen. Their overlapping layers of identity were just the way things were, not a contradiction. At the risk of manufacturing a Hollywood ending to my own story, perhaps their attitude helped me come to terms a bit with my predicament: I can be 'of' Turkey while I am not in it. Geography does not confer identity. It makes us homesick, but it does not define us.

Back in Athens, I met Christos Iliadis, a young Greek political scientist who wrote his PhD on the Greek government's efforts, from 1945 until the late 1960s, to combat 'Turkishness' in Western Thrace. His thesis was, as PhDs go, rather exciting – it was based on a secret government archive declassified in 2002, and shut down a few years after Christos and a few others wrote about it; the archived records described the 'administrative harassment with repressive character' by the Greek government of the Turks.

Christos asked me to meet him outside his office just off Syn-tagma Square, most recently famous for the violent anti-austerity rallies of 2010–11. He corroborated much of what Sabriye and her friends told me in Xanthi, and emphasized that the animosity of the Greek government towards the Turkish minority had been particularly obvious since the 1960s. The timing was a reaction to the efforts of the Turkish government to expel Greeks from Turkey in 1964 (a decade after the infamous anti-Greek race riots of 1955 in Istanbul). Christos discovered some untoward -- indeed, argu-ably illegal – behaviour from the Greek government in the briefly declassified documents he used for his PhD: 'From the late fifties until the seventies – and probably later – the Greek state secretly funded Islamic conservatives in Thrace because they were anti-Turkish and anti-modern – in other words, not in line with the Kemalist (modern Turkish nationalist) agenda. Plus, they have always encouraged non-Turkish Muslim minorities, for example Pomaks and even Egyptians.'

Christos described to me a kind of secret Cold War in Thrace, which was at its height in the 1960s, between the Greek and the Turkish propaganda mechanisms.

'Between 1959 and 1969 a secret council was organized by the Greek foreign ministry. Its archive was found in Kavala [a city near Komotini]. Its members were heads of regional office – deputies of local police, military and intelligence units – and their job was to both implement and formulate minority policy in the region. Per-haps there were similar Turkish councils – who knows?'

The mutual animosity and fiercely reciprocal treatment of the Turks in Greece and the Greeks in Turkey has continued for decades, with little outbreaks of violence, such as the riots in Komotini against the Turkish minority in 1989.

'The reciprocity was a kind of hostage situation,' as Christos put it. 'In the sixties and seventies Greece was copying Turkish admin-istrative efforts against Greeks (of Istanbul).'

Both countries were particularly suspicious of the minority schools in their respective countries. In 1965, the Turkish government downgraded the legal status of Greek minority schools in Istanbul and stopped allowing graduates of Greek schools to teach. Christos found top-secret letters sent between the Greek Ministry of Foreign Affairs and the chief inspector of minority schools in Greece which agreed on reciprocal measures that would 'relieve Greek authorities from spying on these fanatic janissaries [meaning Turkish teachers trained in Turkey before being sent to Greece]'. The tit-for-tat protocol regarding mosques in Greece and monasteries in Turkey shows that reciprocity has endured, half a century on.

Thracian Turks are active in Greek politics, which is not as surprising as it might initially seem since they have an assured voting base of nearly 50 per cent in towns like Komotini, for example. There are four minority MPs in the Greek parliament today, including the MP for Xanthi. There is also a Turkish consul in Komotini in a secret battle with the Greek authorities for local hegemony, according to Christos. 'The Greek Ministry of Foreign Affairs has an office called the 'Office of Cultural Affairs' in Komotini – it tries to counterbalance the influence of the Turkish consulate there, which also operates to some extent in secrecy.'

In 1991, the Greek government decided to appoint local muftis (Islamic community leaders) in Thrace before they could be elected by the local Turkish community, a pre-emptive measure based on the argument that muftis are also judges and, technically, cannot be elected – but the real reason was that muftis had become 'envoys of Kemalism'. When I asked Christos whether the Turkish community objected to this interference, he smiled.

'With the guidance of the local Turkish consul, they [the local Turkish community] just elect unofficial muftis who are de facto community leaders – everyone ignores the Greek government's appointees.'

This attitude mirrored what I had noticed among Sabriye and her friends in Xanthi – a kind of defiance against the status quo. It was clear to me that Sabriye would rather stay in Xanthi and fight the authorities than leave for Turkey; when I ask her why she didn't follow her friend Emre's example, she smiles and shrugs. 'This is our home.'

Aegean Turks

It was only when I started researching this book that I fully realized the ripple effects of the population exchange in both Greece and Turkey today. Almost every Greek and Turk has a family member who arrived after 1923, some dramatic story of loss and love. Christos' grandparents were refugees from Asia Minor to Kavala (Greek Thrace), for example. Electra, a Greek friend of mine, has grandparents from Cappadocia in central Anatolia on one side, and from Istanbul on the other. Many Turks now living in Turkey have relatives who came from Crete, where there was a huge Muslim population. Selin Girit, the BBC's Turkey correspondent, is literally called 'Crete' – an obvious clue to her heritage, since Atatürk only introduced surnames in Turkey in 1934, and people often chose their own based on a detail that vaguely distinguished them (for example, 'Ahmet Son of the Rice Seller', 'Sinan Blond-Beard' – or their place of birth).

My mother told me about a distant relative of ours from Crete who hardly spoke any Turkish but did have an absurdly romantic life story.

'Her husband – your grandmother's cousin – was enlisted into the British army during the Second World War [Cyprus was – in British eyes at least – a Crown Colony from 1914 until 1960]. In 1941, he was captured by the Germans and became a prisoner of war in a camp in Crete, which was occupied by Germans until 1945. When he was in the camp he fell in love with this Cretan girl, who came to give him food through the fence. He married her when he was liberated and brought her to Cyprus – she cried every day wanting to go back to her family.'

Being my mother, she added a few gratuitous details: 'He was very eccentric, it was said that his experiences in the camp made him go mad. I remember he dyed his grey moustache with black shoe polish, which ran when he sweated – like Aschenbach in *Death in Venice*. I remember that very well.'

My friend Ziya the travel agent, who told me the story of his grandmother's flight from Macedonia in 1912, also told me stories connected to the Cretan side of the family – more disturbing because of the relative proximity of Turkey's more recent war with Greece.

'My mother's family were wealthy business owners from Crete. I have no doubt that my family used to be Christian, before they came to Izmir in 1923. Somewhere along the way, they were converted. We have never been conservative Muslims.'

Ziya confirms something I have always assumed – that when people got converted they often practised a mild version of the religion, especially in the frequent cases when the conversion was for pragmatic reasons of avoiding non-Muslim taxes.

Ziya continued: 'I have a friend from Izmir, and her grandmother's nipples were cut out by the Greek soldiers and she was raped, sometime between 15 May 1919 [when Greeks occupied Izmir] and Sept 1922 [when Atatürk routed the Greeks from Izmir]. This was a story that was well known in the family. People like my great-grandmother claimed they didn't remember details of that period but it's because they didn't want to remember. They wanted those painful memories to fade, not to be passed on to the new generations. I could never persuade my grandmother to go back to Crete – she hated that idea. She was afraid to do so.'

On every Greek island of the Aegean, and across much of mainland Greece, one can see the legacy of the Ottomans – there is always at least one mosque, *hamam* or crumbling stately villa built for the local Ottoman governor. Sometimes place names remain, like the Karatepe ('Black Hill') area of Lesbos, where there is now a camp holding around 1,500 refugees. On Kos, the two Ottoman mosques which had stood for 400 years collapsed in an earthquake shortly before I visited in August 2017, leaving alarming piles of rubble cordoned off with tape. That evening, looking for a good restaurant in the main town of Kos, I was surprised to discover Google's recommendation, 'Hasan's Taverna', in a suburb called Platani. Hasan was, as his name suggested, an ethnic Turk, and here were Turkish restaurants aplenty, people talking Turkish in the street, even a functioning mosque. These Turks – about 1,700 of them, I later found out – were definitely not recent immigrants.

It was difficult to enquire about this without sounding

rude – 'Excuse me, why are you here?' Then I remembered that the Dodecanese islands were under Italian occupation in 1923 (in fact, from 1911, when Italy won the islands from the Ottomans, until after Italy lost the war in 1943 and handed them to the Greeks). So today's Turks in Kos were never involved in the population exchange; they have been there since the 16th century, still in a cocooned community, much like the even larger Turkish community in Rhodes – the other major island of the Dodecanese.

Individual families did, however, manage to evade the exchange in territories where it was enforced. In 2012 I met an elderly couple in a village near Trabzon, on Turkey's Black Sea coast. They spoke to each other in Greek, and were, clearly, Greek (the old woman's Turkish was ropey, and she was constantly being scolded by her husband for reverting to Greek) but they took pains to pretend otherwise. There was a large carpet with Atatürk's face on it hanging on the wall, and even a *mescid* (Muslim prayer room) attached to the house. Somehow, these people's parents had managed to remain in Turkey by appearing as Turkish as it is possible to be, but I would never be told the whole story, of course.

Eighteen months after I reported on the refugees returned to Turkey under the 2016 EU deal, I found myself just across the tiny stretch of water from Ayvalık, this time on the Greek island of Lesbos – just south of 'New Ayvalık', in fact. Because of my entry ban to Turkey, I could not go back to Ayvalık, but I could see it, easily – could even pick out individual houses – from the beach near my house. For the first time, I fully understood how heartbreaking it must have been for the Christians taken from Ayvalık to Lesbos to see their old hometown every day, and not to be able to reach it again.

In another instance of strange historical symmetry, the purge conducted by Erdoğan's government against Turks in the aftermath of the 2016 coup attempt has led to huge numbers of middle-class Turks emigrating to Greece, where they have been welcomed with open arms, largely on account of an economy in crisis. In return for paying upwards of 250,000 euros on property, big spending Turks get a 'golden visa' which gives them citizen-like status and the opportunity to send their children to Greek schools rather than Erdoğan's increasingly poor *Imam Hatip* (Koranic) schools. The historical twist is that many of these Turks have settled in the district of New Smyrna in Athens, named after the emigrant Greeks from Smyrna (modern Izmir) who made it their new home in 1922.

Granny Şifa

At the end of my Aegean travels, I went to Cyprus to visit the grave of my grandmother in the north of the island. Because of my entry ban to Turkey, I could not fly to Ercan, the airport in the north, which requires stopping in Istanbul. Instead, I flew to Larnaca in the south and took a bus up to Nicosia (Lefkoşa in Turkish and Lefkosia in Greek), the capital divided by the 1974 border. Crossing that border was an emotional challenge; I was struck by the irony that, as a child, I had never been allowed to cross from the north to the south, which I thought of as an apocalyptic land filled with unknown monsters. The border was a protection. Now, as an adult, I was in the south for the first time in my life, worried about crossing to the north, no longer a place of childhood sunbeams but a place of vague political hostility because it was under Turkish control.

The pedestrian border in Nicosia is busy, right in the middle of town, straddling a street deserted abruptly during the war in 1974 – a kind of 'sniper's alley' full of shuttered windows. The sign on the southern side proclaims the city the world's 'Last Divided Capital' in English, French and German. There is something mesmeric about that sign, the implicit pride of it. Each side fiercely contests the other's sovereignty, but this was almost proof of a perversely shared sense of ownership.

As I passed the Greek guard post and approached the Turkish post, I began to get nervous. After staring at my passport, then back at my face for a heart-lurching moment, an impassive guard waved me through.

I was unprepared for how surreal it would be re-entering the north of the island. It was like being back in Turkey, like actualising my memories – the same adverts on billboards, the same products in shops, the familiar call to prayer, the simple magic of communicating in Turkish. I felt a slight tension this side of the border, a sense that people are less relaxed. I knew from a previous visit I'd made as an adult that many Northern Cypriots feel obscurely embarrassed, emasculated in the case of the men, knowing that their small and precarious republic only exists because of the money and soldiers sent by the Turkish government, which conveys an air of colonial-like ownership. There is a kind of cynicism prevalent, punctuated by outbreaks of frustration, like in 2011, when Turkish Cypriots protested against Erdoğan by gathering in front of the Turkish embassy in Nicosia, demanding reunification of the island and chanting, 'Ankara, get your hands off our shores!'

Since my last visit, there were more grotesque casinos on the coastline, and yet more half-finished buildings dotting the hills. Next door to the cemetery a racetrack had been built, and the whine of speeding cars rang out disrespectfully over the graves. I found my grandmother in the sprawling cemetery with the help of my mother's instructions over the phone and put the flowers I had brought on either side of the marble tombstone, confused memories of her funeral playing in my head. Waiting a respectful distance away were two English friends of mine and a man called Yannis, the Greek Cypriot boyfriend of one of them. We spent the rest of the day driving around my favourite spots in the north of the island. Yannis and I soon clashed, but not in the way I was expecting. Whenever I mentioned 'Turkish Cypriot' or 'Greek Cypriot' he would correct me: 'Cypriot'. Eventually I asked him what his problem was.

'You are perpetuating the nationalist rhetoric used by both Turkey and Greece. We are all just Cypriots. Brothers. Sisters. Whatever. We are not owned by Greece, or by Turkey.'

I saw his point, and agreed, but it was incredibly hard to self-edit in the way he suggested, and particularly difficult to discuss the war, or indeed current politics, without specifying what *type* of Cypriot we were talking about. Eventually we settled on a compromise: 'Turkish-speaking' and 'Greek-speaking' Cypriots, and even that was contentious, as both speak in a dialect much derided by their respective mainland co-linguists.

A few weeks later, I was staying in an apartment on the south coast of the island, owned by an old and grumpy man who seemed suspicious of my face. 'You sure you're English?' he asked me, several times. 'Your face is Cypriot.' Eventually, I admitted that my mother was from the north of the island, and a stony silence followed.

'Turkish? Hmmm,' he said, staring at me.

Here we go, I thought.

'I fought in the war. They took me prisoner and sent me to a prison in Turkey – in Mersin, you know it? For four months, they gave me only four olives a day to eat. Sometimes bread, sometimes no bread. No water. We had to fight to drink the toilet water.'

We sat in silence a while, and on the wall opposite I noticed a faded photograph of a young man dressed in army fatigues and holding a gun, unmistakably my host. Perhaps I had made a terrible mistake, revealing my true identity to this ex-soldier who probably had Post Traumatic Stress Disorder and an abiding hatred for Turks.

The next morning, he came and knocked on my door. '*Merhaba!*' he said awkwardly. I took this as an olive branch, but over the next few days his grumpiness made me nervous and I became convinced that he secretly hated me. Then I took myself in hand – who was being xenophobic and judgemental in this situation, him or me? I've always prided myself on being tolerant and all-loving of Greeks, Turks, everybody, but here I was reading into an old man's moodiness when maybe the paranoia was all mine. Perhaps I have not entirely left behind the suspicions instilled in me from a childhood spent north of the border.

As I spent time in the south, I thought more and more about my grandmother's desperation to make Greek-speaking friends in London, how she clung to Cyprus in that grey, faraway city full of strangers, where she never really belonged. She loved to

sit on a bench near our flat in north London, watching the world
go by. One day, an old man sat down next to her. She looked at
him; he looked at her. Minutes passed before mutual recognition
dawned: here was her old friend Spiros, the father of the boys
who taunted my mother with ham sandwiches. They broke into
excited Greek.

'Spiro! What are you doing here? Do you live here too?' asked
my grandmother.

'Şifa *hanım*, it's good to see you. I'm actually visiting my son in
the hospital up the road, he's not well.'

'I'm so sorry to hear that. How is your other son these days?'

A pause.

'You didn't hear? When the Greeks arrived in '74 he refused to
fight with them. He said he didn't want to kill any Turks, so they
shot him.'

My mother related this exchange to me many years later, a very
simple, searing story of humanity that made me retrospectively
understand the grandmother I had known as a child. She was not a
refugee in the most extreme sense when she came to London; she
was not forced to leave Cyprus, but she left behind friendships that
had existed against all odds, and a community deeply damaged by
war – she was a refugee of political barbarism. Like the exchange of
1923, there was an exodus on both sides of Cyprus after the partition in 1974, and an arbitrary cruelty in the 'solution'. Though
my grandmother remained heartbroken, it was easier for her to
retain her sense of identity hundreds of miles from home than
it has been for the Turks of Thrace to retain theirs in the place
they have called home for generations. Such is the crazed nature

of civilized tribalism, or nationalism, in neighbouring countries with centuries' worth of political grievances to air – or in Bruce Clark's words, the 'perpetually shifting symbiosis' which has existed between these countries since the Battle of Troy.[36]

Minarets in the West

'"This soup is as cold as the sea!" But he was not shouting at the soup. He was shouting at the Turks, at the Venetians, at the Austrians, at the French, and at the Serbs (if he was Croat) or at the Croats (if he was a Serb).'

Rebecca West, *Black Lamb and Grey Falcon*

Bridge on the Drina

On a 500-year-old humpbacked bridge in Mostar, southern Bosnia-Herzegovina, a sunburned man in tiny swimming trunks is collecting coins from tourists. After ten minutes, he hands the money to a friend before stepping on to the crest of the bridge. Breathing deeply and stretching like an Olympic champion, he pauses for effect before simply stepping off and plunging into the green water twenty-four metres below. Robbed of a proper diving performance, the crowd nevertheless bursts into nervous applause as he surfaces from the frothing water, alive.

Spanning the River Neretva near the modern-day border with Croatia, the Stari Most bridge was commissioned by Suleiman the Magnificent in 1566. Impressive even today, it was at its completion the widest man-made arch in the world; the 17th-century travel writer Evliya Çelebi described it in characteristically extravagant terms, 'like heaven's rainbow ... a bridge so high it seems to be connecting two clouds'. Its creator, Mimar Hayrüddin, was a star student of Suleiman's court architect, Mimar Sinan, the Christian designer of iconic mosques across the empire. Walking gingerly over its steep, slippery cobbles in flip-flops, I remember the local story that the original bridge was held together by egg-white mortar, an unglamorous but apparently effective technique, as it lasted for 427 years until deliberately targeted and destroyed by Croat shells in 1993 during the Bosnian war. In 2004, the bridge was carefully reconstructed by UNESCO with its original stones. Now it stands as though untouched while the town itself bears many marks of the 1990s war, riddled with bullet holes and craters. On many of the half-smashed brutalist apartment blocks, I saw '1981' scrawled in red graffiti paint – the date the local Velež football club, which united the town's Croats, Serbs and Bosniaks in fierce support, won the Yugoslav cup, before one of the most horrifically violent wars of the 20th century.

The Yugoslavian history of the town has now been overshadowed by its Ottoman history as tourists flock to see the reconstructed bridge; in the centre of town, the twisted alleyways are packed full of souvenir stands under the eaves of striped black and white, almost

Tudor-looking Ottoman houses. Most of the tourists wandering around are mildly adventurous middle-aged Turks bussed in from Sarajevo to the north. After their excursions, they sit in restaurants by the river, happily eating kebabs and marvelling at the legacy of their ancestors: 'Isn't this wonderful?' they gush. I was to witness a lot of this nostalgic tourism at play during my time in the Balkans, a strange tour of inspection of former territories by modern Turks; a collective basking in reflected historical glory.

From the 14ᵗʰ century onwards, the Balkans made up the long-standing core of the Ottomans' western territories; most of Greece had come under Ottoman control by the end of the 15ᵗʰ century, and Suleiman's Balkan conquests of the 16ᵗʰ century stretched to the gates of Vienna in the west and eastwards to Odessa in southern Ukraine. This regional dominance lasted until the early 20ᵗʰ century when the emergence of the concept of a nation state inspired rebellion among people who were made aware of their 'Bulgarian' or 'Greek' identities. Greece was an early trendsetter, rebelling in 1821 and establishing itself as an independent state in 1830. Nearly a century later, Bulgaria, Crete and Bosnia-Herzegovina declared themselves independent in 1908. Sultan Mehmet V fought desperately to keep these territories in the First Balkan War of 1912 and lost: it was the beginning of the end.

Today, mosques, bridges, caravanserais and *hamams* existing in various states of disrepair across the Balkans are physical relics of the Ottoman glory period and its decline. The bridges have survived best; the Stari Most is one of the most famous of these, but is surpassed in grandeur and cultural legacy by the Mehmet Pasa Sokolovic Bridge in Visegrad, the subject of the historical novel

Bridge on the Drina, written in 1943 by the Bosnian Nobel Laureate Ivo Andric. Surprisingly, the Communist authorities oversaw the building of new mosques in the 20th century, but many of these and the existing Ottoman mosques were destroyed in the Balkan wars between 1992 and 1995. Turkey has come to the rescue, flexing its regional muscles after barely a century's rest.

In the past sixteen years of Erdoğan's rule, the Turkish government has been busy building new mosques, and rebuilding Ottoman mosques and *hamams,* with millions of euros of taxpayers' money. A few hundred yards from the Stari Most bridge in Mostar is a perfectly restored 16th-century *hamam*, oddly sterile, and in Skopje, the capital of Macedonia, the entrance hall of the 15th-century Çifte Hamamı has been transformed into a modern art gallery, light twinkling down through the domed roof on to the exhibits. To give an imperfect Western analogy, this spending pattern is the equivalent of the current Italian government tirelessly and single-handedly restoring Roman ruins across Europe, with a view to promoting both Italy's imperial past and, by extension, its current standing in the world. It seemed absurd and vainglorious as I encountered it at the start of my journey; as I headed south, it made more sense.

The Balkans are a historical twilight zone, unforgiving on first-time visitors confronted with its chequered imperial chronology. As I travelled around the region, I was looking for the legacy of the Ottoman Empire in all its forms – architectural, political and social – and found it in the dungeons of Sarajevo's burned library, the cafés frequented by Turkish-speaking car mechanics in the Kosovan countryside, old tea gardens in Skopje and haunted wooden mosques in Bulgaria. The Balkan landscape is dominated by mountains, rivers and forests, a jagged terrain famously difficult to govern, even for the Ottomans. Like the rest of the empire, the Balkan territories were controlled as *vilayets*, or administrative regions, which were divided into smaller districts called *sanjaks*, ruled – theoretically – from hundreds of miles away by central command in Constantinople. The local government of these districts was entrusted to local *pashas*, who were expected to keep an eye on both the Muslim and more numerous Christian and Jewish subjects. To tackle the challenging mountain districts, the Ottomans chose powerful men to rule their own; two dozen Grand Viziers were chosen from modern-day Albania alone.

The famous 'Bridge on the Drina' in Visegrad was built by the great Mimar Sinan himself, and commissioned in 1572 by the Grand Vizier Mehmet Pasha, originally one of the young Christian boys taken from the area to serve in the Ottoman court in the early 16th century. In his novel, Andric imagines the traumatic experience of these boys, who were seized from their mothers and transported across the River Drina on a decrepit old ferry, eastwards to Istanbul and a life of service to the sultan. Mehmet Pasha Sokollu (the Turkified form of Sokolovici, meaning 'son of the falcon'), who was probably around ten years old when he was abducted from his mountain village, went on to have a glittering career, summarized by Andric like a proud father: 'a young and brave officer at the sultan's court, then Great Admiral of the Fleet, then the sultan's son-in-law, a general and statesman of world renown [. . .] who waged wars that were for the most part victorious on three continents and extended the frontiers of the Ottoman Empire, making it safe abroad and by good administration consolidated it from within.'[37]

Andric's gushing aside, the career progression of this abducted boy was truly extraordinary, and conjures up a Darwinian system in which only the most physically and mentally robust of child conscripts excelled, bringing glory to their place of birth; Sokollu joined the ranks of similarly glorious military figures, Christian conscripts-turned-Viziers from the same region. Andric's perhaps romanticized theory of Mehmet Pasha's commissioning (and personal financing) of the Visegrad bridge was that the great man never lost his painful memories of his birthplace and childhood, despite his later success in the empire. He was seized by a desire to 'join the two ends of the road which was broken by the Drina and thus link safely and for ever Bosnia and the East, the place of his origin and the places of his life. [. . .] That very same year, by the Vezir's order and at the Vezir's expense, the building of the great bridge on the Drina began.'

Missionary Zeal

In the aftermath of the USSR, the decline of the European Union and the rise of religious tensions, the Balkan states are trying to define themselves in the 21st century. Driving across Bosnia-Herzegovina, Serbia, Kosovo, Macedonia and Bulgaria, I noticed half-completed buildings everywhere, and this unrealized construction boom seemed to mirror the semi-constructed, aspirational state of the countries themselves. The region is ripe for more powerful states to carve out influence; Russia and Turkey are currently gaining on the ebbing influence of the EU and NATO in the former Yugoslavia and its surrounding region.

Bosnia-Herzegovina is a study in modern wannabe imperialism; while 500 years ago the country was occupied by Ottoman forces, it is now occupied to a surprising extent by Turkish money, which is poured into schools, media, construction and cultural projects in an attempt to recreate some approximation of past influence. I visited Mostar on a swelteringly hot day in July 2017, and after I watched the sunburned faux-diver performing for tourists, I passed over to the east bank of the Neretva, where a magnificent orange-striped building flies a large red-and-white Turkish flag; this is the Yunus Emre Institute, a governmental organisation set up by then-Prime Minister Erdoğan as a kind of cultural-centre franchise in 2007, with branches all over the world. The single staff member on duty in the Mostar branch – a burly man who spoke Turkish with a strong Bosnian accent – looked astonished to see me. The building was totally empty, the walls plastered with Turkish language charts ('B for Baklava', etc), pristine classrooms awaiting phantom hordes of eager Bosnian students. Despite boasting only twelve Turks, Mostar also maintains a Turkish Consulate well stocked with leaflets about Istanbul's newest museums, and genuine Turkish staff brimming with missionary zeal.

Sarajevo was founded by the Ottomans in 1461 and is a painfully beautiful city of cemeteries, surrounded by hills occupied by Serbian paramilitaries less than thirty years ago, and still haunted by trauma. Today every slope within the city hosts a swathe of white tombstones, many of them the graves of those killed in the recent war, others clearly Ottoman, with the recognizable turban-like headstone of the Sufi Bektashi order. Signs of the war are everywhere: the recently restored town hall was once a library, shelled by Serbian forces in 1992. In the fire that resulted, the one and a half million books, many of them Ottoman, were burned – in the underground archive space, previously used as dungeons, only black-and-white photographs of the collection remain. On the floors and walls of the building itself, almost too perfectly restored, the replicated Jewish Star of David and Islamic-style calligraphic art reflect the multilayered history of the city, visible today because of punctilious archaeologists paid by the EU.

In keeping with the conquering Ottoman modus operandi, the first governor of the city, Isa-Beg Ishakovic, immediately built a mosque, closed bazaar, *hamam*, castle and bridge, which was later the site of Franz Ferdinand's assassination in 1914. He also built a whirling dervish lodge, destroyed by Communist authorities in 1956 and rebuilt by the Turkish municipality of Konya, an uber-conservative town in central Anatolia, in 2013. Trudging up through a cemetery to reach it, I found a spotless Alpine chalet-like building perched above the city on a tiny flower-filled outcrop of land. It was utterly empty and in pristine condition, like the Yunus Emre Institute in Mostar. Inside, bookshelves filled with Turkish editions of the Koran and a silent caretaker who offered me tea; outside, neat flowerbeds and a brass plaque that proudly proclaimed that in 2013, then-Foreign Minister Ahmet Davutoglu (the bespectacled academic, and architect of Turkey's current Ottoman foreign policy), opened this lodge on behalf of the Republic of Turkey.

Turkish politicians take their visits to Bosnia-Herzegovina very seriously; Erdoğan has paid homage at the grave of the country's first president, the unapologetic Islamist Alija Izetbegovic, who died a few months after Erdoğan became Prime Minister of Turkey in 2003. In

2017, Izetbegovic's son Bakir, the Bosniak member of the country's current tripartite presidency, claimed that his father 'bequeathed' Bosnia-Herzegovina to Erdoğan in one of their last conversations: 'He recognized in him [Erdoğan] a future strong leader, and bequeathed him with caring for Bosnia-Herzegovina. I think that Erdoğan has been carrying out that bequest very well. Just look at this new action of his, to build a road between Belgrade and Sarajevo.' In return, Bosnian politicians take their obligations to Turkey equally seriously. In early 2018, the Turkish Nobel Laureate Orhan Pamuk was denied an honorary citizenship of Sarajevo by the city council commission after initial enthusiasm for the idea, seemingly because politicians from Izetbegovic's party feared the repercussions of welcoming a writer who is well known for criticising Erdoğan.

Much more so than Mostar, Sarajevo's Old Town is a Little Turkey, at least in the heady months of summer. On every street in the Old City, I could hear the Turkish spoken by tourists flown in from Istanbul by the national carrier airline on heavily subsidized flights. The Turkish flag is ubiquitous, flying from half-restored monuments, tourist agencies, shops and 15th-century whirling dervish lodges. Near the airport are two major Turkish universities, the International University of Sarajevo (IUS), festooned with suspiciously eclectic strings of flag-bunting advertising its international status, and, just over the road, the Burch University.

The IUS was founded in 2004 by a group of businessmen close to Turkey's ruling Justice and Development Party, and then-Prime Minister Erdoğan himself opened the new campus in 2010. When I visited in July 2017, a large poster hung on the side of the main university building celebrated the upcoming anniversary of the defeated 2016 coup attempt in Turkey, in keeping with the fierce promotion of the anniversary by the Turkish government. I had coffee in the university's drab cafeteria with Professor Mehmet Kovacevic, a softly spoken Bosnian man in his forties who pointed out to me the mountains behind the university where he fought as a young man during the 1992–1995 war. He was hired by the IUS science department a few years after its founding, a rare non-Turkish staff member. He tells me that when the university was founded, almost all the students were Turkish; these days, 65 per cent of the university's students are Turk, and the remaining 35 per cent are mainly Bosnians, with a handful of Croatian, African and Indonesian students. Most of the students are Muslim; a mosque stands next to the central building, and when I visit the girls' dormitories, posing as a prospective student, there is a *mescit* (prayer room) on every floor. There are no rooms with two beds; only three or more, in keeping with the Turkish government's precautions against romantic relationships forming among students of either sex.

Kovacevic discussed the Ottoman-esque aspirations of the university's founders with surprising candour.

'It was very important for [the founders] that Turks were in charge,' Kovacevic told me, candidly. 'All these people looked romantically at the Ottoman Empire. But the irony is that they are very shaped by the secular period [of the Turkish Republic]. They are suspicious of non-Turks – it is extremely difficult to get their trust. The tribal culture is deep-rooted. Yet the Ottomans had a kind of confidence and trust, they trusted their subjects and allowed diversity.'

I agree only up to a point; the diversity Ottoman rulers allowed was closely supervised, and any trust they showed their Christian subjects was hard-won. Yet Kovacevic has a point about confidence – the Ottomans were secure in their own power and ability to control their subjects, at least during the 16th, 17th and even 18th centuries. The Republic of Turkey, on the other hand, has been roiled by coups and political in-fighting throughout its existence and is deeply paranoid as a result. Ironically, a republic which is largely homogenous is more politically tribal than an empire composed of myriad different peoples. At the same time, Ottoman rulers could not dream of the kind of control over their subjects that modern states command – the technology and the surveillance, in particular.

At the risk of creating awkwardness, I asked Kovacevic whether the university's founders have shown the same appetite as the Ottomans for converting their subjects to Islam. Kovacevic, a non-practising Muslim 'despite my name', said he has never sensed any such zeal.

'My Turkish colleagues are very religious, but they are tolerant and careful not to pressurize me to go to the *cami* [mosque]. IUS was started in 2004 to accommodate covered Turkish girls who couldn't study in Turkey [the ban against headscarves in public institutions was overturned by the AKP in 2013] – it has religious beginnings. At first my colleagues were genuinely motivated as good Muslims. It was a pure sacrifice for teachers to come out here, no one had heard of it.'

This reminded me of the Ottoman courtiers sent out to colonize and run the empire; it was both a burden and a privilege, but also a chance to make one's name, the hard way.

According to Kovacevic, Turkish expenditure on Bosnia-Herzegovina, unlike the Ottomans', 'is more emotional than strategic'.

'They like to feel that they are a big brother to a country that needs their help. Turkey was a very attractive role model for countries in the Balkans – it also had a difficult past, but experienced huge economic growth and success. Now these things have changed but the soft power is still sitting on this outdated image. The Turkish tourists love coming to Bosnia because they feel national pride. They see the effects of Ottoman power – they made us all Muslims. We are their ex-subjects, after all.'

Just over the road from IUS is Burch University, affiliated to the US-based Islamic cleric Fethullah Gülen who is accused by the Turkish government of masterminding the failed 2016 coup. Burch University has lost many of its Turkish professors to prison cells in the purge that followed the coup attempt, according to Kovacevic. When I tried to visit the campus, the guard stopped me – peering through the gates, I saw weeds and a generally unkempt air. I wondered if it had enough funds and staff to reopen after the summer. Gülen-linked schools across the Balkans have suffered similar or worse fates; in 2018, I was relatively unsurprised to hear that six Turkish teachers in Kosovo had been kidnapped and forcibly extradited to Turkey to stand trial for treason as suspected Gülenists – Kosovan-Turkish diplomatic relations ranked second in importance to Turkey's determination to weed out the enemy without, as well as within.[38]

At the IUS, I bade Kovacevic farewell, mentioning that I was off to Visegrad, home to the 'Bridge on the Drina'.

'Visegrad,' repeated Kovacevic thoughtfully. 'Will you visit Andricgrad?' I told him yes, and that I intended to interview its creator. The professor's answer was unprintable.

The Art of War Zones

Andricgrad is a model village built as a film set within the town of Visegrad by Emir Kusturica, the film director as famous for his surreal Palme D'Or-winning art as for his political views. In early 2011, he announced he would be making a film adaptation of Ivo Andric's book *The Bridge on the Drina*, and the project is mired in controversy. Sarajevo-born Kusturica is widely despised by his fellow Bosnians for apparently renouncing his heritage and embracing both the Serbian government and its attendant Russian patronage (he converted to the Serbian Orthodox Church on St George's Day in 2005, and received the Order of Friendship from President Putin in 2016) – a bit like the backlash experienced by French actor Gérard Depardieu, so envied by my friend Ivan in Istanbul.

Andricgrad is as much of a political statement as a cultural project. It is first and foremost an homage to Ivo Andric, although his legacy has been twisted since his death. *The Bridge on the Drina*, contrary to popular belief, does not paint Muslims as unmitigated villains, but does begin with the building of the bridge in the mid-16th century and the cruelties perpetrated on the Christian locals forced into slave labour by the Ottoman authorities. Today, the bridge serves as a symbol of tension between Muslims and Christians, and this tension is utterly intertwined with nationalist violence. In 1992, Serbian paramilitaries massacred thousands of Bosniak men, women and children in the Visegrad region. Many of them were shot and then thrown from the bridge, and Bosniak women were systematically raped in nearby hotels. The bridge became a perverse symbol of the retribution of Christians against Muslims, supposedly righting the wrongs perpetrated against their Ottoman-subject forefathers hundreds of years ago on the same spot. In a horrible way, Ivo Andric's book – while not a polemic in itself – can be said to have inspired these reciprocal 20th-century massacres, and Kusturica's film project is a strange, silent seal of approval.

Battles and massacres can sear the subconscious of a people and shape future political narratives; their details can be augmented and twisted to fit nationalistic agendas centuries after the event. The Bosnian historian Edin Hajdarpasic has written about 'authentic fantasies' – grossly exaggerated stories based in historical fact and purporting to carry a central 'truth', like a parable or fairy story – used by Balkan nationalists to fuel hatred of historical oppressors and bolster modern political narratives. Historical legend has been warped to portray the Ottoman rule of Balkan Christian subjects as a black-and-white story of ogre-like Turks terrorizing brave, blameless Christians. Hajdarpasic brilliantly compares the 'authentic fantasies' of the Balkan nationalists to the Trump administration's sharing of Islamophobic fake news on social media (with the bogus justification that the message is true even if the story is not), and notes that 'throughout the 19th century, many Serbian, Croatian, Bulgarian and Greek nationalists developed extensive repertoires – diplomatic memorandums, poems, music, paintings – documenting their struggle for freedom and their suffering at the hands of "the Turks" (a label synonymous with Muslims). [. . .] Many decades after overthrowing the Turkish yoke, Serbian nationalists could revive narratives about Turk-like enemies even in the late 20th century – with catastrophic consequences.'[39]

The Battle of Kosovo in 1389 was fought between the

Ottomans and the Serbs; both armies were decimated, with a narrow but strategic win for the Ottomans that led to their conquest of the whole Serbian region. Hajdarpasic notes that the battle served as fodder for Serbian politicians like the notorious war criminal Slobodan Milosevic centuries later, who restaged the battle on its 600th anniversary in 1989, and thus turned it into a 'rallying ground for fresh nationalist mobilization. Invoking the rhetoric of "revenge against the Turks", Milosevic and fellow war criminals like Ratko Mladic then led genocidal campaigns against Bosnian Muslims in the 1990s.'[40]

President Erdoğan also dredges up ancient battles to glorify Muslim victories against Christian enemies and to bolster his own position as a Muslim strongman standing up to hostile Christians. His favourite is the Battle of Manzikert (modern Malazgirt near Turkey's border with Armenia) in 1071, when the (Muslim) general Alp Arslan led an army of Seljuks, precursors to the Ottomans, in defeating an army of (Christian) Byzantines said to be twice its size. Its commemoration is used to suit whatever political narrative Erdoğan happens to be pushing. On 26 August 2017, the 946th anniversary of the battle, Erdoğan arrived with great fanfare in Malazgirt, accompanied by soldiers in reproduction Seljuk armour, and addressed a huge crowd: 'We faced an assault on July 15th [2016] that appeared to be a coup attempt but was actually aimed at enslaving us . . . [we] fought the same figures as Alp Arslan. [. . .].' These 'same figures' is a reference to Erdoğan's claim that the 2016 coup attempt was backed by Western (Christian) powers. 'With a Turkish flag in one hand and Islam's green banner in the other, our victorious forebears entered Anatolia at Manzikert and marched to the middle of Europe with glory and honour.' Alp Arslan's march to Europe is historically inaccurate but no matter – this is what Hajdarpasic classes as an 'authentic fantasy' where the intrinsic 'truth' of the story is what is authentic: Muslim glory against Christian oppressors – the opposite of similarly tall legends utilized by Christian Balkan nationalists.

The film director Emir Kusturica could not have chosen a more dramatic setting for his most recent contribution to the creation of tangible authentic fantasy. The approach to Visegrad is utterly dominated by the magnificent 180-metre bridge, its eleven arches stretching from bank to bank of the Drina. Unlike the Stari Most, the bridge survived the 1992 war unscathed and stands in its original glory today. As I walked over it, an elderly fisherman stood in his wellies in the shallows below, a peaceful scene utterly at odds with the bridge's bloody history. On the western bank, I turned left and walked on to the gates of Andricgrad, which may one day serve as a film set, but currently operates primarily as an unabashed tourist attraction, complete with a large cinema (showing *The Emoji Movie* and *Planet of the Apes* at the time of my visit), a prominent church, replica Ottoman houses functioning as cafés and a large central statue of Ivo Andric. Serbian tourists throng its streets and large murals of Putin and Communist leaders grace the walls of the cafés, alongside modern Serbian heroes like Novak Djokovic. There is no mention anywhere of the 1992 massacres; it is one of the most astonishing disavowals of history I have ever seen. The encompassing town of Visegrad, largely devoid of Muslims after the massacres, is equally bereft of signs of the conflict – the most infamous 'rape hotel', Vilina Vlas, is now a spa with some glowing online reviews ('four stars – great place to relax').

I tracked down Kusturica just over the Serbian border in his other film-set village, Drvengrad, originally built for his film *Life Is a Miracle* and since used as a venue for cultural festivals. (In 2005, he told the *New York Times Magazine*: 'I'm fed up with democracy. In a democracy, people vote for the mayors. I wanted to build a city where I will choose the citizens.' After meeting him I doubted this was said entirely in jest.) At the time of my visit in July, the village was hosting the Bolshoi Music Festival, sponsored by the giant energy company Gazprom, which is majority-owned by the Russian state and a byword for Russian power in the region. As I approached, a helicopter circled overhead; by the time I had parked, an excited crowd had gathered near a helipad, among them two young Chinese women who had travelled all the way from Beijing for a glimpse of their idol. 'He's here! He's here!' Another fan turned to us, her eyes shining with the euphoria of proximity to Greatness. 'Did you see what he was carrying? A watermelon!' Opinion was divided about the symbolic or pragmatic role of Kusturica's watermelon, purchased that very afternoon in Belgrade, but he would have been furious to be associated with the legendary scene in *Dirty Dancing* that his entrance evoked.

Wandering around the fake village were journalists from *Russia Today* carrying cameras; the crowd seemed composed mainly of Russian press, the musicians themselves, and a few evangelical Kusturica fans like the Chinese women. I was handed a press card and told to stand by for my interview, but first there was a concert to attend: a ten-year-old girl in a puffy white dress, her feet barely touching the pedals, played Scott Joplin on a Steinway piano with great vivacity. The general effect of the fake film-set village, the high altitude, brutally strong Serbian wine and child prodigy made me feel slightly dizzy. In the interval, I was beckoned for my moment with the *maestro*. He stood in commanding fashion on stage as minions milled around him, a Balkan Quentin Tarantino, powerfully built in his shabby suit, with a shock of unruly grey hair. As his PR assistant announced my credentials, he scowled.

'Why should I give you an interview?' he demanded. 'The fucking British press always make me look like a bastard – the *Spectator* called me a child murderer.'

I opted for compliance. 'Mr Kusturica – what would you like to tell the British people?'

Momentarily disconcerted, he launched into a glowing account of the success of his cultural festivals, which continued for some time before I could interrupt to ask him about the legacy of war in the region he chooses to base himself.

'I turn war zones into cultural events,' he declared. 'This is territory which we can say is no-man's-land – as it was during World War One and World War Two. It is a borderline.'

It soon became apparent that Kusturica thinks of himself as the Andric of his time, transforming the legacy of war into art, and the legacy of art into a kind of hybrid homage both to himself and his idol, Andric.

'Since the Drina has such a bloody past, Andric devoted himself to art. Therefore, I wanted to devote a town to Andric.'

But can you make a cultural space that does not acknowledge the past, or rather, which selectively acknowledges the past, as in the case of Andricgrad?

Kusturica frowned. 'We can't forget the past. No – actually, we can.

We have atrocities committed on both sides. We have the Sbrenica story, which is also terrible. The oil fields in the Middle East are also war zones. The list goes on.'

Kusturica is well known for his belief that the West is hypocritical in its criticism of Yugoslavian history, given the Western legacy of colonization and violence. His whataboutery had a note of finality, so I turned to the issue of his reputation among Bosnia-Herzegovinians. While Kusturica is courted in international circles and lauded at Cannes, his countrymen reject him. How does that feel – does he feel any infinity with Orhan Pamuk, the Turkish Nobel Laureate, who is hated by many Turks for publicly acknowledging the Armenian genocide of 1915, and who needs a bodyguard while on Turkish soil?

'Yes, I feel a great artistic affinity.' But what about a political affinity?

'Oh, you mean the threats against my life? I don't care about them. I write, I play music, I get on with my life.'

As I noted this down, Kusturica reconsidered.

'Actually, many Bosnians love me. You could stop a man in Gorazde [a region of eastern Bosnia-Herzegovina where there is a majority Christian, pro-Serbian population] and he would worship me. You don't understand, it's not just the elite who know me.'

As I drove away from this unsettling interview, I began to understand why Kusturica wants to see himself as the champion of the common man. It is a simpler form of popularity, a way of rejecting the complexities of current political discourse, and of his own life choices. Kusturica is still mourning a simpler time and place: Yugoslavia. In October 1992, just six months after its fall, he said:

'I never wanted an independent Bosnia. I wanted Yugoslavia. That is my country.'[41] He no longer has that country – but he does have a cult of personality, and two model villages in which to enjoy it.

Serbia

I headed Russia-wards, north to Belgrade, and on the way, I noticed the minarets which had peppered most of the Bosnian country-side gradually give way to church spires and cemeteries filled with crosses. While Christians in Bosnia-Herzegovina still make up about 47 per cent of the population (the remainder being non-denomin-ational or Sunni Muslim), there are relatively few Muslims in Serbia, something that is reflected in the two countries' foreign policies: while Bosnia-Herzegovina welcomes Turkey and its money, Russia is a long-standing big brother to Serbia, and Putin's popularity is high among ordinary Serbians. Most Serbians I spoke to seemed to see no paradox in wanting to be part of Europe while harbouring a vaguer but more visceral attachment to Russia. Part of this is undoubtedly down to religious affiliation, however mute this is. Even the most secular of both Serbians and Bosnians seem attuned to being *not* Muslim or Christian respectively – not 'the other'. Turkey and Russia both exploit this fault line.

The road into Belgrade betrays Serbia's reliance on Russian and Chinese money – Gazprom and Huawei-branded skyscrapers greet visitors coming into the city, and a new bridge – the 'Chinese Bridge' – has been built over the Danube by the Chinese, in exchange for a massive loan to the Serbian government. Belgrade was once a frontier of the Ottoman Empire; in 1521, seventy years after an initial siege, Suleiman the Magnificent succeeded in conquering the Byzantine fort which still dominates the southern side of the city, in the centre of Kalemegdan Park (from the Turkish words *kale*, 'castle', and *megan/meydan*, 'battlefield/city square'). The Christian inhabitants were transported en masse to the outskirts of Istanbul, to an area which became known as the Belgrade Forest, where rich Turks today play golf and relax in gated villas far from the political smog of the city. The visible Ottoman legacy of Belgrade today is patchy, confined mainly to ruins rather than urban architecture; Zemun, a northern suburb twenty minutes' drive away, was only temporarily occupied by the Ottomans and was indeed a separate village until 1934. You can tell – it is unmistakably Austro-Hungarian, full of picturesque churches and pastel-coloured houses.

Walking around the ramparts of the Belgrade fortress, I couldn't help thinking of Topkapi Palace in Istanbul, dominating the once-forested peninsula on the southern European side of Istanbul. Today, Turkish tourists wandering around Kalemegdan Park are looking primarily for Ottoman ruins, such as the fountain erected in honour of Mehmet Pasa Sokolovic, of Visegrad fame, or the old 'Amam' (*hamam*), erected in the 17th century below the steep ramparts of the fort. I tagged along with one Turkish tour group who grumbled when they discovered the mausoleum of an Ottoman pasha obscured by scaffolding – not quite the gratifying sight of colonial glory they came for.

Despite wielding far less influence in Serbia than in Muslim-majority Balkan countries, the Turks are hard at work here too. In Kalmegdan Park, a large photography exhibition honoured the defeat of the 2016 coup attempt. Looking closely at the blown-up photographs of angry citizens attacking tanks and President Erdoğan attending the funerals of the slain, I noticed the sponsor of the exhibition: TIKA, a Turkish government directorate explicitly devoted to funding projects in Turkic- or Turkish-speaking communities, founded in 1991 after the fall of the USSR. Its website states that 'Turkey and the countries in Central Asia consider themselves as one nation containing different countries'; in the early 2000s, TIKA expanded into the Balkans, and then Africa and even Latin America, pushing beyond its original remit of Turkic- or Turkish-related communities to pastures ever more ambitious: a modern-day empire of influence.

The Kalemegdan photo exhibition, which was produced by Anadolu Ajansı, Turkey's state news outlet, also popped up like a travelling propaganda installation further south in my Balkan travels, for example in the Muslim town of Novi Pazar, centre of the southern Serbian area of Sandzak which was once an important administrative area of the Ottoman Empire. The town itself feels conservative – many women wear the headscarf, and only one bar openly serves alcohol – but the gambling shops on the high street proclaim liberal laws.

Turkish influence is particularly strong near the Serbian–Kosovan border in the Sandzak area (Turkish: *sanjak*, literally meaning 'region'). The usual Turkish-funded mosques are here, along with branches of Turkish banks (including the state 'Halk Bank'), and the Istanbul-based organization Friends of Sandzak, which facilitates marriages, language classes and general support networks between the Serbians who emigrated in large numbers to Turkey over the past twenty years, and Serbia-based, self-identifying Turks. In 2009, soft power hardened when then-Foreign Minister of Turkey Ahmet Davutoglu intervened in a local political dispute, much to the anger of the Serbian government. On buildings and walls just outside the centre of the town, I saw the words 'INDEPENDENT SANDZAK' scrawled in graffiti; many of the residents resent Serbian rule and wish to revert to the city-state identity they held during the Ottoman era. Strangely, here, in the 21st century, the local desire for greater political independence is based in nostalgia for long-gone Otto-man-subject status.

In Novi Pazar, I conducted one of the most bizarre interviews of my life with Alija Sahovic, the president of the Novi Pazar branch of the Friends of Sandzak. I had first tried to track down the group's headquarters via Facebook – I sent a message in Turkish, and received a response in Turkish, inviting me to come and visit. Then, when I tried to ask about precise directions, I found myself inexplicably blocked.

I decided to go anyway, based on the map shown on the Facebook page, but could find no trace of the place in the sleepy river-side neighbourhood. As I stood rather helplessly outside a butcher's shop strung with calf carcasses, a sixteen-year-old boy wandered out. He was called Elhan, and spoke excellent English thanks to a passion for American films. To my relief, he decided to help me – 'I don't want a salary,' he said solemnly. 'But you must buy some beef sausage from my father's shop – no pork, we are Muslims here.'

After an hour of knocking on doors, a middle-aged bald man with a large beak of a nose poked his head out of the upper window of one house. 'What do you want?' he demanded, in Serbian. This was

Alija Sahovic, and this was his house, aka the HQ of the Friends of Sandzak. He answered my Turkish greeting in kind – '*merhaba*' – so I continued my pleasantries, only to be informed by Elhan that Sahovic could not actually speak Turkish – the local version of Serbian had incorporated a few Turkish words since Ottoman times, hence my confusion.

'We took Turkish words, like *merhaba* and masturbated them into Serbian,' declared Elhan. I kept a straight face so that he would continue to translate for me, craning his head up at the upper window where Sahovic's face still poked out warily.

'Alija apologizes for blocking you on Facebook – he was worried you were a Gülenist [follower of Gülen].' I had no idea why Sahovic thought a Gülenist might be trying to infiltrate his group, but his attitude mirrored the paranoia of Turks in the aftermath of the attempted coup. Apparently, he had translated my Facebook message and sent a reply with the help of a Serbian friend based in Turkey, who also advised him to block me. I think I was the first non-Serb to ever contact the group.

Assured that I had honest intentions, Sahovic led us round to the back door through his garden. To my surprise, the terrace was strung with AKP bunting – Turkey's ruling political party – and large flags with President Erdoğan's face on them. We went into the house, where Sahovic showed me further stashes of AKP bunting and stationery, Turkish Korans, and even AKP-branded versions of the decorative wands wielded at Turkish circumcision ceremonies – an extravaganza of nationalist merchandise packed into boxes in his basement because there was not enough space to display it all in his house.

Upstairs, my host insisted on fetching me tea prepared in the Turkish style, leading me into the kitchen to show me the samovar. '*Türk çay!*' he said proudly, beaming as I accepted my tulip-shaped glass. In the sitting room, we sat on a leather sofa in front of a flat-screen television showing TRT, the Turkish state news channel – incomprehensible to Sahovic, but he enjoyed having it playing constantly in the background, and occasionally being treated to the sight of Erdoğan's face.

I was overwhelmed by this Serbian man's passion for the modern reincarnation of the empire that had subjugated his ancestors. It was almost as though he was suffering from a historic case of Stockholm syndrome – a version of the 'Make America/Britain Great Again' nostalgia, but from the point of view of the colonized, rather than the colonizer. Why did he feel such an affinity for Turks?

'He thinks everyone should feel Turkish because the Ottomans made us, they gave us Islam,' Elhan translated. Apparently, Sahovic considered himself, fundamentally, a Turk. Not so long ago, his family members grew up under Ottoman rule, speaking Turkish.

'Alija's mother's grandfather knew Turkish as well as Serbian,' said Elhan. 'And his wife's grandfather only knew Turkish. Here, until 1912, Turkish was the native language.'

Sahovic was clearly regretful that he himself could speak only Serbian, which he insisted on calling 'Sandžakian'. Listening to him desperately trying to convey his admiration for President Erdoğan, I was struck by how powerful Turkish influence had become in this region during the last fifteen years and in particular, how important the Islamic element of Sahovic's Ottoman self-perception was. Before Erdoğan's Justice and Development Party (AKP) took power in 2003, no Turkish government had been so explicitly religious – indeed, most were much more secular. Erdoğan has been the first Turkish leader to effectively wield the Muslim card in pursuing a foreign policy which essentially seeks to resuscitate an Ottoman sphere of influence. The Muslim card was the common denominator between the Ottomans and the Turks – the denominator which Atatürk had temporarily erased when he created a secular Republic, and which Erdoğan had effortlessly reintroduced shortly after he came to power, knowing it would have enormous resonance far beyond Turkey's borders.

For Sahovic, the Christian Serbs were oppressors, and the Turks were true and rightful overlords. 'Serbia is pushing out the Turkish influence,' he told me, seemingly oblivious to the last century of history. As I left, I asked him to pose for a photograph in front of the flags in his garden. He stood, proudly, making the Islamic Rabia sign adopted by Erdoğan when he addresses his rallies of the faithful – right hand held aloft, fingers spread, thumb tucked in. As I waved goodbye and walked away, slightly dazed, I reflected that Alija Sahovic was almost certainly the most historically confused middle-aged fanboy I would ever encounter.

Kosovo and Skopje

To get from Novi Pazar to Kosovo, you have to drive via Montenegro, because Serbia regards Kosovo not as an independent state but as Serbian territory occupied since the war of 1999, during which NATO forces intervened to stop the killing of the country's large ethnic Albanian contingent by Serb forces. The route is incredibly dramatic – up and down winding, heavily wooded mountain roads, via suspicious border guards who demand unnecessary 'insurance' to let you pass. The Kosovan landscape is flat, a kind of war-ravaged basin encircled by hills. My first stop was Peć [Albanian] or Peja [Serbian], a sleepy town with the usual Ottoman bridge, mosque and bazaar I had come to recognize in the towns of Bosnia-Herzegovina and southern Serbia. Like most of the mosques in Kosovo, the Bajrakli mosque was damaged during the 1999 war; in this case, the interior was burned to a cinder and restored with the financial help of the Italian government. Outside it, men sell Albanian flags as well as flags depicting maps of Kosovo with wildly ambitious borders, encompassing Sandzak, Albania and even Corfu – a kind of fantasy Albanian mini-empire. In each sub-section of the Balkans, I was to find unique self-declared identities such as this.

A few hours south-east of Peja is Prizren, a beautiful town dom-inated by a citadel and a lofty Orthodox church, now cordoned off and sporadically guarded by KFOR (NATO's Kosovo Force) since 1999. Mosques and churches throughout Kosovo were tar-gets during the war; the church in Prizren town was torched and a gloomy Serbian guard told me that the tiny Christian community was 'dead' – his church had become a lacklustre tourist attraction, not a functioning place of worship. Outside, a sign obscured by deep scratches proclaimed: 'This building site is protected by law. Any act of vandalism and looting will be considered as criminal offense of the utmost gravity.' In the town centre, KFOR soldiers patrolled, in slightly aimless fashion, and from the Byzantine citadel above the town I watched Black Hawk helicopters circle – the stern eye of the West still obvious amid simmering tensions nearly twenty years after the conflict. Later, I tried to get into the American army base outside Prishtina, improbably called 'Camp Bondsteel'. A gale-force dust storm was gathering as I waited at the heavily guarded gate for the permission that never came, chatting to the soldiers above the howl of the wind.

'The Kosovans seem to like you,' I shouted, remarking on the abundance of American flags flying from ordinary civilian homes.

'They'd better,' a red-haired soldier shouted back, in a Texan drawl. 'They wouldn't be here if it wasn't for us.'

The 17th-century Sinan Pasha mosque fifty metres away from the vandalized church in Prizren has been restored to its former glory by TIKA money, according to a brass plaque proudly bearing the Turkish flag and seal of the Turkish presidency; an Albanian-language newspaper claimed the renovations cost 1.2 million euros. Inside, as I gazed up at the calligraphy on the inside dome of the Sinan Pasha mosque, a young man came up to me, sensing I was not a local. He addressed me in English, but on an impulse, I answered in Turkish.

'You speak Turkish!' he exclaimed. 'Yes,' I said. '. . . As do you?'

Ilaz, as he introduced himself, was visiting family in Kosovo; he had settled in Switzerland, in common with many Kosovans who had fled there during the war. He explained that most people in Prizren had spoken Turkish since Ottoman times, having not been as effectively 'Serbified' as the inhabitants of Novi Pazar, including the unfortunate Alija Sahovic. To me, someone used to standard mainland Turkish, the version that had persisted in Prizren sounded like a peculiar dialect. Later, I spoke to a newsagent who compared it to the Turkish spoken by people in the Black Sea – not a separate language as such, but with idiosyncratic pronunciations and grammar. He introduced proudly himself as Unal – 'a totally Turkish name'. He claimed that the 'modern' Turkish he and I were speaking was different to what he spoke at home with his family, and which I heard snippets of as he spoke to his daughter on the phone – 'It is an old Turkish, Ottoman.' This seemed to me a romantic view – I could discern no archaic words, just an odd pronunciation, but it was interesting that Unal thought he was speaking Ottoman. Remembering Sahovic's adoration of Erdoğan, I asked him what he thought of Turkish politics.

'We are just happy that Turkey is strong at the moment. No doubt if we lived in Turkey we would support some party or other – my relatives live in Izmir, they like the CHP [Turkey's main opposition party] – but as it is, we just like the fact that Turkey is strong. It's like supporting Turkey in a football game – you don't care which club the individual players are from. You just support Turkey.'

His analogy stayed with me: here was a more long-standing feeling of kinship than Sahovic's frenzied worship of Erdoğan's brand, and I believe the key to this was language, which produces perhaps a more enduring umbilical cultural connection than religion, at least in Kosovo: Turkish had been spoken here since time immemorial, so a feeling of affinity with Turkey was not so explicitly linked to Islam or politics (although, admittedly, Turkey's perceived ascendance under Erdoğan's rule made it more attractive, like a star striker enhancing a national team). Kosovo is, unexpectedly, less politicized than Serbia, in the sense that it is more or less homogenously Muslim, as opposed to a Christian state with a fiercely independent and resentful Muslim minority in the south. In Serbia, Turkey can exploit ethno-religious tensions and promote Turko-Islamic identity in people like Alija Sahovic; in Kosovo, a sense of Ottoman heritage is well established, without the frenzy of a recent awakening.

A few kilometres outside Prizren I found an even more Turkish enclave: Mamusha (originally 'Mahmut Pasha'). Essentially an open-air car factory, it is the only ethnic Turk-majority town in Kosovo, and a gate at the entrance of the town welcomes you in Turkish: '*Hoşgeldiniz*', with Albanian and English signs underneath, almost as afterthoughts. Its streets are lined with car part-replacement stores, garages and kebab houses full of mechanics eating lunch. Unlike in Prizren, I heard no Albanian at all. I also saw no women – a young man I met in the park told me they come out at weddings and *bayrams* (festivals), and indeed a wedding party passed by as I walked down the main street, cars trailing white and red streamers, horns honking incessantly and women waving shyly from inside the cars.

Clearly, in Mamusha the Erdoğan brand is big, as in southern Serbia, due largely to ties created with Turkey by the mayor, Arif Butuç, who welcomed Erdoğan in 2010 to open the 'Anatolia' primary school, and who supported him through the anti-government Gezi Park protests in 2013. The local park is full of benches donated by Keçiören Municipality in Ankara, with 'Keçiören' painted on to the wood. It's as if the town itself has been branded, and the locals are more than happy with that. 'We are Turks, from long ago,' a waiter in the Genç Osman ('Young Osman') restaurant told me. I asked him if he felt Kosovan. 'My heart is Turkish.'

On 23 July, shortly after my visit, the Ottoman Tomato Festival would be celebrated with much pomp and ceremony – 'flags and drums, there is a big procession', the young man in the park told me. 'Turkish vegetable suppliers come and try the tomatoes, then they pick the best ones and order imports. We produce many tonnes of tomatoes.' An extensive internet search confirmed my suspicions that there was no such Ottoman tradition, which meant that a local trade festival had been retrospectively 'Ottomanized' and jazzed up for maximum nationalistic impact.

At this point in my travels, I made a realization: nouveau-Ottomanism is not purely a construct of Erdoğan's, or the AKP's. Muslims in the Balkans are aware of their Ottoman heritage and already identify with Turkey – there is a ghost empire here ripe for the taking and it just needs to be brought to life. There is no actual continuum between the Ottoman Empire and modern Turkey's power in the region, and other countries (Russia in particular) could claim former domination, but Turkey seems to be the country most aggressively courting influence – not always unchallenged. In 2012, Macedonia's Information and Society Minister announced that the broadcasting of Turkish soap operas would be reduced on national channels because Macedonia's own shows were being pushed past midnight as Turkey hogged the prime-time slots. 'To remain under Turkish rule for five hundred years is quite enough,' he semi-joked.

Kosovo is a good example of Turkey swooping in for the spoils of recent war; Erdoğan was one of the first world leaders to congratulate the newly declared independent state in 2008, nearly a decade after the 1999 war of independence. In October 2013, he visited Prizren and announced with characteristic paternalism that 'we all belong to a common history, common culture and common civilization; we are the people who are brethren of that structure. Do not forget,

Turkey is Kosovo, and Kosovo is Turkey!' The Serbian government furiously called his statement a 'direct provocation'. Some Kosovo-based Albanian language newspapers are also not fans of Turkish quasi-intervention in the country; in 2015, a Prishtina-based newspaper claimed that Erdoğan's business associates laundered money by building mosques in Kosovo tax-free via TIKA, which had restored at least thirty religious Ottoman structures in four years – if true, this conjures up a kind of mosque-building mafia empire.

Turkey has competition in the form of Saudi Arabia, particularly in Macedonia. In 2010, the *Sunday Times* reported on a Macedonian investigation into a network of extremist imams and Islamic terror cells allegedly funded by Saudi money; this was echoed by a Bulgarian journalist I met later in Sofia who told me that many ordinary Macedonian locals no longer go to mosques because of the extremist rhetoric preached by the new Saudi-funded imams – 'You can always tell the Saudi-built mosques' (something that is also true for some of the mosques around Sarajevo). Turkey's relatively moderate form of Islam seems to have been more naturally absorbed in the Balkan region; the fall-out between Turkey and Saudi Arabia over the Qatar crisis in 2017 intensified the proxy Islamic Balkan war that has been playing out since the 1990s.

From Kosovo, I went south to what was still then the Republic of Macedonia – in June 2018, an accord was signed to change its name to the 'Republic of North Macedonia', solving a thirty-year dispute with Greece over their respective claims to Macedonian ethnic and territorial identity. Unlike much of the Balkans, where the countryside is dominated either by Muslim or Christian villages, Macedonia is dotted with churches and mosques in quick succession.

The country felt almost Soviet, with street signs in Cyrillic, and socialist-style housing blocks even in the villages. On the banks of Lake Ohrid, hotels built in the 1960s reminded me of abandoned Soviet holiday homes on the banks of Lake Sary-Chelek in Kyrgyzstan, Central Asia – one of the other limited holiday destinations for Russians during the Cold War. The Ottoman past life of Ohrid itself, a town described by tourist operators as the 'Jerusalem of the Balkans', is obvious in its distinctive white houses with black-edged, jutting windows next to the remaining Byzantine churches. The overwhelming air is of a once-magical town gone to seedy tourism.

Macedonia's capital, Skopje, was conquered by the Ottomans in 1392 and remained under its control until 1912, when Macedonia joined the Balkan League in fighting for independence from the empire. After a massive municipal splurge in 2013 (207 million euros according to official sources, around twice that amount according to opposition figures), the visible narrative of the city is hideously ugly; some inexplicable bronze horses burst upwards out of a fake fountain, and gargantuan statues of Alexander the Great alongside Balkan nationalist heroes like Gotse Delchev and Pavel Shatev, who led rebellions against the Ottomans at the turn of the 20th century, dominate the centre. In fact, only pre-Christian and Christian leaders from Macedonia's past have earned their bronze form in Skopje's centre, with a strange gap coinciding with the 500-year period of Ottoman rule.

Despite the public denial of its Ottoman past, Skopje's social Ottoman legacy is strong, like Prizren's. Around 10 per cent of the community are ethnic Turks, concentrated on the eastern bank of the River Vardar, and even non-Turks speak the language brokenly.

The signs on mosques are in Turkish, as is random graffiti – 'Özlem [a girl's name], I'm so sorry', declared one anguished love-struck message scrawled on a garage door. A short way away from the old bazaar, I found surprisingly peaceful little tea gardens with old men sitting and chatting in Turkish over glasses of tea. In the bazaar itself, now given up almost entirely to tourists (many of them Turkish), I passed one baklava shop with an enormous faded poster of Erdoğan's relatively youthful face called 'Turkish Angela Merkel Baklava' – presumably established in the height of the politico-romance between the two leaders circa 2011 (and sadly lapsed since then), and noticed the lira–Macedonian denar exchange rate displayed prominently at the top of the bureaux de change. Skopje's architectural narrative may say one thing, but the reality of tourism is perhaps more eloquent – Turkey still has more than a foothold in a country it ruled for 500 years.

Minarets and Muftis

Bulgaria felt the most Soviet of all the Balkan states I passed through, and the most Christian; almost all the country's mosques were destroyed during the Russian–Ottoman war in 1878. To avoid the wrath of Muslim Bulgarians, Russians went about this destruction with an impressive level of subterfuge: they planted dynamite in the minarets of seven mosques and waited for a stormy night in December to set them off, later blaming lightning. Sofia is the accidental capital. It was chosen after it was liberated from Ottoman rule by the Russians in 1878, a modest town of 12,000 people, on the basis that it would also be the capital of Macedonia; as 20th-century history played out, however, and Macedonia achieved its own state, it lies not in the centre of Bulgaria but towards the edge, across the border from Serbia.

Bulgaria has the highest number of indigenous Muslims in the EU – around 1 million, or 15 per cent of the population: 75 per cent of them are ethnic Turks, the remainder Roma and Pomak, a Slavic ethnicity which converted to Islam during Ottoman rule and remain a very distinct, traditionally dressed and self-sufficient community. Despite the high number of Muslims, there is only one functioning mosque in Sofia, the russet-coloured, modest Banya Bashi Mosque, built by the great Mimar Sinan in 1576. Most Bulgarian Muslims (who are usually classified as 'Turks', regardless of whether they are ethnic Turks or not – an Ottoman throwback) live outside Sofia, where they feel more welcome – recent reactions to the refugee crisis have led to unprecedented levels of Islamophobia, as I was to find out.

A hundred metres away from the Banya Bashi Mosque is the city's only functioning synagogue, built in 1909 at the very end of Ottoman rule; it is strikingly beautiful, almost art deco. Just inside the hall is a wedding tent, and on the walls are commemorative plaques of deceased members of the congregation and boards of donors' names for a recent renovation project. The Bulgarian journalist Anthony Georgieff took me here; a prolific author, and the former editor of Bulgarian *Playboy*, he has amassed a huge amount of knowledge about Balkan history. As we walked to dinner, he kept stopping to point out items of interest – 'Look! Here are the fountains where residents can get mineral water for free – so healthy, the Germans would love this' – 'Ah, there is the house of the last Ashkenazi rabbi of Sofia, most Jews here are Sephardic of course.'

We went to a restaurant near Georgieff's house, where he insisted we sample several versions of the local spirit, *rakia*, made variously of apricot, figs and quince. Suitably fortified, he told me the story of the ethnic Turks of Bulgaria, in particular about the intensified anti-Turkish feelings during the Communist era. In 1986, when Bulgaria was under Soviet control, authorities, worried by the high birth rate of the 10 per cent Turkish demographic, decided that they should be Christianized and forced to assimilate, and part of that involved the imposition of Christian names – Mustafa became Michael overnight, whether he liked it or not.

'But no one knew this was happening. The American Embassy found out only when their [Turkish] driver informed them his name had been changed.'

The atmosphere worsened, and in 1988, a thinly disguised Soviet propaganda film was released, *Time of Violence*, which the Bulgarian writer Kapka Kassabova describes in her book *Border: A Journey to the Edge of Europe*:

'*Time of Violence* [was] the must-see event of the season and, bafflingly, remains Bulgaria's favourite film to this day, indicating a neurotic fixation on a doctored version of the distant past, the kind of fixation that drove murderous nationalists next door in Yugoslavia.'[42]

This 'doctored version of the distant past' echoes what the Bosnia-Herzegovinian historian Edin Hajdarpasic calls the 'authentic fantasy' of Ottoman oppression in the Balkan region.

'It was a fictionalized portrait of the Islamization of the Rhodope region in the seventeenth century, complete with the country's finest actors, soulful music, and impalement scenes to haunt your lifelong nightmares. Its message was as simple as the production was sumptuous, and the message was: the good guys (Christian Bulgarians) were quietly heroic and their women were pure. The bad guys (the Turks) were sadists with shaven heads whose women signalled their moral turpitude by eating baklava. The main villain was a janissary, once taken from the same Christian village he was now converting by fire and sword. People gobbled it up with a masochistic relish, and collective self-pity lubricated the exodus of the ethnic Turks.'[43]

This exodus came in 1989, only months before the end of the Cold War, and was carefully PR-managed: Bulgarian-born Turks were 'allowed' to return to Turkey (and indeed, were invited to do so by the Turkish government at the time, who immediately handed them passports) but Georgieff says that, in reality, many were expelled by the Bulgarian authorities.

'Secret police told them they had twenty-four hours to move out – these poor people left with only what they could carry across the border. My German wife at the time was travelling near the border and saw these refugees and thought they were traders, they had carts full of bits of furniture, and most didn't have horses so they pulled the cart themselves. No one [outside Bulgaria] knew what was going on.'

Some of these Bulgarian Turks returned in due course because life in Turkey was too hard. 'They couldn't integrate. For example, they spoke a kind of Ottoman Turkish, not modern Turkish.'

Georgieff, a Bulgarian of relatively typical heritage, can understand Turkish thanks to a childhood spent chatting to his grandmother. 'Like almost everyone else in Bulgaria at the time, my grandmother had many friends and neighbours all of whom spoke their languages, including Turkish. Language purity was not – and still is not – a

Balkan virtue.' At this point in our dinner, he had relaxed and started
telling me about his travels in Turkey, a country he loves.

'I can make myself understood, but my limited vocabulary of
Bulgarian Ottoman-style Turkish can lead to some unfortunate
incidents. I was in a restaurant, and every time the waiter brought
something I said "*aşk olsun*" – in Bulgarian Turkish, that just means
"how lovely". But the waiter kept taking the dish away!' I tell him
that in modern Turkish, the expression is one of emphatic disagree-
ment. 'Yes, a man on a table next to me told me that, so finally I could
eat.' Later, to further illustrate his point about language, he sent me a
trailer for *Game of Thrones* made by Bulgarian fans who, in his words,
'wanted to make fun of the kind of bogus Turkish Bulgarians think
is actual Turkish'. I could understand less than half of it.

Before we parted, Georgieff's buoyant mood deflated as he
described the increase in Islamophobia in Bulgaria in the wake of
the refugee crisis, and the 'extreme nationalist' government of the
last few years. 'The deputy Grand Mufti of Bulgaria was beaten up
with his wife and daughters the other day. It is disgraceful – this
country is a house of straw, it just needs a match to set it alight.'

I asked if the deputy Grand Mufti was an ethnic Turk. 'Yes. His
name is Birali Birali. You want to interview him? Here's his number.'

Birali Birali (the name is particularly comic to a Turkish ear) is a
very busy man – luckily, he had a spare half-hour between meetings
to see me the following day, so I went to his office near the mosque.
He welcomed me with a gentle inclination of the head – no shaking
hands with a strange woman. To my surprise, his office was full of
Dali-esque paintings, featuring strange objects half-sunk in sand, and
when I remarked on them he smiled – 'I love art,' then pointed to

himself: 'Bir Dali!' It took me a moment to realize the holy man was making an unexpected pun on his own name, and claiming authorship of these artworks, or so it seemed. Swallowing my surprise, I got to business: why the recent increase in Islamophobia in Bulgaria?

'There is fear in some parts of Bulgaria, a restlessness. They say we Muslims will bring sharia law, that we will become radicalized. They have made a building [of Islamophobia] on the foundations built in the Communist era. They learn in school how the Ottomans oppressed them for five hundred years, there is a sense of resentment towards the Muslims, the heirs to the Ottomans, supposedly.

'Then, of course, there are the refugees coming in, and sadly there is propaganda in the news, plus news of ISIS and so on – these ideas are thrown around and Bulgarians start thinking, "Will our Muslims become radicalized?" Vigilante groups are rounding up refugees at the border with Turkey. Generally, in this country we get on very well with Christians, but in Sofia in particular it has got very bad.'

Birali experienced this first-hand a few weeks before our interview, when his headscarf-wearing daughters and wife were attacked by a group of teenage girls in the street as he parked their car nearby.

'My daughters tried to protect my wife, so they got beaten badly. When I caught up I tried to protect them, I was also beaten – here,' he showed his arm, 'bruises all along my arm. But the media said my daughters lied – that in fact they started the fight. This is really the bit that hurt us. My daughters are very traumatized by this; perhaps they would have got over the attack itself but really, when someone accuses you of lying . . .' His voice trails off.

He believed his family were attacked simply for being visibly Muslim – the teenagers did not know of his position of deputy Grand

Mufti. In 2011, outside the mosque at Friday prayers, far-right Bulgarians burned the prayer mats of worshippers. Georgieff had told me about this incident; he had been present with the Turkish Nobel Laureate Orhan Pamuk, and when the attack started, they had run off to take refuge in the synagogue nearby.

As with the Turkish community in Serbia and Kosovo, I felt compelled to ask Birali what he and his congregation thought of Turkey's ruling AKP, and Erdoğan. His answer was circumspect.

'In general, the Turks in Bulgaria feel close to Turkey – we receive a lot of support, for example for our schools. So we support Turkey in turn.' As I thought.

In March 2017, the Bulgarian government cancelled a previous agreement with the Turkish government which had allowed it to pay the salary of imams in Bulgaria via the Diyanet (Turkey's religious body). The reason was that Turkey's government was seen to interfere in Bulgaria's snap parliamentary election on 26 March, encouraging Bulgarian Turks to vote for Muslim candidates.

As it happened, I had been in southern Bulgaria in March that year, at the time of an incident when Bulgarian border guards turned away busloads of Turks, based in Turkey but with Bulgarian citizenship granted to them in 1989, who had been bussed in to vote for AKP-sanctioned Bulgarian candidates. This was also in the lead-up to the referendum in Turkey, in April 2017, in which Turks narrowly voted for President Erdoğan to gain executive powers, amid accusations of vote-rigging. I had crossed into the country from Greece, at the Makaza checkpoint. There had been an immediate change in the landscape, from the rolling, grassy hills of Northern Greece to more dramatic forested hills dotted with rather bleak-looking villages, and a darkening horizon as a thunderstorm rolled in. By the time I got to my destination, the 600-year-old wooden Yedi Kizlar mosque near the village of Podkova, the rain was torrential and flashes of lightning cracked out of the sky. Looking up at the wooden minaret of the mosque as I sat in my car in the rain, it seemed incredible that it had withstood six centuries of thunderstorms and lightning bolts – I hoped it would survive one more.

The Yedi Kizlar or 'Seven Girls' Mosque is an object of religious-touristic pilgrimage for Turks today, its Facebook page alive with selfies. Its little cemetery has seven gravestones to represent the seven girls who, in legend, built the mosque, preferring to perish through hard labour rather than marry, and whose spirits are said to haunt the mosque even today. Most tombstones in formerly Communist Bulgaria have neither crosses nor the Bektashi turban-tops present in most Ottoman-era cemeteries throughout the Balkans, so the presence of the Bektashi tombstones alerts you to an emphatically Turkish village such as Podkova, which is easily the most depressing place I've ever been.

After my rain-soaked and slightly spooky mosque trip I needed food and friendly faces, and in Podkova I found neither; as I drove through the village I noticed an emaciated cow eating from a skip. The signs were not good, and sure enough, I had a futile search for food before finally discovering a shop whose owner would sell me bread and *sucuk* (a typically Turkish beef sausage, such as the one I bought from Elhan in Serbia in return for his translation services). At the back of the shop was a smoky enclosed terrace in which several Slavic-looking, middle-aged, ethnic Turkish men were discussing the upcoming referendum in Turkey, which was to decide whether

Turkey should switch from a parliamentary to a presidential system to solidify President Erdoğan's power. The men fell silent and stared as I sat near them; as in Mamusha, Kosovo, I had not seen another woman in public. After an excruciatingly long time they looked away and picked up the conversation again.

'He will steal the votes,' said the eldest of them, a man with a cynical, scowling face. 'Of course he will. This is his chance to become president forever – why *wouldn't* he?' 'He won't get away with it,' said another, younger man, with faux assurance. The first man cast him a pitying glance. While the conversation progressed in this vein, Bulgarian national television played quietly in the background – none of the men were watching, engrossed in the question of whether Erdoğan would win eternal presidency in a country none of them lived in, but felt utterly invested in.

Unlike Alija Sahovic in Novi Pazar, or Birali Birali in Sofia, these Podkovian Turks did not consider Erdoğan some kind of modern, paternalistic sultan, but a power-hungry politician. They were in a minority. Erdoğan and his AKP government have always been aware of the political advantages of resurrecting influence in the Balkan region, especially for trade, but there has always been a more emotional impetus behind this: Erdoğan identifies as an Ottoman leader in troubled modern times, leading the faithful, and his self-belief has translated into a strange reality. Sometimes he signals his Ottoman credentials with heavy-handed symbolism, sitting in his newly built, 1,000-roomed White Palace in Ankara with all the trappings of a modern sultan, and other times explicitly, such as when he lamented the precise loss of Ottoman territories at the fall of the empire in 1923.

'In 1914, our land covered two and a half million square kilometres. Nine years later it fell to seven hundred and eighty thousand
square kilometres.'

'Our land' is the key: Erdoğan and the fellow founders of the AKP
both assume and actively promote a political continuum between the
Ottoman Empire and modern Turkey which does not exist. During
the liberation of Mosul in 2016, Turkish state TV channels broadcast
maps of a new, enlarged Turkey encompassing northern Iraq, an old
Ottoman territory. If the Balkans were as militarily vulnerable, perhaps the map would have included those territories too, but given
Turkey's current sway in the region, such graphics are unnecessary.

On 20 May 2018, I found myself in a roaring crowd of 10,000
Erdoğan supporters in an Olympic stadium in Sarajevo, nearly a
year after my first visit to the city. While the Turkish president paced
the stage, microphone booming, the Bosniak leader Bakir Izet-
begović stood respectfully to one side, a host supplanted by his
guest. As I looked around at the adoring Turkish diaspora, most of
whom had travelled hundreds of miles to attend Erdoğan's only rally
on European soil, I realised that Alija Sahovic was almost certainly
somewhere in there too, waving his flag with as much gusto as any
Turkish voter, and not understanding a word.

Spires in the East

'The air over Jerusalem is saturated with prayers and dreams like the air over cities with heavy industry.

It's hard to breathe.'

Yehuda Amichai, 'Ecology of Jerusalem'

'The fact of simultaneously being Christian and having as my mother tongue Arabic, the holy language of Islam, is one of the basic paradoxes that have shaped my identity.'

Amin Maalouf

Jerusalem and the West Bank

The Turkish towns near the Syrian border, on the edge of the Arab world, have an echo of the centuries of life that existed before modern Turkey ironed everything out into homogeneity. In their

synagogues, mosques and churches of various denominations, congregations are tiny but still congregating. Before Syria's civil war,
Aleppo and Damascus would have been the logical points on my
journey further south. Instead, I went to Palestine and Lebanon, both
part of what was regarded as Greater Syria, an important region of
Ottoman control from 1516 until the end of the First World War,
when the territories were lost to the Allies. Fractious, racked by war
and hopeless politics, these are still places where Muslims, Jews
and Christians – not forgetting ancient peoples like the Druze and
Samaritans – have lived together for centuries. Lebanon's recognition
of religious minorities is perhaps the nearest modern equivalent we
have to the Ottoman *millet* groups, while Israel and the Occupied
Territories of Palestine show us some of the most disturbing consequences of the creation of the nation state.

Travelling through the Holy Land can be an unholy experience
for an atheist. There is something perverse about the atmosphere
of reverence still shown by millions of religious tourists every year
to a place so brutalized by war and apartheid. In Hebrew, Jerusalem
means 'City of Peace'; its Arabic name, Al-Quds (the 'Holy City')
is less obviously incongruous, but perhaps its most eloquent epithet
is from the medieval Arab scholar Muqaddasi: 'a golden goblet full
of scorpions'. Throughout its history, conquering crusaders, sultans
and 20th-century generals have marched through its gates; dominant
religions have been periodically foisted on it. In 1517, Selim the
Grim gained control of the city but it was his son Suleiman the
Magnificent who ordered the rebuilding of the city walls in 1536
and ensured that all faiths had access to places of worship within
these walls. In 1980, Israel absorbed Jerusalem and today the city is

carved up between east and west. The latter is officially part of the state of Israel, and the east is the cusp of the West Bank, Palestinian land controlled by Jordan and Egypt prior to the Six-Day War of 1967, and now controlled by the Israeli military.

Jerusalem is pockmarked by conflict and heavy with tension, but commercial and domestic life continues; on the winding streets of the Old City, between signposts marked in Arabic, Hebrew and English, hawkers sell everything from carved wooden figurines of Jesus Christ and miniature tinsel Christmas trees to carrot juice and freshly shelled walnuts. I went in November 2017, just before Trump's recognition of the city as the capital of Israel drew thousands of Palestinians to the streets in protest. The air was laced with a mix of winter street food: roasted chestnuts, Turkish coffee and frying meat, overlaid with the occasional waft of cheap frankincense. Most passers-by are tourists, pilgrims or a mixture of the two, transported by the busload from Tel Aviv airport. Herded by guides, they have the energy of children on a school outing, adding to my impression of Jerusalem as a kind of religious Disneyland, and wear signs around their necks denoting their affiliation to evangelical churches across the world: Houston, Manila, Taipei, Belfast.

Locals weave purposefully through the crowds – black-robed priests with long beards and aged nuns hobbling down the cobbled alleyways to hidden churches, ultra-Orthodox Jews making their way to the Wailing Wall, and Palestinian housewives buying vegetables. The scrum becomes particularly hectic on Friday afternoons, at the approach of Friday prayers and Shabbat. At a particular spot on the Via Dolorosa, said to be the path that Christ took on the way to his crucifixion, and now home to barber shops and souvenir stalls, pilgrims gather for reasons unknown to the casual observer. They stand with eyes closed, gently swaying as they sing holy verses, oblivious to the shouts of nearby shopkeepers advertising the price of cauliflowers. The chaos of Jerusalem's Old Town evokes the Grand Bazaar of Istanbul, but this cast of characters is like some vast Hollywood studio with extras mingling from several different sets. As a reminder that this is far from fiction, however, groups of soldiers from the IDF (Israeli Defence Force) stand silently at every junction, guns at the ready as they survey the crowd. Further up the Via Dolorosa is the seat of the Armenian Catholic Church, the joyfully named Church of Our Lady of the Spasm, but the focus of the route is the Church of the Holy Sepulchre, believed to be Christ's resting place and in many ways a microcosm of Jerusalem's divisions.

In high season, the Holy Sepulchre is alive with the flash of cameras as religious tourists jostle for space. Their guides lead them bravely through the fray, flags held aloft as though for benign Crusading armies. Several local Orthodox and Catholic denominations own particular sections of the church, ascribing authentic status only to their own territories and maintaining a fierce rivalry that seems comically petty to an outsider, like a real-life version of Monty Python's *Life of Brian*: 'Are you the Judean People's Front?' 'Fuck off! We're the People's Front of Judea!' Monks stick prissily to their sections, carefully cleaning the floor with mops that dare not transgress into the neighbouring patch. In 1187, quarrels over ownership of the church were so serious that Sultan Saladin of Egypt entrusted the key to a Muslim family, in the same year he defeated the Crusaders; today, Adeeb Jawad Joudeh al-Husseini, a descendant of the same Ghodayya Hashemite family, unlocks the church at 4 a.m. every morning and locks it at 8.30 p.m. every night.

One Sunday morning in early November, I sat at the back of the 9 a.m. service at Christ Church, the oldest Protestant church in Jerusalem, trying to work it out. The church was built in 1849, a decade into the Tanzimat reforms introduced by Sultan Mahmud II. This church was one of the many foreign missions that took advantage of the reforms to stake out a presence in the Holy Land. I was puzzled to find no iconography inside the church at all; even more curiously, all the script was in Hebrew, and a menorah (the Jewish seven-branched candelabra) stood on the altar. A priest from New Zealand was giving the sermon, in Anglican low-church style, to a packed congregation of mainly tourists.

None of it added up until I talked to the Ukrainian evangelist manning the museum next door, who explained that the church was founded by London-born Messianic Jews – i.e. Jews who believe that Christ is the Messiah – and who were eventually folded into the Protestant Church because they were rejected by Orthodox Jews. I took a moment to appreciate the news that Sultan Mahmud II indirectly enabled these Londoners to eke out a stake in the religious real estate of the most holy city in the world while the market was down in the mid-19th century.

Hundreds of tourists flock every Sunday to flagship churches like the Holy Sepulchre and Christ Church, and the services can seem oddly formal and performative. Visiting priests from across the world are given special billing, sermons are posted online and members of the congregation are urged to download the official church podcast (available on iPhone and Android) to enhance and preserve their religious experience.

The services in smaller, local churches are far more relaxed – for example, the Greek Catholic church by Jaffa Gate was entirely dominated by tiny, noisy children running down the aisles. The church was a riot of colour, its walls covered in images of saints in pastel blue and yellow. The service was attended by a small but loyal local crowd; they sang hymns from memory in their mother tongue of Arabic, and the badly behaved children were never shushed. At one point, a particularly disruptive roving toddler was scooped up by a woman as he scuttled past her, and kept occupied while the priest got on with his animated sermon, a natural gesture I very much associate with Middle Eastern communities, including Turkey. I understood none of the Arabic and was wondering why the priest kept lifting his robes and wailing like a demented spectre when he uttered the English word 'Halloween', and I realized he was mocking the derivative of the Christian festival of All Hallows' Eve that had taken place a few days earlier.

There are around 165,000 Christians in Israel and around 53,000 in the occupied territories of Palestine – 50,000 in the West Bank and 3,000 in the Gaza strip. I went to two Muslim-majority but traditionally Christian towns in the West Bank – Bethlehem and Ramallah. The latter is now the de facto capital of Palestine, a collection of three villages still home to a roughly 30 per cent Christian minority, mainly Catholics, who often take European names. I was given a lift to the church of St George by a couple called Renée and Anton, who told me they were from the 'Latin' church; when I asked whether they meant the Roman Catholic Church they denied this vehemently, thinking I meant 'Rum' or Greek Orthodox (from the Byzantine Church of 'Rome'), but in fact the Latins are Catholic. Ramallah is largely propped up by development money and is home to a significant community of Western expats; these expats and the Christian community create an excuse to allow residents more license than is usually found in Palestinian towns – alcohol can be found relatively easily, and a popular café in the centre of town is a discreet haunt for the city's LGBT community.

Entering the West Bank gave me a glimpse of life under occupation – enough to make me realize that it is difficult to talk meaningfully about coexistence in Israel and the Occupied Territories, in places so marked by separation, inequality and displacement. I crossed the Qalandia checkpoint near Ramallah and the Bayt Jala checkpoint near Bethlehem on municipal buses; at both, Palestinian commuters trying to cross into Jerusalem are corralled into crushing queues at rush hour, sometimes for hours at a time. As a foreigner, I was told to stay on the bus while locals got off to show their identity cards to armed IDF soldiers. Even more than in Jerusalem, I felt deeply uncomfortable at the passage of tourists (myself included) flocking to Bethlehem to take photographs of the birthplace of Christ, passing blithely through what is effectively an open-air prison.

What I witnessed was a manifestation of much deeper divisions, of a state of apartheid that started with a decision made a century ago by the British government. I arrived in Jerusalem on 2 November 2017, exactly a hundred years since the Balfour Declaration, an event that destroyed Muslim–Jewish relations in Palestine. It took the form of a letter, sent by British Foreign Secretary Arthur Balfour to Lord Rothschild, head of the Zionist movement in Britain at the time, pledging the government's support for the creation of a Jewish state with the understanding that 'nothing shall be done which may prejudice the civil and religious rights of existing non-Jewish communities in Palestine.' Two years later, however, Balfour wrote to his successor Lord Curzon explaining that 'in Palestine we do not propose even to go through the form of consulting the wishes of the present inhabitants of the country . . . The Four Great Powers [the US, UK, France and Italy] are committed to Zionism.'

Today, Jews make up 75 per cent of the state of Israel, while Muslim and Christian Arabs are 20 per cent and the remainder are non-Arab Christians. In 1917, in the last days of Ottoman control, Arabs made up 90 per cent of the population of Palestine, while Jews made up just under 10 per cent and owned just under 2 per cent of the land. When the Balfour Declaration was officially announced in Palestine – which was not until the end of 1919 – it did not go down well. The country was under British military administration and still recovering from the famine that had lasted over the past few years of war and reached its height in 1916, claiming 300,000–500,000 lives in Greater Syria. In 1915, this famine had been exacerbated by a plague of locusts which had annihilated the region, taking two hours to pass over Beirut alone. In December 1915, no flour remained in Jerusalem or Beirut, causing riots in ransacked shops. News of the Balfour Declaration caused panic, and protests soon broke out in Jerusalem, especially among Arabs, but, more interestingly, also among Jews who were ambivalent about Zionism, particularly the (majority) Sephardic Jews who were wary of European Zionism creating a new state which excluded Arab Jews, as they counted themselves (local Muslims often considered their Jewish neighbours as fellow natives or 'sons of country' [*abnaa al-balad*] and as 'Arab Jews' [*Yahud awlad Arab*]). By 1922, the anniversary of the Balfour Declaration became an annual day of mourning and protests marked by black flags; even women attended.

Jerusalem was at its most genuinely cosmopolitan in the late 19th and early 20th century, at the tail-end of the Ottoman Empire, as a consequence of the Tanzimat period of reforms (1839–1876). Public services were completely overhauled, state schools introduced and religious communities mixed as they had never done before. The Western missionaries such as the Messianic Jews who came to Jerusalem to take advantage of these reforms, set up organizations that brought the local Jewish and Arab communities together by shaking up the status quo – even Orthodox sects played in mixed football tournaments, copying the example set by the newly established St George's Anglican College club. There is no such Orthodox team now, and indeed the Israeli football scene is mired in racism directed at Arab-Israeli players, most notable in the 2005 attacks against Abbas Swan, an Arab-Israeli midfielder who was one of the most successful players in Israeli history.

Writing about the shared culture between Ottoman Jerusalemites in his book *Lives in Common: Arabs and Jews in Jerusalem, Jaffa and Hebron*, the Israeli scholar Menachem Klein paints a very different situation from the Jerusalem of today: 'There was no mental boundary separating Muslim and Jew. The walls of language and culture were low ones, and Jews and Arabs who entered the physical or linguistic zone of the Other felt no sense of being alien.'[44]

In the early 20th century, Jewish and Muslim families socialized together, attending the same bathhouses and cafés, inviting each other into their homes for meals on religious holidays, even marrying each other. Klein also mentions the performances of the Ottoman puppet show *Karagoz waHajawat* in Arab cafés frequented by Jews during the month of Ramadan in the early 20ᵗʰ century. Karagöz and Hacivat is still performed in Turkey during Ramadan, and throughout the year in Greece, as I discovered in Lesbos. Overlap of culture was as common with the Jews and Muslims of Palestine as it was with the Greek Orthodox Christians and Muslims of Anatolia, including in the religious – or, more accurately perhaps, superstitious – spheres.

'Both Jews and Muslims believed that rabbis could work wonders, and that demons and spirits residing around or in their common courtyards could hurt them. It was in this context that the members of both faiths, of all ages, shared their fears and their ways of coping with them. [. . .] When Muslims returned from their pilgrimages to Mecca, their Jewish neighbours congratulated them and the Muslims shared with them dates from the holy city.'[45]

Klein does not paint a utopia; there was mutual suspicion and tensions not just between Jews and Muslims but also Christians. But, says Klein, this 'does not obviate the wealth of evidence for a local Arab–Jewish identity. Members of the two nations conducted their web of daily interactions on a different plane from that laid out by official theology.'[46] One very obvious symbol for co-existence before British Mandate was that the Muslim, Christian and Jewish quarters of Jerusalem were not strictly kept; people lived across these borders, whereas now the Israeli and Palestinian sides of town are, residentially at least, deeply segregated.

In Jerusalem, there are walls within walls, and communities that remain completely hidden from sight. One evening by Jaffa Gate,

I arranged to meet George Hintlian, an Armenian scholar. I arrived early for our rendezvous and was scanning the crowd when he hove unhurriedly into view – I instinctively picked him out, a man with the confidence of a seventy-two-year-old who has long enjoyed local respect, the endearing scruffiness of an eccentric bachelor and bushy grey sideburns which reminded me of a bonvivant character from a French film of the 1960s.

'So,' said George without preamble, fixing me with a friendly but scrutinising eye. 'You're Turkish? *Hoşgeldin* – welcome!' To my surprise, I found myself speaking Turkish with a first-generation Jerusalemite Armenian as we strolled by the walls of the Old City; he spoke fluently, telling me what a joy it was to speak the language he'd learned from his parents, who escaped the Armenian genocide in their twenties. Both witnessed terrible things, losing family members in the death marches; George's father acted as court translator in the British trials of the Young Turks who had ordered the genocide. But somehow, they never lost their love for Turkey, and passed it on to their children. George tells me how he grew up being regaled with stories about life back in the good old days, and listening to Turkish songs his father sang for him and his sister. He visibly enjoys himself as we talk, laughing as we trot out particular idioms, commenting on my British accent, asking about his own, congratulating both of us on our flawed fluency.

'Listen to us! Not perfect, but *şöyle böyle*, we're alright. I miss Turkish. Sometimes I speak it to myself, not to forget.'

That night over dinner, he told me how for most of his life he had studied accounts of the Armenian genocide and interviewed survivors like his parents, consumed with the injustice of both the genocide itself but, more importantly, the Turkish government's refusal to admit it. In 2015, however, the year of the centenary, he suddenly gave up. He realized Turkey would not acknowledge the genocide during his lifetime, and after half a century immersing himself in its history, 'drowning in its blood', as he put it, as he relived its events with the 800 survivors he interviewed, he felt it was all for nothing. 'I have looked into hell,' he told me, then shrugged expressively. 'Now what?'

Only semi-joking, he told me that he was glad to have met me now, when he no longer hates Turks. Privately, I reflect that it is also lucky that I've met him after visiting the Genocide Museum in Yerevan. George's hatred dissipated with the anniversary in 2015, and he has begun to feel sorry for the Turks living through Erdoğan's regime. He says the bridges he had just begun to build with Turkish historians have all been destroyed in the purge of journalists, teachers and academics since the coup attempt of 2016, because these academics are either in jail or in exile, and he himself can't return to Turkey because of his lobbying.

'Maybe in ten years' time the present generation of Turkish intellectuals will come to understand what exile means,' George ruminated. 'Maybe, it will bring us [Armenians and Turks] closer together. Of course,' he added rather touchingly, 'I am not so egotistical as to expect these people will be worrying about the Armenians. They have enough to worry about at the moment.'

We talked about the psychological toll of exile on a diasporic people. 'The Armenians are similar to the Palestinians,' said George. 'Obsessed with their lost homeland to the point that it occupies all their mental energies.' He clearly includes himself in this classification. As we part, he gives me an article he wrote about some of the stories he has heard over the last fifty years from genocide survivors in Jerusalem; reading it later, I find it almost unbearably painful. What is almost more painful, however, is the way George has always cherished his family's oral history with barely anything to connect him to his ancestral homeland:

'My family came from Talas, near the birth place of Saint Sabbas [a Syrian 5th-century monk], in Cappadocia, but I had never seen any picture of Talas, nor was there any picture of my grandfather and the family. I have never seen a picture of my uncle who died on the death march at the age of four, nor of the house which they left behind. What hovered in my mind was only graphic and vivid descriptions.'

Two days after our dinner, George took me on a tour round the monastery of St James Cathedral, where he has lived all his life along with many other families of those who escaped the genocide and were taken in by the resident Armenian Orthodox community of Jerusalem at the time. The monastery is vast, a grand medieval maze of cloisters, high walls and unexpectedly spacious courtyards. As we passed people, George called out theatrically to them in Turkish, introducing me. 'This is Alev. She is a Turk.' He was clearly a local beloved 'Uncle George' character; they greeted him with a wide smile and nodded at me curiously before moving on.

'Her family is from Maraş – and that man is from Kutahya. See that girl? She's from Kayseri.' I noticed he used the present tense. George pointed to a group of children playing by the walls of the church: 'They have been brought up to hate the Turks because the Turks are the deniers of the genocide. People like me, first-generation

Jerusalemites, and second generation, we don't hate the Turks. We know from our parents how fond they were of Turkey. If you speak the language, you can't hate the people. But these kids – Turkish is just another language to them like French or Spanish.'

Again and again on my travels, I saw this – language is the key to a shared culture, and to understanding people. In the library of the monastery, George showed me stacks of records from each town in Anatolia detailing family stories and village life – Ottoman journals, newspapers, including the first periodical published in Armenian, in 1746 in Madras, India. Looking at the stacks and stacks of books and papers, and momentarily distracted by the twin Siamese cats who roam the library, I wished passionately that I could read Armenian.

Upkeep of such a library is expensive – the entire monastery complex is funded by the foundation of Calouste Gulbenkian, the famous Ottoman Armenian philanthropist. Gulbenkian was born in Istanbul in 1869 and made a vast fortune by discovering oil in Mesopotamia – modern-day Iraq – for Sultan Abdul Hamid II. In 1896, however, he and his family had to flee as Armenians were massacred in the aftermath of the recent wars with the Russians in the east of the empire, a harbinger of the genocide to follow twenty years later. Gulbenkian went on to become one of the richest men in the world, advising European governments on oil fields in the Middle East, and amassing a huge art collection. He gave away much of his money to Armenian charity projects, including the St James Cathedral and monastery in Jerusalem, as well as the St Sarkis church in London, which he intended as a sanctuary for 'dispersed Armenians' like himself.

The 12th-century Cathedral of St James is a living museum of

Ottoman Armenian history. When I arrive with George, young men in slightly sinister black hooded cloaks are singing near the altar. While we wait for the service to finish, I look around at silver filigree lamps hanging from the beams of the church and the beautiful wooden doors to hidden rooms – the church is a bewildering mixture of styles from Damascus, Istanbul and Greece. I have a brief but genuine moment of quasi-religious peace in an alcove lit with long tapered candles, rudely interrupted when George points out to me the traditional blue-and-white Iznik tiles on the pillars, in particular the small crosses in the design, denoting that these were a batch destined for Armenian churches, while others were shipped off to be fixed in mosques. A wooden board hangs from chains outside the door of the cathedral, and is still hit by wooden hammers to call the faithful to prayer, a continued custom from Ottoman times when church bells were banned – 'We had to keep a low profile,' as George put it.

This 'low profile' reminded me that, for all the friendship and cultural ties between Muslims and non-Muslims in Ottoman Jerusalem, there was still hierarchy which subdued non-Muslim worship in public life, and that led to resentment towards the authorities who policed them. On one wall inside the church, a series of Iznik tiles forms a storyboard showing scenes from the Bible; the sultan's soldiers, the janissaries, are depicted harassing Jesus and his disciples, even though they were several centuries early for the time of Christ. As George explained, janissaries were the bogymen in the consciousness of these Ottoman Armenian artisans, just as they were for their Balkan subjects, hence their inclusion in art, regardless of anachronisms – another example of the 'authentic fantasies' created to enshrine victimhood.

While Turkish overlords loomed large for their Ottoman subjects hundreds of years ago, President Erdoğan is an important figure for Muslims in Palestine today. Walking into a corner shop in East Jerusalem, I was surprised to be met by the sight of the President of Turkey cupping Obama's face tenderly on a poster above the till; another poster showed him shouting at an unseen audience, his contorted face crimson with rage, with Arabic script underneath. The images were so ridiculous that I suspected they might be satirical, but when I asked about them, the shopkeeper explained that they showed how Erdoğan both pities Americans and defies them. I judged this a good moment to drop the bombshell: that I am half-Turkish.

'You? Turkish?! No.'

'It's true. I swear on my mother, who is a hundred per cent Turkish.'

A moment of stunned and respectful silence. Then, 'Come with me' – the shopkeeper beckoned me to a backroom, and opened the door with a theatrical flourish. A Turkish flag was painted across an alcove.

'We love Turkey very, very much.' The sincerity in his voice was unmistakable. By now, the other shop workers – his sons and nephews – had stopped stacking shelves and gathered round, adding their voices in agreement. When I asked one of his nephews why he liked Erdoğan so much, he said he admired him for berating then-Israeli president Shimon Peres at the Davos forum in 2009 for Israel's Gaza offensive, while another cited the Mavi Marmara incident as another golden moment, when a Turkish Islamic NGO sent a flotilla of aid ships to break the Israeli blockade of the Gaza strip in 2010; nine Turkish activists were killed when Israeli soldiers stormed the ships. As a result, diplomatic relations between the two countries were ruptured until 2016, and are still uneasy. In August 2014, Erdoğan appeared in the last session of parliament before the presidential elections wearing a Palestinian *keffiyeh* (scarf), an act of solidarity with the victims of the Gaza bombardment.

'Erdoğan is strong. He is an Islamic leader, like an Ottoman leader,' insisted the shopkeeper.

'No,' said his son, the boring voice of reason. 'Not as strong as a sultan, Dad. But still strong.'

Other Palestinians I spoke to told me Erdoğan's popularity was on the wane from the once-feverish pitch after the Mavi Marmara incident; in 2010, posters of his face had been pasted in shops across East Jerusalem and towns all over the West Bank.

Erdoğan invokes his Ottoman predecessors at every opportunity. In July 2017, protests broke out among Palestinians after Israeli authorities introduced new security measures at the al-Aqsa Mosque on Temple Mount. Erdoğan urged Muslims to visit the mosque in defiance of Israeli restrictions, and, with much poetic licence, contrasted Israel's intolerance with the tolerance shown by the Ottoman sultans to non-Muslim subjects of the empire, pointing out that the empire had ruled over the Al-Aqsa Mosque, Islam's third-holiest site, for four centuries: 'Our ancestors had acted with such great delicacy and sensitivity that it is impossible not to remember them with gratitude and longing given today's cruelty [in Israel].' He vowed to defend their conquests with his usual brand of grandiose Islamic fighting talk, stopping short of any actual threat: 'Let's defend [Al-Aqsa Mosque] as if we are defending Mecca and Medina.' After President Trump's recognition of Jerusalem as the capital of Israel, he announced that Turkey would be opening an embassy in East Jerusalem to recognize Palestine's claim to the city as their capital.

Erdoğan's attitude to Islam could hardly be more different from that of the founder of the Republic himself. One of Atatürk's main concerns after establishing the Turkish Republic in 1923 was instilling secularism in the public life of a Muslim population. Looking back at the fall of the empire, and at what Atatürk created out of its ashes, it is tempting to think that this was how Turkey was fated to develop. The historian Banu Turnaoğlu has noted that various forms of republicanism were competing in the last century of the empire, however: an Islamic form, a Liberal form and lastly the victorious Kemalist form. The historian Ben Fortna points out that the Liberal vision of a Turkish republic would have accommodated the minorities of the empire in a way that Atatürk's Republic certainly did not: 'The Liberals ... may well have produced an attempt at a decentralized empire that could have afforded a degree of regional autonomy for the main ethno-national groups in the empire, such as the Rum [Greeks] and the Armenians.'[47]

When I met the historian Menachem Klein in Jerusalem, he was adamant that the demise of the empire 'killed coexistence. Today, you can see the same [resulting] problems from the Balkans down through Greece to Cyprus and here to Palestine.' This is, of course, a contentious claim –the empire allowed for coexistence between ethnic and religious groups, but was beset by tensions in its last century, making it more difficult to make comparisons to the nation states that replaced it. Abdul Hamid II imposed stricter Islam on his own people and frustrated the burgeoning reforms which preceded his reign in the 19th century and which would have granted minorities greater freedoms in the dying empire. Just forty years after the Tanzimat reforms ended, a combination of his paranoia and the Great War stopped any future version of Ottoman coexistence in its tracks. The problems that Israel and the Occupied Territories have witnessed in the past century are too complex to be blamed on the collapse of the empire, however, and even towns held up as models of coexistence are not entirely what they seem.

The Hanging Gardens of Haifa

The bus to Haifa was just pulling out of Jerusalem Central Bus Station when I scrambled on board. Young IDF soldiers had already taken all the seats; I found myself in the awkward position of having to sit in the aisle at the top of the emergency exit steps, side by side with an ultra-Orthodox Jew. He sat on his suitcase, opened his Torah and began to pray; I browsed Twitter on my phone, bracing myself to avoid impact at every swerve. At the end of the two-hour journey we exchanged weak smiles as we parted.

Jerusalem is a wearying place; I had been told by several friends who'd visited Israel that Haifa, a town on Israel's northern coast, is the opposite – laidback, religiously diverse and, very unusually for Israel, famous for its Arab culture. The town was a minor port until the British took it from the Ottomans in 1918 and chose it as a strategic hub for transporting crude oil from the Middle East, making it the most important Mediterranean port north of the Suez Canal. Today it is a picturesque town spread over the slopes of Carmel Hill, and utterly dominated by the Baha'i gardens – 'The Hanging Gardens of Haifa' – cascading down the hillside in a series of eighteen terraces comprised of immaculately manicured lawns and flower beds covering 200,000 square metres of land. The gardens are dramatically lit at night; during the day, a small army of gardeners patrol at all times, armed with hoses and clippers, working in respectful silence.

The gardens, and the Baha'i shrine (where I was not allowed to enter, as a non-Baha'i unluckily visiting at the wrong time of day), are a good representation of the minority cultures of Haifa; the Baha'i faith is an offshoot of Islam whose members have been persecuted as heretics since the religion was founded in 1863 in Iran. There are around 6 million Baha'is in the world today, and Haifa is the centre of their faith, although they are not actually allowed to live here thanks to Israel's notoriously restrictive residence laws for foreigners (reminiscent of Ottoman rules allowing non-Muslims from outside the empire to visit for a specified period of time only). Instead, Baha'is make a nine-day pilgrimage every nine years, and only the staff of the shrine and attendant buildings stay permanently, with special dispensation from Israeli authorities.

The Ahmadiyya, another relatively niche Islamic sect, came to British-controlled Palestine in the 1920s, specifically to the Kababir area of Haifa, after being persecuted in Sunni-majority Pakistan; Israel is in fact the only place they can practise in the Middle East (their headquarters in Morden, South London, is the biggest mosque in Europe). The Druze are a more long-standing resident community, and, along with Muslim Arabs, make up a significant proportion of the student body of Haifa University. The Druze faith was born in AD 986 in Egypt, from within Islam; they self-identify as 'Unitarians', taking elements of religious teachings from all three major Abrahamic religions as well as the Greek philosophers, as I was to discover when I visited some religious *sheikhs* in southern Lebanon. There are over a million Druze people worldwide, and about 140,000 in Israel, most of them living in the north near the Lebanese border in towns like Haifa.

I heard much more Arabic in Haifa than I did elsewhere in Israel, especially in the music-filled cafés between the lowest slopes of Carmel Hill and the port. One night, I walked to the German Colony, established in 1868 by the German Templars at the foot of Mount Carmel (and now a glamorous district comprised almost entirely of open-air cafés). I sat in a garden festooned with fairy lights outside one of these restaurants, Fattoush, and ordered the eponymous Lebanese salad; as the waitresses bustled past me they talked to each other in Arabic, their voices mingling with the Arabic pop music, a strangely counter-intuitive sound in Israel. A short walk from the German Colony is the famous Wadi Nisnas ('mongoose valley'), a traditionally Christian area with a market patronized by the full plethora of Haifa residents. As I wandered along the bottom of the Baha'i gardens late one night, I passed the Jewish Arab Culture Centre, proudly displaying three symbols on its facade: a cross, Star of David and Islamic crescent.

While the surface appearance of Haifa seemed to back up what people had told me – it being a city of coexistence – I became aware that I could not see the whole picture. While Arabs in Israel enjoy far more freedom than the Palestinians who live in the Occupied Territories, it remains a fundamentally unequal society. Here, as elsewhere in Israel, the Arab community bears the legacy of having had their homes and land taken from them, and when the Jews of Haifa celebrate the anniversary of the Israeli victory in the 1948 war against the Palestinians, there is no local Arab participation for obvious reasons. In some pockets of town, like Masada, young Jews and Arabs mix in hipster cafés, but that social integration is not representative of the norm. Some Jewish and Arab children mix in school but most attend their own schools, with separate curricula. Even the mayor, Yona Yahav, admitted in the run-up to the 2018 celebrations of the 70th anniversary of the 1948 war that he prefers to talk of 'shared existence rather than coexistence'.

The mayors of Haifa have acted as a barometer of shifting power: the first mayor was Hassan Shukri, who held office from 1914–1936, and insisted on appointing a Jewish deputy mayor despite the fact that Arabs were the majority; in 1921, he expressed support for the Balfour Declaration in a telegram to the British government that is poignant today:

'We do not consider the Jewish people as an enemy whose wish is to crush us. On the contrary. We consider the Jews as a brotherly people sharing our joys and troubles and helping us in the construction of our common country.'

Since the early 1940s, when Jews became the majority in Haifa through the forced displacement of Arabs, the roles have switched: the mayor has always been Jewish, and the deputy mayor an Arab from the Israeli Communist Party. This is not a rule, but an organically adopted custom, and a highly unusual one in Israel – even to be a deputy official is relatively unusual for the Arab community.

Part of the reason I came here was to meet Professor Edy Kaufman and his fifth-generation Jerusalemite wife. The couple left Lisa's hometown of Jerusalem in 2013 because they had had enough of the tensions of the city and moved to the very top of Carmel Hill, looking out over Haifa with a view of the Mediterranean Sea stretching towards Cyprus. When I arrived at their apartment, I was delighted when Edy offered me coffee in a *'fincan'* (pronounced 'finjan') – the Turkish word for cup (derived from Persian via Arabic), although Edy used it to denote the little brass pot in which he had brewed the coffee. This started a discussion about the way Ottoman Turkish words crop up in the Hebrew spoken by Israeli Jews, particularly domestic words. I asked Edy whether an Israeli in New York would use these words – 'Certainly not – these words are local.' It is strange to think that the Hebrew spoken in Jerusalem, which I would have assumed to be the purest form of Hebrew, is Turkish-inflected. I thought of the similar phenomenon of Turkish words in the Greek language, and in particular in parts of Greece with high proportions of the 1923 population-exchange victims, like Lesbos.

Edy has a Spanish accent which initially bewildered me; he was born in Argentina to Ukrainian parents, and came to Israel as a teenager with the rest of his family to work on a kibbutz. His wife, Lisa, is from an old Jerusalemite family; her mother was a Moroccan Sephardic Jew, and her father an Ashkenazi Jew from Russia, killed before the outbreak of Israel's War of Independence in 1948 when he was part of an ambushed medical convoy going to the Hadassah hospital in Mount Scopus. Lisa tells me her grandmother had a 'milk brother' – an Arab boy who was breastfed by her great-grandmother.

Klein writes about this too, as something that often happened between Jewish and Arab families in the early 20th century, when a new mother found she could not breastfeed and asked a friend to help, resulting in Jewish and Arab 'milk siblings'[48] – a practice that was also common in Jewish-majority Ottoman Thessaloniki.

I was surprised when Edy mentioned that he was a fan of current Israeli prime minister Benjamin Netanyahu's original party, the 'Pact of Minorities'. This party's ethos was based on the theory that the Middle East has always been a mosaic of minorities which exists separate from empires, and that if all the minorities band together they are more numerous, and more powerful, than the Muslims. Knowing what we do of Netanyahu's nationalist policies today, it is hard not to view such a party cynically, as the precursor to a harder anti-Palestinian agenda.

In large swathes of the Ottoman Empire, for example in most of the Balkan states, and particularly in parts of Greece like Salonika, non-Muslims formed the majority of the population for hundreds of years (and even as late as 1912, after the massacres of non-Muslim subjects in the 19th century, there were more Christian than Muslim subjects in eastern Anatolia). In the Middle East, the existence of religious communities like the Druze, Zoroastrians, Yazidis and Samaritans alongside the Christians and Jews contributed to a larger non-Muslim population than often assumed. The Ottoman Empire survived for half a millennium because of the efficiency of its administration and law enforcement; but when non-Muslims were galvanized by the notion of nationhood to break free from the empire in the 19th century, it worked.

As someone who has worked on conflict resolution in Israel and

Palestine for decades, Edy is particularly attuned to the language in which we talk about coexistence. He dismisses the 'melting pot' as an unhelpful metaphor – identities do not simply melt into each other. He also disapproves of the word 'tolerance'. 'If I just tolerate someone, that is not very positive. Likewise, diversity is not enough – we have to be *united* in diversity.' This makes me think of Klein's depiction of pre-1948 Jerusalem as not a mixed but a 'shared' community which preceded the nation state, an abstract construction consisting of a flag, a map and an anthem, as the great historian Benedict Anderson points out in *Imagined Communities* – 'shared community' was also the term favoured by Haifa's current mayor.

Unsurprisingly, Argentina, where Edy grew up, is a place where Jewish and Arab diaspora communities get on much better than locals in Israel and Palestine, and this occurs in the rest of Latin America; in fact, in October 2017 a declaration was signed between several Church organizations, the Latin American Jewish Congress and the Islamic Organization of Latin America and the Caribbean declaring a 'region of interreligious coexistence'. It is easy to coexist away from the backdrop of war. While diasporic communities often become more entrenched in their attachment to a distant homeland and a corresponding, theoretical, hatred for 'the other side', day-to-day coexistence often flourishes more naturally than it could in a home setting plagued by conflict – I found this later when I interviewed Turkish and Greek Cypriots living and working side by side in north-east London.

I wanted to find more harmony in Haifa than I did, but one story did stick with me – that of Maxim Restaurant on the corniche, co-owned by a Jewish and an Arab family. In 2003, an Islamic militant suicide bomber walked in and blew herself up, killing twenty-one people and injuring fifty-one, including family members of both proprietors. The aim was to target a place famous for its coexistence, and the terrorist herself was someone whose life had been devastated by political oppression; her fiancé was killed by IDF soldiers when she was twenty-one. What is remarkable about the tragedy, however, is that the surviving Jewish and Arab proprietors reopened the café just seven months later, with a plaque honouring the many dead, and vowing to continue the restaurant in their honour. Today, it is as busy as it was, apparently, before the bombing.

Beirut

As a nation state, Lebanon is a manifestation of semi-organized chaos. It is unique among Middle Eastern countries in its Ottoman-esque recognition of eighteen official minorities, but is liable to break into civil war at a moment's notice (13th April, the day that civil war broke out in 1975, is still marked every year, but not the date it ended). Its politics are bewildering and unpredictable, the Saudi kidnapping of Lebanon's prime minister, Hariri, in 2017 being a recent case in point. The Arab Spring passed without a Lebanese revolution, although one nearly started over abandoned garbage. It is an attention-hogging diva of a country.

The soundtrack of Beirut is dominated by car horns and the thunder of drills from ubiquitous construction sites. At night, bars in the quarters of Gemmayze and Mar Mikhael pump out music; the defining cliché of Beirutis is that they are famous for partying through war. There is a fatalistic hedonism to the nightlife that is a direct response to decades of conflict; Middle Eastern ostentation coupled with relatively liberal mores give the city its exaggerated 'party while you can' attitude and diamante-studded style. Away from the clubs, the more low-key focus of the city is the corniche. As the sun sets over the sea, especially on weekends, men bring plastic chairs down to the rocks and play cards while smoking shisha; on the walkway above, Christian and Muslim families parade in their Sunday best.

The ancient centre of the city – misleadingly called Downtown Beirut – has been renovated in faux-old but obviously modern style by a construction company founded by the billionaire Hariri family (former prime minister Rafik al-Hariri, assassinated in 2005, was the father of current prime minister Saad al-Hariri) and largely consists of pristine malls encased in sandstone-coloured concrete, with glass facades displaying Chanel handbags worth many times the yearly income of most Beirutis. The remains of a Roman Forum are scattered in a shallow depression in the centre of this district, surrounded by churches and mosques which give a warped indication of the city's proportional Muslim and Christian demographics. There is no Shia mosque, for example; those are to be found in the parts of the city held by Hezbollah, the Shia militant group which controls large swathes of eastern and southern Lebanon as well as much of southern Beirut.

The St George Maronite (Eastern Catholic) Cathedral, built in 1894 right next to the forum, has a neoclassical facade and booming interior, and has been restored since being bombed and defaced in the 1975–1990 civil war, as has the rival St George Cathedral opposite, built in 1772 for the Greek Orthodox community. These are the seats of the Maronite and Greek Orthodox dioceses of Beirut and both are trumped in size by the adjacent Mohammed al-Amin Mosque, a Sunni mosque built in 2005. Looking at the three buildings, there is definitely a sense that the superior size of the mosque is deliberate – if anything defines Lebanon, it is competition among its religions, and indeed a bell tower was constructed for the Maronite cathedral in 2016 exactly matching the height of the minarets of the Mohammed al-Amin Mosque.

Synagogues are notable by their absence in Beirut, considering the once-sizeable Jewish community. There is only one left, the Maghen Abraham Synagogue, built in 1925 in the Jewish quarter of Wadi Abu Jamil which was targeted, ironically, by Israeli shells in 1982 following rumours that Yasser Arafat's Palestinian Liberation Organization was storing weapons there. The damaged synagogue was restored in 2010, so I set out to visit it, confidently following directions on Google Maps. As I approached, I found a road block guarded by a gendarme – this is not unusual in Beirut, especially in the newly renovated Downtown area, so I tried walking past, only for the gendarme to stop me. The synagogue was closed, inaccessible to the public. For how long? I asked. The policeman shrugged. 'Always.'

Later, I found out that the synagogue has never been reopened since the civil war, unlike the churches and mosques similarly damaged. Until the 1960s there were sixteen synagogues in Beirut, for a Jewish community several thousand strong. Lebanon was a magnet for Jews in the Middle East since the 1839 Tanzimat reforms of the late Ottoman Empire; like Jerusalem, Beirut flourished under more liberal laws for religious minorities, and Jews continued to benefit after the First World War when Lebanon came under the control of the French, who continued the tradition of power-sharing among minority communities. After the creation of Israel in 1948, although some of the city's Jews left for the promised land, Beirut's Jewish community actually grew as Jews from other Arab countries chose the relative tolerance of Lebanon's multidenominational state over the increasingly hostile majority-Muslim states that had been their home for centuries.

After Lebanon's Six Day War with Israel in 1967, however, anti-Semitism began to rise in Lebanon, and became exponentially worse after the Israeli invasion of 1982. The Jewish community in Beirut is now reduced to a few hundred who keep an extremely low profile – as the political scientist Paul Tabar puts it, 'they have chosen to live as discreetly as possible'. A Syrian Christian I interviewed in Beirut told me about a Jewish friend of hers who gets together with other Lebanese Jews every Saturday in a kind of informal, secret Shabbat; this friend refused (politely) my request for an interview.

The presence of ubiquitous gendarmes and roadblocks in Beirut, coupled with the IDF patrols of Jerusalem, made me think about how minorities viewed 'the authorities' in the Ottoman Empire. The line has always been thin between law enforcement and repression, whoever is in charge. In Istanbul, the sultan's janissaries represented power, of course, but not occupation, as the IDF represents in Jerusalem (although, if its name is to be believed, the Israeli Defence Force acts only in 'defence'). However, when the empire was violently unravelling during the early years of the First World War, there was a similar resentment towards Ottoman soldiers in

Greater Syria, especially among those subjects who saw themselves primarily as 'Arabs', and who resented the Turkification of the empire instigated by the Young Turks, which included the enforcement of Turkish as the official language taught in schools. As a result, previously loyal Arab subjects who had supported the Young Turk revolution began to turn against the empire, and, as had happened in the Balkan states, so too in the south-eastern reaches of the empire, nationalism took hold at the turn of the century with violent consequences.

The Maronites of Beirut were among the most prominent of the Arab nationalists who wanted a dual Arab–Turkish nation in which Arabs and Turks had equal rights and responsibilities. The historian Eugene Rogan makes the sage point that these firebrands tempered their ideology with pragmatism: they still wanted to be part of the Ottoman Empire because they feared that otherwise they might become part of a European empire (as indeed transpired under French rule, when the Maronites again showed their pragmatism by forging strong ties with the French).[49] The Young Turks were having none of it. In April 1913, the Beirut Reform Society, the foremost of the Arab nationalist entities, was closed down and some members taken prisoner; a strike ensued, and Beirut entered a political crisis until the prisoners were released and the strike brought to an end. The Young Turks made a pretence of listening to the Arab nationalists, inviting delegates to Istanbul for an 'Arab Congress' apparently for the purpose of discussing compromise, but within three years several of the delegates had been executed in Beirut. Rogan has unearthed an obscure play called 'Beirut On Stage', published in 1920 by the Maronite Georges Mourad about the events of the First World War. The Lebanese characters are victims of the 'venality and cruelty of the Turks' – notable scenes include local Red Crescent units blackmailing Maronite victims of typhus in Beirut, Ottoman authorities requisitioning their houses, and a rape attempt by an Ottoman Turkish soldier on a Maronite girl. While the play is melodramatic and contains hints of Hajdarpasic's 'authentic fantasies', there is certainly plenty of evidence for Ottoman cruelty – for example, Beirut's Union Square became known as Martyrs' Square (as it still is today) because in 1916, twenty-one notable Arab nationalists were hanged for treason, singing Arab hymns as they were led to the gallows. Cemal Pasha, who as Governor of Syria was responsible for these executions, became known as 'Cemal the blood-shedder' thereafter.

Unsurprisingly, many Lebanese subjects were glad to be free of Ottoman rule. The French Mandate (1923 until independence in 1943) continued a version of the Ottoman *millet* system with recognized minorities; the Lebanese constitution of 1926 states that Christians and Muslims should have equal representation and rights, something that theoretically holds today – with big caveats.

While the Lebanese diaspora is vast – around 14 million – the country itself is home to roughly 6 million, including more than a million Syrian refugees and around 175,000 Palestinian refugees. Demographics are hazy, since the last census was conducted in 1932, but there are eighteen official minorities, including various Orthodox and Catholic denominations, Shia and Sunni Muslims, the Jews, and the Druze. Seats in parliament are allocated on a 50/50 basis for Christians and Muslims. Parliament is headed by a troika: the president is a Maronite Christian, the Speaker of Parliament a

Shia Muslim and the prime minister a Sunni Muslim; this division of power is growing more controversial as Sunnis are now assumed to be the largest minority in the country, including refugees. Elections present a divisive form of democracy based on partisanship. The representation of minorities is theoretically but not in reality proportional; voting blocs are based on long-standing family and community-based loyalties – essentially tribalism – and there is no real incentive to cooperate for the greater good of all minorities. 'But compare to other Arab countries!' some say, in Lebanon's defence. A comparison to Syria, Yemen or Egypt does not obviate the country's problems.

Social restrictions follow from political ones. Walking around Beirut, I noticed four or five posters in the windows of travel agencies featuring happy-looking couples against a beach backdrop; looking more closely, I saw that these were adverts for wedding trips. Only religious marriages are recognized and performed in Lebanon, and the laws governing marriage between people of different sects are complicated; for example, a Sunni or Shia Muslim man can marry a Christian or Jewish woman, but a Muslim woman cannot marry a Christian or Jewish man unless he converts to Islam. The laws governing the religion in which the children should be brought up are equally complex; in the light of this confusion, couples who belong to different sects often travel abroad for a civil marriage – nearby Cyprus is the most popular choice, and is often advertised as a convenient three-day package.

In February 2009, Rana Khoury, who was born into a Maronite family, and Rayan Ismail, born a Shia, decided to stage a mock wedding in a bar to protest Lebanon's laws prohibiting civil marriages.

They got married legally in London two years later but continue to campaign.

'We set up a solidarity group for civilly married couples. It was to say: "We are many, we exist, so why can't we just get married here in our country?"' Rana told me.

I met the couple at a popular Armenian restaurant in south Beirut. Rana is the step-daughter of Samir Kassir, an outspoken journalist who was assassinated in 2005, and she has continued his legacy of activism, founding the political platform Beirut Madinati ('Beirut, My City') in 2015 to challenge Lebanon's archaic voting system.

The group grew out of the infamous 'You Stink' 2015 garbage protests, during which over 100,000 people took to the streets to protest the failure of the Beirut municipality to deal with a closed refill site. The garbage symbolized a greater problem: corruption, mismanaged resources and the laziness of an unfairly elected government. Less than a year after Rana co-founded Beirut Madinati, the party managed to get 40 per cent of the vote in the municipal elections of 2016, winning one electoral district but losing the other two. They got no seats.

The dynamism and outlandish optimism of Beirut Madinati reminded me of the Peoples' Democratic Party (HDP) in Turkey, before the party was effectively dismantled. With a 50:50 gender ratio, a strikingly young rostrum of parliamentary candidates and a huge support base among Kurds in the south-east of the country, as well as with secular voters in the big cities (neither group is the AKP's favourite), the party stormed into parliament with eighty seats in the general election of 2015 (the same summer, incidentally, as the 'You Stink' protests in Beirut). That was, arguably, the beginning of the end for Turkey, at least for the foreseeable future – the moment when Erdoğan's Justice and Development Party lost their ruling majority and decided to put a stop to all opposition, starting with the HDP: many of its members are now in jail. That has not yet happened to Beirut Madinati; perhaps it would if it gets more successful, but Rana remains stubbornly optimistic, saying that she and the other founders are changing Lebanese politics in a way that is only positive, and irreversible.

In a bar in the popular Gemmayze district of Beirut, I met Ayman Mhanna, another young political activist setting out to change his country.

'I dream of the day when sect-specific positions in government are not needed and it is entirely secular, but of course I recognize this is not feasible at this stage.'

Ayman reminded me of Midhat Pasha, who dreamed up the Tanzimat reforms in the late 1830s, envisaging an Empire where 'there would be neither Muslim nor non-Muslim but only Ottomans'. This oddly modern dream has always struck me as the equivalent of John Lennon's 'Imagine', much more so than Atatürk's dream of a secular republic (although a Muslim identity has always been a presupposed component of the Turkish identity). Ayman told me of the increasing sensitivity among Lebanon's minorities to the language in which they are spoken of, and how that relates to their political treatment.

'It is no longer politically correct to say "minorities", for example. They are "religious groups".'

Why?

'Because the Sunnis don't like being the majority [biggest

minority], as though it cheapens life. They feel that the smaller, favoured minorities – for example Christians – are protected but a Sunni life is cheap.'

Again, I think how typical of Lebanon that there is even competition among minorities to be, if not the most special, at least not the most common, the most overlooked.

Many of Lebanon's institutions are shackled by imposed religious strata. In theory, the armed forces, like parliament, should consist of 50 per cent Christians and 50 per cent Muslims, but the French-imposed system gave more power to the Christians, who have traditionally had little interest in sharing power with other religious groups; by the time civil war broke out in 1975, there was an entrenched imbalance across the armed forces. The commander of the entire army – around 72,000 strong – is traditionally a Maronite (like the president), while the Chief of Staff was a Catholic until 1959, at which point Muslim officers complained and a Druze commander was appointed in response, a tradition that has continued to today. I found myself wondering about the Ottoman predecessor to the modern Lebanese army: the janissaries, formed in the 1380s as the Sultan's special cohort. 'Recruits' were Christian boys taken by force from their parents in newly conquered lands, like the Bosnia-Herzegovinan boy who went on to become Grand Vizier Mehmet Pasha in the mid-16th century. They were sent to the homes of Turkish families to be schooled in Islam, were expected to be fiercely loyal to the sultan, given decent pay and food and organized within a scrupulous hierarchy – the result was an astonishingly effective elite force. Over time, Muslim recruits were taken too, and by the mid-17th century janissaries were conscious of their enormous power and had begun to mutiny over pay. In 1717, Lady Mary Montagu wrote to a friend that 'the government here is entirely in the hands of the army. The Grand Signor [Sultan Ahmet III], with all his absolute power, is as much a slave as any of his subjects, and trembles at a janissary's frown.'[50]

Subsequent sultans endured this humiliating state of affairs for another century, but in 1826, Sultan Mahmud II announced he was disbanding the janissaries, a decision based on his need to replace an increasingly unbiddable army with one that was more modern and – crucially – loyal, to help him implement the Tanzimat reforms. The maverick soldiers did not go down without a fight – a revolt led to an apocalyptic fire and thousands of executions, known as the 'Auspicious Incident'.

If the janissaries were too powerful, the Lebanese army is arguably not powerful enough, racked by infighting like many of the country's institutions. I had a chance to observe the Lebanese army life first-hand when I joined a unit of soldiers near the town of IS-held Arsal, near the Syrian border in the Beqaa valley.

An Islamic State Enclave

In May 2017, I travelled with the artist Richard Mosse, who was taking thermographic photographs of the refugee camp of Arsal from the army outpost on a hill above the town. Because the region was so volatile, we would never had been allowed permission to visit the area alone. Instead, we went under the protection of Nora Joumblatt, the Syrian, non-Druze wife of the warlord Walid Joumblatt, who is the de facto head of the Druze minority in Lebanon.

Nora is a prominent patron of the arts and Richard was donating his art to her refugee charity, but it was still far beyond the call of duty for her to personally escort us to an area prone to gunfights between the army and local IS militants. She cut an incongruously stylish figure in a bright lemon silk shirt, cream slacks and immaculately coiffed hair as she shook hands with the officers in their dusty fatigues at the outskirts of the town: the embodiment of explicitly feminine power in a military-macho setting. I had met her in Beirut the previous evening, and she stood out even in that superlatively glamorous city – here, she moved with incredible assurance among the tanks and sandbags as though viewing exhibits at the Venice Biennale, where she had been a few days earlier. She had spent much of the journey relating recent military developments to us as we set off at the crack of dawn from Beirut in an ungainly motorcade: the three of us in a non-armoured Range Rover driven by her bodyguard, joined by open-topped jeeps full of armed soldiers as we approached the outpost.

Listening to her explain the troubled relationship between the Shia militant group Hezbollah and the Lebanese army, and the political obstacles she encountered with her local charity work, it struck me that she should make the leap from warlord-wife to world leader at the earliest available opportunity – it would be a continuation of the political family tradition that saw her father Ahmad al-Sharabati negotiate Syria's transition from French rule between 1946 and 1948, just as the 1948 Arab–Israeli War broke out.

The Beqaa Valley has traditionally been controlled by Hezbollah;

just across the nearby hills from Arsal is Syria. Driving through the surrounding villages, it is impossible not to notice the posters of Nasrallah, the Hezbollah leader, plastered on every lamp post. In 2014, IS forces took Arsal and at the time of my visit were still in control since Hezbollah withdrew, leaving the area to a small outfit of Lebanese soldiers who kept well out of town. I noticed that the soldiers were even more nervous than I was. They refused to take us into the town itself, or the camp (which held around 120,000 Syrian refugees); predictably, there was a burst of gunfire directed at the outpost while we were up there, making sense of the sandbags. Many of the refugees in the camp were the families of IS fighters, who stored their weapons in the tents before going to fight over the border.

Two days before our visit, a local woman had been kidnapped and knifed in the neck by IS because they suspected she was a spy for Hezbollah – the mayor showed me horrible photos on his phone. He seemed bowed down by his responsibilities: 'If there is no gunfire for a day or two, I get worried – maybe something bigger will happen'. The mayor before him was dismissed over fears he was colluding with the group. His deputy, Rina Krounbi, is a Communist and the first woman to win the post by popular vote; she told me she received daily anonymous death threats because she refuses to wear the headscarf. The two of them met our party with a group of local village elders, who wanted to petition Nora to apply pressure on her husband Walid to lobby for extra government funding for sanitation and education. Within days, Nora had managed to get the ministry of education to allocate money for a new school; so, a Muslim majority town had successfully appealed to a powerful

Druze-aligned woman to intervene on their behalf, having drawn a blank with their own political representatives – one of many signs that 'representative' tribal Lebanese politics do not work.

Up at the army outpost – a bleak, sandy, sun-blasted outcrop of land with no shrubs for miles around, and no internet or phone coverage – I noticed lovesick graffiti etched in to the barrack walls: 'Ahmet <3 Nadim'. Sentry duty is a lonely job, particularly without access to the internet. As I waited for Richard to take his photo, a lengthy process requiring a 120kg military-grade thermographic camera which aroused the suspicions but also the respect of the soldiers accompanying us ('Wow, how much is the CIA paying you?'), I got chatting to Joseph, an officer who spoke excellent English thanks to the Lebanese army's practice of sending officers to America and Europe on a kind of military Erasmus exchange programme.

Joseph revealed himself to belong to the Greek Orthodox Church; he claimed that among the lower ranks of his particular division, 90 per cent of the men were Muslim and 10 per cent Christian, and that the latter only socialize among themselves. He did concede, however, that most officers were, like himself, Christian. As we talked under the beating sun he gradually revealed his ambitions to rise up to Greek Orthodox division general. I asked him if he had ambitions beyond that. 'Higher than that?' he smiled at the ludicrous question. 'Well, I could be the defence secretary in the cabinet – that is also reserved for a Greek Orthodox.'

Again, the paradox of Lebanese society struck me: that in a bid to accommodate various religious groups by ensuring each has some role in public life, some worthy position of responsibility, there is in fact a bizarre system of segregation that all too often teeters into entrenched discrimination. No single group ever thinks they have got the best deal; everyone envies the lot of others, like a playground game in which children fight over whose turn it is to play the hero. It is, in fact, an infantile system dressed in adult garb and policed by old men.

Ain Dara

I wanted to see Lebanon's religious coexistence in a less political setting, so one morning I headed to the village of Ain Dara, about an hour east out of Beirut, halfway to the Syrian border. It lies at 1,300m above sea level on a hill, an unpretentious collection of little houses with vine-covered verandas overlooking tilled fields and vegetable patches; originally a Druze village, it is now predominantly Christian, with three Orthodox churches, two Maronite churches and an Evangelical Baptist church.

I arrived with Richard and our translator Suzan, a diminutive woman in her fifties, who wore impressively shiny gold platform shoes and a leopard-print top, a cursory white scarf for our church visits, and arresting red lipstick. Her look is pure Beirut, and failed to raise any eyebrows but mine – I felt like a frump in comparison, in my standard baggy 'places of worship field trip' outfit. First, we wandered into the St George Melkite church, built in 1890, where I found an Iraqi Christian sweeping the floor, from one of the twenty-five Iraqi Christian refugee families in this village. He told me he was from Qaraqosh, a Christian town near Mosul, and came to Lebanon to join relatives after IS invaded his home in 2014. I have noticed non-Muslims have much stronger ties with their extended and far-flung families than Muslims in the Middle East, probably a relic of *millet* groups in Ottoman times looking out for each other and managing family businesses across the empire.

On a hill above the rest of the town is the newest of the three Eastern Orthodox churches, its foundations laid in 1974; the civil war started the following year and construction was put on hold until 2012. Now it appeared to be finished, but we found it locked. On the roof of a house opposite the church, an elderly couple were sitting at a plastic table shelling beans and watching us with amusement. Suzan called out and the old man – Yusuf, as he later introduced himself – disappeared and returned with a ladder which he placed between his roof and the porch of the church, above a twenty-metre drop to the street below. 'No!' we cried in unison, as he prepared to cross. He chuckled, settling his 'Australia!' cap firmly on his bald head and clambering over despite our protestations, as his wife placidly continued to shell beans.

Yusuf produced a key to the church. The cavernous interior had the unmistakable empty smell of a building that had never been used. 'It's nearly finished – we are still waiting for some decorations,' Yusuf told me, via Suzan, who was perched on a pew, resplendent in her white scarf. I asked him about his cap – did he get it from Australia?

'No – my relatives in Australia visited and gave it to me.'

Later I learned from Yusuf and his wife that their Eastern Orthodox community used to be the majority in Ain Dara but many emigrated to the US and Australia. All of the roughly one hundred families that remain here pay eighty dollars to the church every year, and relatives abroad often pay more, proportional to their greater income,

reflecting the sense of community spirit of many diasporic communities I encountered. Yusuf's family came to the village in 1860,
soon after the Tanzimat reforms which dramatically improved life
for Ottoman subjects in this part of the world – although Yusuf the
Elder may well have had his own reasons.

Father Ghassan Haddad oversees all three Orthodox churches,
and is also the principal of the Ain Dara school. He is a handsome
man in his fifties, his black beard tinged with grey, and welcomed us
expansively into his office above the St George Orthodox Church,
insisting we take some of the bread he gives out in Sunday service
– it smelled and tasted, disconcertingly, like lemon cologne. Walking
around sedately in his long black robes, he talked about his congregation with touching enthusiasm. He has been the resident Orthodox
priest since 1994, and in 2016 set up a YouTube channel where
he livestreams Sunday services to the Ain Dara Orthodox diaspora
across the globe. He says it's particularly popular in America and
Canada. 'My parents in Los Angeles watch every Sunday.' I find some
archived videos of Easter services stretching back to 2011, plentifully
attended by smartly dressed locals (the regular Sunday services are
less well attended, but still dutifully streamed to some of Lebanon's
vast Christian diaspora).

The internet sensation of Ain Dara jokingly attributes his You-
Tube prowess to his degree in electrical engineering. After leaving
university, Father Ghassan received Canadian immigration papers in
Cyprus but at the last minute decided to return to Lebanon; when
I ask him why, he replies, 'Ask God.' The former star student now
teaches English and French to 165 children in his school, including
local Druze children (because 'there is no Druze school'). Most of

the local Druze children, however, go to the smaller Maronite school in the village which also accommodates the handful of Catholic children. I sense some local politics, just beyond the bounds of polite enquiry. He is more forthcoming about the 'roughly one hundred' Syrian refugee families who have come in recent years, all of them Sunni Muslim.

'They come and live twenty-five in one room. Maybe in fifty years, the Muslims will be more than Christians in Europe. They have too many children.'

My interest is piqued when Father Ghassan insists that 'there is peace between the Maronites and Orthodox people here' before returning to the subject of the 'cold and closed' Druze community.

'The Druze went to Africa in the 1940s, looking for diamonds,' he says darkly, refusing to elaborate (I drew a blank on a subsequent Google search). Clearly, the Druze keep to themselves; luckily, I soon had an opportunity to find out more about them when Nora Joumblatt invited me to dinner with her husband Walid, leader of the Lebanese Druze.

Warlords and Sheikhs

Some of the old men who police Lebanon's political system are more heavily guarded than others. The Joumblatts live in the Armenian district of Beirut, near the Apostolic Church (there are roughly 156,000 Armenians in Lebanon, many of them descendants of those who fled Turkey during the 1915 genocide). To reach the Joumblatt residence, I pass two checkpoints at either end of a deserted street;

I'm late, and walk as quickly as I dare, clutching a bottle of champagne under the gaze of armed guards.

Walid Joumblatt has the air of quiet dignity which befits a retired warlord with nearly half a million Twitter followers. He greets me under a life-size portrait of his younger self, his enormous blue eyes and hawk-like nose unchanged at the age of sixty-seven. Dinner follows: a riot of anecdotes about the Lebanese Civil War, in which Joumblatt controlled a sizeable militia, which at one point rained shells on American marines sent by President Reagan to Beirut in 1983. 'Ah, *la belle epoque*,' he sighs, topping up his tiny cup of sake. 'Those were the days.' Now, Joumblatt follows Middle Eastern politics less actively, from a Twitter account rich with emojis and photographs of his beloved dog, Oscar – who also serves as his alter ego in written communications, as I later discover.

Despite formally handing over power in March to his son, Taymur, Walid is still the de facto political leader of the Druze, who form one of Lebanon's eighteen minorities. There about 300,000 in Lebanon, and Druze politicians act as kingmakers in parliament, navigating between the Christian and Muslim blocs. The Joumblatts have represented the interests of the Druze both politically and militarily for decades; in 1977, Walid took over in true feudal style after his father, Kamal, was murdered at the hands of Bashar al-Assad's uncle, Rifaat al-Assad. In an interview given to *Playboy* in 1983, Joumblatt gloomily accepted the likelihood of his own future assassination – hence the checkpoints.

Joumblatt is a curious mixture of idealist and weathervane. Despite representing a religious minority in a far from socialist country, he is an avowed socialist and secularist. He speaks passionately about particular events like the 1982 Israeli invasion of Lebanon, or Trump's eye-wateringly expensive 2017 visit to Saudi Arabia, yet he is pragmatic in his alliances and highly cynical about the theatre of politics. In the *Playboy* interview, which took place in Geneva during infamous peace talks which failed to resolve Lebanon's civil war, Joumblatt admitted freely that the negotiations were a total waste of time – 'rubbish', in fact. 'Maybe I'm crazy!' he tells his interviewer, laughing. Despite this levity, he was a serious player in the war – his well-armed militia forces were accused of multiple atrocities, and of driving thousands of Christians from their homes. He comes across as a kind of Macbeth-like figure, ambitious and ruthless, but, somewhere beyond the surface, horrified by the inevitability of conflict – and perhaps by his own part in it.

'Who is not bloody and ruthless in Lebanon? Who is not? Everybody in his own way is bloody and ruthless. We are all ruthless; everybody is a warlord! Who is not responsible for crimes and destruction?'

During dinner, I soon become aware that my host is still heavily prone to both cynicism and intellectual excitement, sometimes in the same breath. 'Ba'athism was the worst thing to ever happen to the world!' he shouts at one point, referring to the secular Arab nationalist movement that emerged in Syria and Iraq between the two world wars. 'The Ottoman Empire was fantastic because it was the East standing up to the West,' he declares later, sounding not dissimilar to Erdoğan, and indeed many Muslims across the Middle East – I am surprised by this unusually hackneyed opinion from a maverick who quickly moves the conversation on to the origin of bananas ('I am convinced they came from Latin America' [they do not]) before moving on to his visit to Bobby Sands's cell in the Maze, and, finally, his enduring disappointment that the Playmate on the cover of his famous 1983 interview was 'not very beautiful'. As he said this, I glanced over at Nora who was smiling with regal unconcern. Joumblatt is known for his love of beautiful women – his wife is the ultimate testament to this – and her equanimity amuses me.

After dinner, I pluck up the courage to ask for an introduction to the religious elders in the south of the country, who are notoriously wary of outsiders. Joumblatt nods gravely before picking up the phone, and within minutes, everything is arranged: tomorrow Richard Mosse and I will head to the foot of Mount Hermon on the Israeli border, to meet Sheikh Saleh Abou Mansour and his brethren.

Unlike their decidedly candid warlord leader, the Druze are known for their pacifist, puritanical faith and the fierce secrecy with which they protect it. Persecuted since the founding of their religion a thousand years ago, and scattered across Syria, Lebanon and Israel, the Druze may only marry other Druze (a rule most famously flouted by Amal Clooney, née Alamuddin), and outsiders cannot convert or be taught their doctrine. As well as following the teachings of the Bible and Koran (officially classed as Muslims, they call themselves 'Unitarians'), the Druze believe in reincarnation and give the teachings of Plato and Pythagoras equal weight to those of the Abrahamic prophets. I am optimistic that Sheikh Saleh, who is surprisingly forthcoming over WhatsApp, will tell me more.

The sheikh – 'call me Saleh, please' – proves to be a genial man in traditional Druze garb: a high-collared, black tunic, baggy shalvar trousers and a white skullcap. In a mild American accent, he describes himself as 'a liberal and a progressive' who has studied extensively abroad; he is also the youngest president of any federal administration in Lebanon, the Jabel Sheh Municipalities Administration of the south-east. When I arrive at his office, he is engrossed in a meeting with government representatives, discussing how to democratize the archaic local councils of the region.

'I am thirty-six, leading a council of men in their fifties and sixties,' says Sheikh Saleh, wearily, when the representatives have left. 'Imagine! There is a lot to change.' I ask how he got his position. 'I was put forward by a minister who is a friend of the Joumblatts.'

As I hoped, the young sheikh is unusually open; our conversation veers between the personal, the political and the religious. I ask him why he is being so open – I have heard that the Druze are very secretive about their faith, bringing to mind Muslims who are permitted by the Koranic principle of *taqiyya* to conceal their faith if threatened.

'I am a liberal,' he says proudly, before telling me about his education in America ('the food almost killed me, can you imagine – coming from Lebanon') and his progressive views.

But why are the other Druze so secretive?

'Our progressive faith has not been welcomed. Also, we believe knowledge has to be reached step by step. Faith can be misunderstood, so faith is only taught gradually to the Druze. Outside the Druze community, there is no point sharing the deep secrets of the doctrine. You cannot become Druze, you can only be born Druze.'

At one point, the sheikh informs me that Judgement Day is coming soon. 'We know this because of how quickly humanity is changing, with technology and so on – we are expanding our humanity. Soon it will be time.'

I ask how I, a non-Druze, will fare on Judgement Day.

'Sadly, you will not be saved. You are not a Druze because of the choices you have made over the past hundreds of millions of years – yes, we believe the Earth is that old, not what the Bible claims. We are reincarnated according to the choices we make in these many lives.'

Could I not be reincarnated as a Druze in my next life?

'No,' says the sheikh, with gentle finality. 'It is too late.'

There is an awkward silence after this, so I change the subject – I want to know why the Druze generally do not worship in mosques or indeed in any kind of obvious place of worship, just a room in an unmarked building with a piece of fabric dividing men and women. Nora Joumblatt had told me about this and hazarded a guess that it was a legacy of having been persecuted for hundreds of years and wanting to escape notice. Sheikh Saleh respectfully disagrees with Mrs Joumblatt:

'No, it is not for secrecy, it is more because we do not like to be showy. We have a culture of saving money for good works – instead of spending money on a mosque we give it to the poor. However, we have begun spending on big domes and burial grounds for the prophets recently and, personally, I disagree with this.'

How does the Druze community view the Joumblatts?

'Religious leaders are not political and vice versa. He's doing good for the community, I'd say sixty to seventy per cent of the Druze respect him, while the others support his rivals. But sixty to seventy per cent is good! American presidents only have fifty-one per cent popularity after all. And Mr Joumblatt is not a conventional politician.'

Later, Richard and I have lunch with his deputy and the state-issued policemen who follow the sheikh wherever he goes – apparently for his own protection, though he seems irritated by their presence. During the meal, which to my surprise involves blobs of raw liver, he is delighted to discover that Richard is a Quaker, and by the end of the meal has developed a theory that Quakers are the Western equivalent of the Druze – passive, tolerant, modest and misunderstood, both eschewing the pomp and ceremony of decorated places of worship in favour of a bare room, and communing directly with God instead of doing so via priests.

To illustrate his point, the sheikh decides it is time to show us the *khalwa* – a monastery-like centre of worship – where he studied for several years. We drive several miles further south before climbing a steep winding road and reaching a gate where we are told to go away, as there is a secret meeting of the elders taking place.

'Never mind,' says the sheikh cheerfully. 'We will go and see my teacher.'

Sheikh Majed Abou Saad lives in the nearby village of Hasbaya and greets us with plump benevolence as we arrive at his white-washed, modest house. The policemen troop in, too, awed by the honour of the occasion – I have not realized they were Druze until this point – and we all sit, cross-legged, on the floor with our backs against the walls of a large, empty sitting room. Sheikh Majed's wife, shrouded in a white sheet which covers her mouth, hands me a sheet, too – I wrap it awkwardly around my lap, and she goes to sit in the furthermost corner of the room, only her nose and eyes visible in a diamond-shaped wedge of face. I keep looking at her silent form while her husband explains the respect accorded to women in the Druze faith. The genders are equal, he insists. Really?

'Yes. But they are not the same, of course. Sperm has the same sixteen minerals as earth – it is the most important agent in creating new life. We must not forget that. Also, we refer to God as Him. That is significant.'

I hesitate and quail at the prospect of challenging the surreal logic of this ancient wisdom, and instead ask the sheikh why the Druze have been persecuted for so long.

'There are two reasons. The first, which we are not responsible for, was that people were suspicious of the Druze keeping their doctrine secret. The second, which we are responsible for, is that the Druze do not concentrate enough on ritual, too much on theory. That is why there is now a new focus on building mosques.'

Later, as we're leaving, he poses for a photograph with Richard, shaking his head regretfully when I step forward. Living in Turkey for years, I got used to the conservatism of certain men who would refuse to shake my hand when I held it out to them; I quickly learned not to offer my hand. Similarly, I learned not to take it personally when men would not meet my eye, or talk directly to me, instead addressing any man I was with. I understood their behaviour as a complicated cocktail of respect and misogyny, exacerbated by Islamic doctrine. But there was something uniquely annoying about the attitude of this sperm-obsessed Druze sheikh, who lectured me about the equality of the sexes while his silent wife sat swaddled in a modesty-sheet in the corner, and who refused to appear in a photograph with that totally equal but dangerously immodest of creatures: woman.

We depart for the *khalwa* again, up the winding mountain roads, passing villages shelled by Israeli forces a decade ago. Sheikh Saleh informs me that these villages in fact got off relatively lightly, because religion trumped the nation state; the Druze soldiers serving in the Israeli Defence Forces were reluctant to bomb their own (the presence of the Druze in the IDF is a factor of their status as a 'favourite' minority in Israel, another reason they are often viewed with suspicion by other Arabs). By the time we arrive back at the *khalwa*, the meeting is over and at the gates I'm given a black robe to wear before we walk up into a kind of bucolic open-air monastery. Men wander round the gardens, looking like Greek Orthodox priests. Three women gather round me silently like Biblical Graces in their white sheets; one of them leads me into a doorway and up to a table laden with food; she presses biscuits and dried fruit into my hands insistently. I am an alien, but the laws of hospitality hold strong. Sheikh Saleh steers me discretely away from the central prayer hall, where I glimpse seated figures; just outside is a stone circle, and the policemen accompanying us take their shoes off and step inside to pray.

'This circle is a *howeita*, it is believed your prayers are heard more clearly inside it,' he explains. 'Even if they are silent.'

Driving through the village on the way down from the *khalwa*, we pass houses with Druze families sitting and eating on their terraces. Most adults wear the traditional black tunics and white sheets, while the children run around in Western clothes, and one young man strolls out of a pastry shop in a wife-beater. It is a strange splicing of the ancient and the modern, like the landscape – we pass mosques flanked by centuries-old churches and concrete apartment blocks where Shia, Sunni, Maronite and Orthodox Christian denominations live side by side.

Individuals like Sheikh Saleh are the future of Lebanon – community leaders who understand that it is important to cooperate with representatives of other faiths. The sheikh even seems mildly apologetic about the strictures that some of the Druze still impose upon themselves; compromise, he implies, is necessary for survival. No one understands that better than Walid Joumblatt, a former warlord who poses with the Pope and posts the photo on Twitter to the delight of hundreds of thousands of followers across the globe.

After my trips to Palestine, Israel and Lebanon, I found myself wondering what to make of the troubled overlapping of the region's minorities; having been eager to find Ottoman parallels in the social frameworks of the countries I visited, I realized there was too much overlaying the past hundred years – imposed borders, huge numbers of refugees and internally displaced people, meddling from neighbouring countries like Saudi Arabia as well as Western colonial powers and, more brutally, war.

There is no real equivalent of the Ottoman *millet* system today, but I still came away with one conviction: that its social and cultural legacy is most obvious in the Levant, not in Turkey, Greece or the Balkans. Perhaps this is because the Levant has the greatest significance for the three Abrahamic religions. The earliest churches, synagogues and mosques are here, and with them the oldest legacy of coexistence – and of conflict.

In his book *The Jews of Islam*, Bernard Lewis identifies a particular kind of symbiosis between connected religion and culture, arguing that Jews have historically flourished only 'under the aegis of one or the other of the two successor religions of Judaism – Christianity and Islam [. . .] There were occasional Jewish settlements in areas dominated by other civilizations and religions, such as India and

China, but – despite the very large measure of tolerance they enjoyed – they did not flourish.'[51]

Lewis seems to have identified the same reason as Klein for why this was: shared culture.

'They had no great share in the life and culture either of those countries or of the Jewish people, and appear to have produced nothing of any real importance for the one or the other. In India, it was only with the advent of Islam that the small Jewish communities of that country received a modicum of attention and played a small part [. . .] The main center of Jewish life and activity since the early Middle Ages have always been in the lands of Islam and Christianity.'[52]

Today we can see a Western version of multiculturalism in cities like London and New York, but these, however successful, are comprised of geographically displaced minorities. Diverse Ottoman communities were based on a common geography and background, giving a kind of coherence and shared culture which is difficult to identify in the former empire today.

What made the *millet* system work? One tentative conclusion is that harmonious coexistence between minorities is all about a practicable power balance, which under the Ottoman system of course meant a form of (generally) benign tyranny. It worked because all non-Muslim minorities were on the same footing – none of the governed minorities had a stick with which to beat the others, and it was in no single group's interests to cause trouble. The Ottoman *millet* system was tough – it kept a variety of ethnic and religious groups living in relative peace, but only because dissent was met with the severest of punishments. The result was a working mix of people.

Clearly, we need something different for our times; we can aim higher than the *millet* system, the apartheid system of Israel–Palestine and the bogus pluralism of the Lebanese system. New movements like Turkey's HDP and Lebanon's Beirut Madinati – Icarus-like though they may be, for now – show that we could be on the brink of a new form of representative power and cohesion. But for now, the world is frustratingly resistant to change.

Memleket

Homeland

'Memleketim, memleketim, memleketim,
ne kasketim kaldı senin ora işi
ne yollarını taşımış ayakkabım,
son mintanın da sırtımda paralandı çoktan,
Şile bezindendi.
Sen şimdi yalnız saçımın akında,
enfarktında yüreğimin,
alnımın çizgilerindesin memleketim,
memleketim,
memleketim . . .'

'My country, my country, my country,
I no longer have a cap made in your lands,
No longer have a shoe that carried your roads,

My last shirt was long ago shredded on my back,
It was from Şile fabric.
You are now only in the whites of my hair,
In the dead tissue of my heart,
In my forehead lines, my country,
My country,
My country . . .'

Nazim Hikmet, died in exile 1963

Perhaps the inevitable consequence of crossing so many borders for this book was that I began to imagine what preceded them: how people used to say 'this is our space; that is yours'. As I handed over my increasingly cluttered passport, I thought about people who lack this privilege to cross borders freely, about those who have never left home, those who can never return, and those who identify with an ancestral land they have never seen. What is 'homeland' – a place or an idea? The more I travelled, the more powerful and yet obscure I found the emotional connection between geography and identity.

A *memleket* was not always marked with passport controls – it was merely where your people happened to be. Before nationality was a part of the public consciousness, Ottomans lived in little pockets of urban or rural life across the vast lands of the empire, and what primarily defined them was their community. *Yurt dışında* ('abroad') is a phrase in Turkish that means literally 'outside the yurt [tent]'. The phrase is a throwback to a time when Turkic tribes considered the outside world to be anything outside the confines of their tiny tented community, and when life was nomadic, so that 'home' actually moved. In Turkish, the word *memleket*, from the Arabic ةكَلْمَمْ (*mamlaka*), is loosely translated into English as 'homeland' but in fact it is untranslatable. Its primary, implicit meaning is Turkey – the shared *memleket* of most Turkish speakers (hence 'my country', in the words of the poet Nazim Hikmet, above). But speaking to a Turk within Turkey, the word transforms into something different: *memleketiniz neresi?* becomes 'which part of Turkey are you from?' – the particular region, town or village. The word adapts to context, zooming in as the focus narrows, but it means, essentially, where your roots are.

There is a similar word in German: *Heimat*, which has more negative connotations, at least to those who are conscious of the racist sense with which it was used in 1930s Nazi Germany, when Adolf Hitler popularized the 'Blood and Soil' conception of German nationalism. In early 2018, the German government controversially announced it was creating a 'homeland ministry' ('*Heimatmin-isterium*'), to be headed by a representative of the conservative, anti-immigration Christian Social Union in Bavaria.[53] Words matter – the announcement worried those who fear the blurring of the line between patriotism and xenophobia in the age of the refugee crisis, and who look askance at the most visible global role model for a 'homeland ministry' – the Department of Homeland Security in the US, notorious for the ferocity with which it guards its borders.

Patriotism is separated from nationalism by linguistic nuance; it sounds more acceptable, suggesting a "homeland" rather than a nation state. Significantly, English has no equivalent for *Heimat* or *memleket*. There is no word to denote that tribal sense of belonging to a particular community located in a particular place, perhaps because of the unique, conglomerate nature of Great Britain and what preceded it. Yet we still try to pinpoint where we think people 'belong', picking up on clues like accent and asking new acquaintances questions like 'Where did you grow up?' to avoid the less politically correct 'Where are you from?'. The more specific the question, the more factual and therefore acceptable it is. In English, this quest to locate people's origins is often surreptitious. In Turkey, the question is asked openly, because it is a much more homogenous society, and there is less concern about offending non-natives – although, as I hope this book has made abundantly clear, no one is a native if you look back far enough.

Fenced Life

If no one is a native, who gets to decide where other people should live?

Europe is connected to the current wars of the Middle East most obviously by the refugee crisis at its borders – the political debate rumbles on, ugly and polarising, as displaced families wait indefinitely. Visiting refugee camps first as a journalist and then while researching this book, I thought about the connection between the breakdown of the Ottoman Empire, the nation states that replaced it and the conflict that we are seeing today. I met Sunni Muslims fleeing Bashar al-Assad's Alawite regime, Christians fleeing Sunni extremists, and other refugees who had abandoned their homes for a variety of reasons, but often because of religious or ethnic divides. The Ottoman system accommodated different religious groups far from perfectly, but there was no mass exodus of minorities from the empire in the way we are seeing in the 21st century. Likewise, the population exchange and forced assimilation of minorities at the dawn of the Republic of Turkey was wrong in many ways, and we are seeing the results of that today – but a relatively homogenous society like Turkey is unlikely to see the kind of splintered, sectarian civil war that Syria or Lebanon has experienced.

When people have lost everything, their basic and most urgent need is to create something approximating a home, however difficult or temporary that may be. The Greek authorities no longer allow journalists inside Moria, the camp on Lesbos, and I saw why when I squeezed through a hole in the fence in November 2017: the camp was built to hold a maximum of 1,800 people and held around 7,000 at the time of my visit. Flimsy two-man tents of the type that Europeans take to summer festivals hold families of six, set up higgledy-piggledy in the middle of paths connecting different sections of the camp. Just outside the camp's fences, three shanty-cafés provide warm pockets of life preserved inside plastic zip-up walls. Inside, the air is thick with sickly sweet smoke: young men sit on low chairs with legs spread macho-wide, puffing on shisha pipes propped up beside their rickety tables. Each table is reserved for a different group of men, from Yemen, Egypt or Syria, and each has a crackly stereo blaring out their own music so that the space is filled with competing sound. A cocoon of nostalgia, this is the only place approximating home for these men, an illusion of familiarity segregated by region and shared by necessity, with the kind of reluctant community spirit that emerges in adversity.

Women are notable by their absence, performing domestic tasks in their own approximation of home back in the tents. Some refugees sit in the rain playing musical instruments they have carried thousands of miles, singing songs that others crowd round to hear, whether or not they can understand the words. Turkish is often the broken lingua franca between disparate groups of people who have spent months in limbo on Turkey's Aegean shoreline, waiting to cross to Europe; unsurprisingly, children are often the most fluent.

The better-funded asylum centres of Western Europe, the holy grail of people fleeing the overstretched camps in Greece, are in some ways more alien environments to refugees from the Middle East and Africa. The weather is colder, the landscape more unfamiliar, the culture more remote – and the need for familiarity correspondingly more desperate. Take the rickety city-link train from the centre of Amsterdam for thirty minutes and you reach Almere, a suburb town which hosts many of the Netherlands' asylum seekers in a 1,000-person camp on its outskirts. The identical bedsits in Lego-like blocks of red brick set in featureless fields have an atmosphere of impermanence and reluctant schedule, housing a collection of people thrown together for the common purpose of waiting. Around the camp wander Eritreans, Afghans and Iraqis, young mothers pushing prams, slouching adolescents, middle-aged men carrying shopping bags. The ground floors are reserved for men and the first floor for women, two rooms to a unit, two people to a room.

I visited the Almere camp in 2015 to meet a Syrian doctor called Samer, who showed me into the unit he shared with three other men – an Egyptian, a Yemeni and Christian Syrian from Aleppo. A traditional Arab breakfast was in full swing when I arrived, and I was invited over to join in – flat bread and *labneh* (strained yoghurt) with fresh mint, *zaatar* (thyme, sesame seeds and salt) and olive oil were spread over the tiny table. At the time, I wondered where the men managed to find these ingredients; later, I realized that local shops soon learn to stock the refugees' favourite ingredients. What struck me at the *labneh*-laden breakfast table was how spick and span everything was in this quasi-Middle Eastern setting, despite the lack of women. In honour of my arrival, a shisha pipe was brought from a nearby unit and 'top-quality' apple tobacco proudly produced by the Yemeni man, Maagdi, who translated for me. Word soon spread of a visitor in Block D and at various stages of the interview new faces appeared to take a puff on the pipe and offer their stories to me.

I learned from these refugees that a sense of home can be reclaimed in the imagination, or in domestic ritual, if not in reality. But as the 21st century becomes both more nationalistic and more fractured, the reclaiming of a collective homeland – real or imagined – becomes harder than ever. We are becoming a world of nomads, obsessed with the nation state.

Conjugations

The word *memleket* has sailed effortlessly into the 21st century despite its old-fashioned brand of nostalgia. It forms a bridge between two people, though they may not share the same *memleket*, simply when one speaks it and the other understands, because language is perhaps the greatest unifier of all.

My Turkish friend Nur lives in London, and when we meet, we usually speak in English. Once we met for lunch in a private members' club in Piccadilly, and sitting at the other tables were white-haired Englishmen tucking into guinea fowl. Instinctively, we started speaking in Turkish, first because it allowed us to freely comment on the oddities of our fellow diners, but also because, in hindsight, we needed a moment of solidarity. Turkish became a spoken form of kinship: the two of us were inhabiting a verbal *memleket*.

That lunch made me think of the Turkish proverb Ziya Gökmen quoted to me in his Istanbul office: *Bir lisan bir insan* – 'Each language is a person'. When Nur and I spoke Turkish, we were not only creating a sense of home but also slipping into different personas. I am certainly a different person when I speak Turkish. I have a more limited but more hard-wired vocabulary thanks to a childhood spent nattering away to my grandmother. Turkish phrases pop into my head when I am angry or surprised, or when I talk to animals. My sense of humour tends more towards the absurd. Sometimes, only an English phrase or a Turkish phrase will do in a particular context; at those moments, it is a liberating as well as a mildly schizophrenic experience switching between the two languages with another person who can understand both.

In every country I visited, I saw that language can divide as well as unite people, and in southern Serbia I saw that it can be used as a tool even when it is incomprehensible to the person using it. Alija Sahovic, the Erdoğan fanboy, was a master of linguistic appropriation. He spoke no Turkish, yet derived great satisfaction from the sound of it playing on Turkish state TV all day long: for him, it was a form of Wagnerian music representing a historical legacy that he worshipped. By calling the language he spoke 'Sandžakian', he gave it a rarefied Ottoman status despite it being basically the same language spoken by about 20 million others living across Serbia, Croatia, Bosnia-Herzegovina and Montenegro. Thus, he used both a language he didn't speak, and one he did, to self-identify as an Ottoman. In the Kosovan village of Mamusha, the men I spoke to in Turkish identified as Turks in a much more instinctive way, and had done since childhood, largely because of a 'native' tongue that had been spoken for hundreds of years, hundreds of miles away from the Turkish heart of the empire. In Bulgaria, Anthony Georgieff's strange Ottoman-era Turkish, absorbed from his grandmother, informed a significant part of his affection for Turkey but also led to him being misunderstood when he travelled there: a full-scale version of the 'false friend' British students are warned against when memorising GCSE French vocabulary. In Istanbul, a young Sephardic woman told me that her community was disintegrating partly because Ladino 'died with our generation'. Because language serves as a powerful tool of identity, when it dies, so does a part of the community that used it.

I found Turkish words scattered like Ottoman souvenirs across the countries I visited, and this was one of the most striking indications of the empire's social legacy. Greetings like *merhaba,* and culinary terms (*dolmades* and *boreki* in Greek, *findjan* and *bardak* in Hebrew, *džezva [coffee pot] in Serbo-Croat)* were all relics of the centuries of coexistence of Ottoman subjects, and of an even deeper overlap of Arabic, Turkish and Hebrew in the region. My own name causes confusion; Jews sometimes think I am Israeli because my name sounds like the first letter of the Hebrew alphabet – *aleph (alpha* in Greek, and other Semitic scripts, also meaning the number one).

Arabic words used by Muslims of various ethnic and geographic backgrounds – *inshallah, mashallah* – also create a sense of shared identity. I am guilty of gratuitous use of these words to ingratiate myself in some of the Muslim communities I met while researching this book. Using them provides an immediate bond, a way of saying 'I relate to you'.

Strangely, though, the death of a shared language can also create bonds as well as destroy them. The Afro Turks of the Izmir region are united in mourning the lost African languages spoken by their ancestors that were never passed on to them because of the pressure to assimilate into the Republic. In Jerusalem, seventy-two-year-old George Hintlian revealed the full emotional legacy of a more recently lost language when he told me how much he missed speaking Turkish: 'Sometimes I speak it to myself, not to forget.' For him, it represented not the language of oppression associated with those who killed his relatives in the genocide, but the adored home of his parents that he was taught to love from afar. His eagerness to keep hold of it created a bond with me, another Turkish speaker. 'If you speak the language, you can't hate the people.' Cynics will point out that this is easy to disprove in the context of historical conflict, but the sentiment of Hintlian's observation struck a chord with me, particularly when I thought of my grandmother. In her case, language was much more of a unifying than a divisive force, because her ability to speak Greek was both a consequence of and a contributing factor to her affinity with Greek Cypriots, wherever she found herself. The Lebanese writer Amin Maalouf believes language can carry equal if not greater weight than religion as a marker of cultural identity, and both can be used as divisive forces. In his essay *On Identity*, he notes that: 'When two communities speak different languages a common religion is not enough to unite them: take for instance the Catholic Flemings and the Walloons, or the Turkish, Kurdish and Arab Muslims. Nor does a common language ensure that Orthodox Serbs, Catholic Croats and Muslims can coexist in Bosnia-Herzegovina.'[54]

While this is true, it would be miraculous if language alone could prevent our hunger for conflict, and Maalouf points out that language, unlike religion, is a necessary component of someone's identity. 'If the Israelis are a nation today it is not only because of the religious links, powerful though they are, that bind them together, but also because they have managed to make modern Hebrew into a genuine national language. A person who lived in Israel for forty years without ever going into a synagogue would not thereby exclude himself from the national community. The same could not be said of someone who lived there for forty years without attempting to learn Hebrew.'

Language can unify, but is that always to the good? In the crumbling years of the Ottoman Empire, the feminist writer Halide Edip helped to carry out a programme of forced assimilation in the 'Turkification schools' under the instructions of Cemal Pasha in Beirut in 1916. In these schools, orphaned Armenian children of victims of the genocide were stripped of their Armenian names, given Turkish names and punished if they were heard to speak Armenian rather than the Turkish literally beaten into them. According to Halide Edip and her colleagues, this was all in aid of the 'unification' of Ottoman citizens – for the Armenian community, it was part of the overwhelming tragedy of the genocide and its aftermath. A few years later, in the new Republic of Turkey, language was key to breaking with the country's Ottoman past. As part of Atatürk's nation-building, he introduced sweeping, 'westernizing' reforms that included an overhaul of the Turkish language. In 1928, he replaced the Arabic script of Ottoman Turkish with the Latin script in which it is written today; the present government has painted this as an act of gross negligence – 'he made his nation illiterate overnight!' – but in reality, only around 8 per cent of the population were literate anyway. The new Latin alphabet was introduced on 1 November, as well as the Turkish replacement words for the Arabic and Persian vocabulary which had dominated Ottoman Turkish. Atatürk gave the country only three months to acclimatize to this modernized language. On 1 January 1929, the new Turkish alphabet became obligatory in public communications and the Republic came one step closer to the West – at least for the time being.

Minced Words

In February 2018, while walking in the Old Town of Nicosia in Cyprus, just north of the border crossing, I found a hefty, bright orange dictionary in one of the stalls of the old Ottoman caravan-serai. Its title was printed in both Turkish and Greek, as were its contents: *The Shared Dictionary of Cypriot Turkish and Greek Dialects* – a compilation of the words that have spread between the two languages over centuries of mutual use. For me, this was a manifestation of the overlap of culture that often goes unnoticed, the Greek Cypriots not realising that words they use daily are Turkish in origin, and vice versa. The dictionary was more than a dry reference book; it was proof of linguistic bonds forged by coexistence. Much of Cypriot geography has been revised – villages with Greek names in the north have been rebranded with Turkish names (Ipsil – now Sütlüce – in the Karpaz region, for example) or alternative names officially discarded (the village known as Bodamya by Turkish Cypriots is now officially named Potamia, because it lies south of the border), but little can be done about the way the two dialects have merged like vines over centuries of use. Vines are hard to uproot, or disentangle.

Opening the dictionary halfway through, I found the last page of the Turkish section. Even *vallahi*, literally meaning 'in the name of Allah', has an equivalent in the dialect of the church-going Greek Cypriots: *ballaci*. Unreasonably excited by my find, I thought back to my conversation with Yannis, the young man I had met on a previous visit who had refused to differentiate between Cypriots. His only compromise was to label them 'Turkish-speaking' and 'Greek-speaking', which I now recognized as a great irony as I leafed through the dictionary. The outside world has never really registered the linguistic overlap of the Cypriot dialects, bent on emphasising differences rather than commonalities. A pamphlet produced by the British Foreign Office in 1920, when Cyprus was under British administration, displays the government's disproportionate focus on the Greek Cypriots of the island, and a corresponding misunderstanding of the Turkish Cypriots and their language, exemplified in this far-fetched claim: 'The Osmanlı [Ottoman] Turkish spoken by the Moslems is considered very pure.'

When I was a child, the border was closed between the two halves of the island, which had a shuttering effect on my mind. Now the border is open, I have developed a fascination for crossing it. After finding the dictionary in the Old Town of Nicosia, I hired a car and drove along the mountainous backbone of the island up to the most remote tip: the spectacularly beautiful tongue of land known as the Karpaz. As I headed north-east, the scratchy Greek pop music emerging from the radio gradually fuzzed into Turkish; suddenly I could understand the words, but the music stayed the same. I left behind the urbanized area of casinos and resorts in Nicosia and Kyrenia to find that spring had already emerged in the north: fields of bright yellow and purple flowers, bordered by olive trees. The island got narrower; golden beaches appeared on either side of the road ahead of me. Herds of aggressive donkeys replaced the tourists, patrolling the road to the 12th-century Greek Orthodox monastery of Apostolos Andreas at the furthermost tip of the Karpaz. At the most photogenic point of the drive, on a cliff high above the beach where turtles lay their eggs and tourists stop to gawp, a stubborn mafia emerged into the path of my car, forcing me to stop. I had nothing but an orange to give their ringleader, who seized it through the window, splattering juice over the dashboard before I could drive on.

The village of Rizokarpaso, or Dipkarpaz in Turkish (*rizi* means 'root' in Greek, and *dip* 'end' can be used to mean the same in Turkish – perhaps referring to its position at the end of the Karpaz), considers itself the most beautiful in Cyprus – so beautiful, and so self-contented, that after the 1974 war its entirely Greek Cypriot population refused to leave, defying the UN decree to move to the south of the island. The result was a unique social enclave; there is no equivalent community of Turkish Cypriots in the south, although here and there a few families remain, as I was to discover. Forty-five years on, there are only 300 Greek Cypriots left in Rizokarpaso (numbers fluctuate as families come and go from the south), while the Turks number around 2,000. The dominant Greek history of the place is explicitly challenged. The 12th-century Ayios Synesios church takes centre stage in the square but directly opposite, Atatürk sits astride his horse, with his most famous quotes inscribed on adjacent blocks of stone: it is a face-off between ancient and new identities. Twenty metres away from the church is a mosque, the Turkish and Turkish Cypriot flags flying at the base of its minaret, a phenomenon peculiar to Northern Cyprus, where nationalist branding is everything. It was built, belatedly, in 1992 for the Turkish citizens who were shipped in from the mainland after the war in an attempt to counterbalance the Greek presence in the village – mainly former inhabitants of Trabzon, a town on the Black Sea, or Kurds from the south-east of Turkey. Above the mosque are the Turkish primary, middle and senior village schools, and above the church are the Greek equivalents. Children are, theoretically at least, segregated, as are their fathers and grandfathers, who traditionally congregate in separate coffee houses down in the square. I found this depressing until I realized that in practice, everyone mixes. I stopped to watch some children playing football in the square and heard them shouting to each other in a mix of Turkish and Greek. This was the first time I had heard Greek spoken in Northern Cyprus and it was strangely unsettling. When they saw me, they stopped and waved, trying out a mix of greetings for this unidentified stranger: '*Yassou!* [Greek] *Merhaba!* [Turkish] HELLO!'

Away from the square, the village is bucolic in the extreme: cows wander around amid the cabbage patches, and near the mosque I encountered a strutting herd of presumably Orthodox turkeys who gabbled in furious response to the call to prayer. Women occasionally emerged from their houses to sweep a porch. Men drove around in tractors, or repaired them in muddy backyards. There was very little sense of time. Down the road from the central square was a 500-year-old, stone colonnaded house, transformed into a guest-house by a couple from Trabzon. I made friends with the wife, Emine, a hardworking mother of three with hidden reserves of humour, and spent a lot of time in the kitchen with her as she prepared food, occasionally stirring a pot for her, occasionally reading aloud from my new dictionary. At first Emine feigned interest, then asked me to look up some words she remembered from the dialect she had spoken as a child in Trabzon. Much of the Black Sea area was traditionally Greek before the formation of the Republic, its lexicon heavily infused with the Greek that Emine's grandparents spoke fluently. She had unconsciously cross-referenced these words with the Turkish Cypriot dialect over time, and sure enough, her hunches were spot on. Inspired, she picked up a teaspoon with a flourish.

'*Kutali* – we called this *kutali* in Trabzon, and we call it *kutali* here!' (*Koutali* is a Greek word not used in standard Turkish.) 'And this [brandishing a fork] is a *piron.*' I had never heard this in Turkey and consulted the dictionary to discover that *piron,* or *pirounin*, is a Cypriot word of Venetian origin used in both dialects. Emine beamed in satisfaction when I told her, then hitched up her long skirt and started stepping rhythmically backwards and forwards around the kitchen, still grasping the *kutali*.

'You've probably seen this – the *horon* dance of the Black Sea.' *Horon* is actually a Greek word related to *chorus* (meaning 'dance'), and Emine told me that a Greek guest of hers had once shown her the same dance being performed in his hometown, immortalized on a YouTube clip. Next, she put down the spoon and retied the lilac headscarf that she wore in a practical fashion over her hair. She wrapped the ends around the top of her head like a kind of tasselled tiara: 'This is how both the Greeks of Trabzon and the Cypriot women tie it – the Turkish Cypriot women too, I suppose they copied it from the Greek women.' The pressure to prepare dinner on time put an end to further anthropological ruminations, but I did discover later some Turkish words that unexpectedly came from Greek – most impressively, 'cabbage' (*lahana* or *lacana*), used by the comedian Aristophanes over 2,000 years ago.

Emine was clearly fond, on a personal level, of what she called her 'Rum' neighbours (the standard Turkish word for a Greek living in Turkey). She pointed out that, like the inhabitants of Rizokarpaso who refused to leave in 1974, many Greek Orthodox Ottomans refused to leave Trabzon in 1923 during the forced population exchange. While describing a Greek neighbour in the village, she bestowed what she clearly thought was the highest form of praise – 'a wonderful woman, decent, kind . . . In fact, *Türk gibi* – like a Turk.' However, this personal warmth did not stop her resenting the benefits this woman enjoys as the recipient of significant financial and food aid from the Cypriot government (delivered, of course, by the UN as a tolerated third party). She also felt the injustice of her neighbours exercising their freedom to go south whenever they please – a freedom Emine herself does not enjoy as the holder of a Turkish passport. It was a delicate balance of friendship and resentment.

Coffee Cups

The next day, I headed to the all-male preserve of the Greek coffee house in the village, which stands opposite the Turkish coffee house. A slight bearded man with nervous movements and a smile that flickered on and off introduced himself as Yosef Nikolas and welcomed me, his Turkish heavily Greek-inflected. The other men in the café – an unshaven, brooding Clive Owen type, and an ancient man swaddled in scarves – eyed me silently from a nearby table before I engaged them in conversation, at which point they became extremely friendly, although their Turkish was almost incomprehensible. It occurred to me that these men could get by without speaking much Turkish both socially and financially, thanks to the Cypriot government handouts. Sitting at my table was a man in his late thirties with leathery brown skin, light blue eyes and a slow voice. Recep, originally from Trabzon like Emine, was a tyre-fitter by trade. Whenever Yosef struggled to find a Turkish word, Recep would supply it, and the two would occasionally lapse into Greek – as I was to discover, many of the Turks in the village speak unexpectedly good Greek; as the majority, their only reason to learn it is for the purposes of sociability.

After some comfortable small talk, I asked Yosef why his fellow Greek Cypriots stayed here after the war of '74.

'The war was further south, there was no war here. We had no reason to leave.'

What caused the war?

'It is Greece who caused all the problems in the sixties, and the war. There was no problem between us before that.'

I wondered if he was saying that to please me, or whether he had genuinely aligned his loyalties with the North. I also wanted to know, conversely, how far Recep's affinity for Greek Cypriots extended – did he vote in favour of unification of the island in 2004? He hesitated before answering, picking at some mud on his knee.

'I did. But it is not a promising situation. Last year, ELAM [an ultranationalist Greek group] attacked some of our middle-school kids here. There is hatred, still.'

Yosef nodded gravely in agreement. Recep turned to me.

'You want to talk to some more *Rum*? Go and see my neighbour, Gagou *hanım*, she lives next to the mosque. She will tell your fortune.'

Hanım roughly translates as 'lady', so my Turkish–English brain automatically computed her name as Lady Gaga as I walked up to the house. I was welcomed warmly by her husband Christos, a cheery chain-smoking man in his sixties, and two of their adult daughters. Christos fiddled unsuccessfully with an ancient television aerial as we waited for his wife to appear – 'this is an antique' – before giving up and taking me to inspect his animals in the backyard. Among them, to my shock, were two pigs, oinking loudly in the shadow of the mosque. When I asked my host if anyone minded this, he laughed.

'No! No one cares around here. Aren't they beautiful?'

The pigs were merely the warm-up act: finally, Lady Gagou made her entrance, an elderly woman wreathed in smiles, with dyed jet-black hair, dressed in farm clothes and boots. Stepping into the house, she immediately took off her muddy trousers to reveal pyjama bottoms underneath. As if reading strangers' fortunes was a daily occurrence, she nodded cheerily to me, ordered one of her daughters to make coffee and sat at the kitchen table, scrutinising my face. Suddenly, a jeep pulled up outside and two enormous young men dressed in brown camouflage emerged, stomping over the threshold with guns and bags of recently slaughtered songbirds. This Tweedledum and Tweedledee pair of hunters turned out to be Kurdish brothers from Turkey. Elated by their combined haul of thirty-five birds, they had come to give some of them to Gagou's family, because Greek Cypriots are not allowed gun licences in the Karpaz and so cannot join in the hunting that takes place every Sunday and Wednesday. The brothers were clearly part of the family – one immediately seized Gagou's six-month-old grandson and tossed him into the air, cooing, while his gargantuan brother sat on a worryingly spindly chair and regaled everyone with an account of his hunting exploits, mostly in Kurdish-inflected Turkish with snatches of Greek, drawing guffaws from the daughters, who had already started plucking the birds for dinner.

Amid this mayhem, Lady Gagou had not forgotten her fortune-telling duties, and motioned to me to finish my coffee. I had not had my *fal* read since I was a child, but knew in advance that this Greek Cypriot woman would read it exactly as my grandmother had. I placed the saucer on top of the cup, swirled it round three times and tipped it over so that the upside-down cup drained on to the saucer. We waited for it to cool. Then, like my grandmother, Lady Gagou peered inside the cup before sighing and reporting a finely balanced blend of obscurely tragic and joyful news based on the shapes she pointed out in the dregs. 'In three weeks – or three years, I'm not sure – you will be given some money, or a field . . . There is a jealous woman in your life, avoid her evil eye' . . . etc. As I left, she gave me her number and kissed me warmly. 'Any time you need me to read your future – from London, wherever – just call me. I'll make some coffee and read the signs for you. Any time, honey.'

The Greek Cypriots and Turkish Cypriots of Rizokarpaso are a family. Like all families, there are tensions, but the underlying love is steady, born of proximity and continuity – as Yosef explained, they lived only on the periphery of the war, and its repercussions. I wanted to talk to Cypriots who did live through the war, and who are still determined to be friends. The most defiant of these are undoubtedly the members of the Traitors' Club of Cyprus, who have been meeting for coffee just north of the border crossing in Nicosia since it opened in 2003. These men – both Greek and Turkish Cypriots – see themselves merely as 'Cypriot', thus 'traitors' to the nationalist segments of their respective communities.

I returned to the ancient Büyük Han caravanserai, where I bought my dictionary, to meet the Traitors. As their name would suggest, they treat life with a certain levity. Coffee progressed to a boozy lunch, at the end of which each boozer placed several empty beer bottles in front of the only person not drinking, chiding him for his alcoholism. They speak in English, although one of the founders, Andreas, took Turkish lessons for three years in an effort to speak to his Turkish Cypriot friends in their native tongue – 'But the bastards just spoke back to me in English.' Jokes flew back and forth, their camaraderie deliberately mocking, as though to parody the more serious tensions between their respective communities. The day after the border opened in 2003, Andreas crossed over to the south to track down his old classmates, Turkish Cypriots who had attended the English high school with him in Nicosia and whom he had not seen in decades; he never managed to find them. About nine years ago, he tells me, his son was serving in the Greek Cypriot army; at the same time, the son of one of his fellow founders, Suleyman, was serving in the Turkish Cypriot army – these young soldiers could have been facing each other at opposite military outposts while their fathers sipped coffee together in Nicosia.

Dimitri grew up in the Greek enclave of Famagusta, which is now on the Turkish side. No Greeks were allowed to stay behind after 1974, so Dimitri is technically a refugee. He told me, 'I identify more with other refugees – others who had to leave their homes after the war, from either side – than I do with Greek Cypriots.' Like Yosef in Rizokarpaso, Andreas holds Greece, and the nationalist segments of Greek Cypriot society, responsible for the war: 'I feel that we bear more responsibility for what happened – we were, and still are, the majority, so we must solve this.' Needless to say, there are many Greek Cypriots who do not share this view – hence the majority who voted against the Kofi Anan unification referendum in 2004.

What struck me most about these men was, frankly, how old they are. I've met pro-unification Turkish and Greek Cypriots before (they usually refer to themselves as 'bi-communal') but they were all young, in their twenties and thirties, and I'd assumed, from my mother's example, that people of her age and over would not be pro-unification. The members of the Traitors' Club lived through the war, as my mother did, but either they have less bitter memories of it or the act of continuing to live in Cyprus for decades afterwards has softened them. There are certainly more politicized bi-communal groups in Cyprus, such as those supported by Easyjet's boss Stelios Haji-Ioannou, who has donated nearly 3 million euros to bi-communal projects in the past decade, but the Traitors' Club's low-key brand of defiance is the real deal.

Before I left Cyprus, I made one last trip, this time south of the border to Potamia (Turkish Bodamya), a tiny village which still hosts three Turkish Cypriot families whose relatives have lived there from long before the war. Unlike Rizokarpaso far up in the north, Potamia was geographically in the thick of the war but refused to take part – most of its Greek and Turkish Cypriot residents were, and still are, Communists and rejected the right-wing nationalism of both sides. They considered themselves 'brothers, always brothers', according to an old man I chatted to in Turkish in the village café (as surreal an experience as hearing Greek in the north of the island).

'It was impossible that those bastards would separate us – impossible, impossible, IMPOSSIBLE!' he shouted, banging his fist on the table. Seeing my startled face, he smiled. 'We still live all together, thank God.' Later, I walked down from the café through the sleepy village to find two cemeteries – the larger one Greek Orthodox, the smaller Turkish, with the crescent and flag picked out in red on the tombstones, another astonishing sight to anyone used to the ubiquitous blue and white colours of the Greek flag in the south of the island. To a Greek nationalist, this would be anathema.

These tombstones were my abiding memory of a trip that overturned many of my childhood preconceptions, but I was also conscious that I had deliberately sought out the Cypriots who are comfortable living side by side, and who are in favour of unification, at least in principle (many Cypriots, particularly in the south, object to the political solutions proposed so far). There are contingents on both sides – in Cyprus, and in the diaspora – who will never vote in favour of unification, and who cannot forget or forgive horrific acts of war. My mother is among them.

When I was a child, we used to go to a Turkish Cypriot supermarket called Yaşar Halim on Green Lanes in North London. We would stock up on pastries – *börek, simit, çörek*, baklava – so that even when we did not make it back to Cyprus, the smells and tastes of the food in this grey little corner of London kept the connection alive until the next opportunity to fly home. When Turkey beat Senegal in the 2002 World Cup quarter finals, my decidedly un-sporty family drove down Green Lanes with all the other Turks celebrating and honking their horns in fierce excitement. It was around this time that I noticed the Greek script on the shop fronts and cafés and realized that Green Lanes is not just the preserve of Turks and Turkish Cypriots, as I'd thought – the six-mile-long road is also home to Greek Cypriots in its upper reaches, near Palmers Green. Communities have settled in close proximity here since the 1960s, before the UN-drawn Green Line cut Cyprus in half. I did not fully absorb this at the time, but wondered vaguely how strange it was that mortal enemies (as I understood Greek and Turkish Cypriots to be) would choose to settle in the same stretch of London, with the whole of the city open to them.

On a snowy, grey day in February 2018, I walked down Green Lanes both as a nostalgic experiment and to see how the mixed Cypriot diaspora in London compared to the mixed community of Rizokarpaso. Perhaps the freezing weather was the reason for people's relative unfriendliness, and not for the first time I wondered about the role weather plays in the character of a community. In

Rizokarpaso, I had felt so welcome that I had broken the habit of a lifetime by entering the male-only preserve of the village coffee house, something I had never dared do in my years of living in Turkey. Emboldened by that success, I did the same thing in Newington Green, walking brazenly into a scruffy basement coffee house where old men playing cards and snooker stopped and turned to look at me in chilling unison. They all wore woolly hats, Turkish to the core in their determination not to catch pneumonia indoors. I sat down at an empty table, smiling vaguely to appear brave. After about a minute, a middle-aged Eastern European woman emerged from a kitchen (I suspect a Turkish woman would not be allowed to work here) and came to tell me I was not a 'member' of this establishment. I looked at her in mock surprise.

'Is this a members' club?'

She looked at me sternly. 'Yes.'

'Should I leave?'

The stern gaze did not soften, but there was a pause. 'I will bring you one coffee.'

My coffee arrived, and before long, the disapproval of the old men was overcome by curiosity and we were soon discussing manly subjects such as the economy. One hailed from Kayseri, a city in the centre of Anatolia, which he had left to come to London in 1965; another was from Istanbul, and a third from Cyprus, and they too had arrived in the 1960s. I soon realized these men were stuck in a time warp. 'England is much nicer than Turkey – you know why? The interest rate here is five per cent, versus eighty-five per cent in Turkey.' Cocooned in London for the past few decades, they had not caught on to post-currency-devaluation Turkey, which I found sadly comic, given the numerous reasons they were – unwittingly – much better off in England in 2018. I had told them I recently lived in Istanbul, but it did not occur to them to ask me what the current situation was; they preferred their own fossilized reality, like Norma Desmond in *Sunset Boulevard*.

As I progressed north, towards Palmers Green, the exclusively Turkish and Turkish Cypriot cafés and shops began to be mixed with Greek Cypriot signs. In the windows of a couple of pharmacies, I noticed a Turkish sign advertising vaccines for the Haj, something that spoke of the increasing numbers of Turks joining the more secular Turkish Cypriots. I was relieved to find my favourite childhood supermarket still thriving; the queues of people included Greek as well as Turkish Cypriots stocking up on obscure items like *kolokas*, a strange root vegetable I have never seen anywhere other than Green Lanes and Cyprus. In Wood Green, I asked a Greek Cypriot baker in his forties, who had the accent of a born and bred Londoner, whether he had ever crossed to the north of Cyprus on his trips home. 'I'd like to, it's the most beautiful part of the island, but out of principle I wouldn't want to have to show my passport. It's ridiculous – we are Cypriots, not Greeks. Cyprus is an independent island'

This man had an extra reason to be pro-unification. 'My father is Greek Cypriot and my mother is Irish, so both are from segregated islands. I've had enough of that shit.'

Sixteen years on from the mystery that puzzled my adolescent mind – that of 'enemies' inexplicably congregating in this pocket of North London – I have realized why the Greek and Turkish Cypriots live here together, and it is pretty simple: people naturally gravitate to those who are like them, who share a similar background and culture. All Cypriots need easy access to *kolokas*, after all. My mother will never agree with me on this one, and neither will many others; indeed, it is a common feature of diasporas that they are often more ferociously nationalistic and unforgiving of their nation's perceived enemies than the people who stay behind. In a strange, paradoxical metaphor, those who stay behind move with the times, while those who leave are stuck in the past. Nevertheless, I believe communities like Green Lanes prove that a shared culture will naturally win out over the political differences imposed by jingoistic nation states like Greece and Turkey, especially away from the battle-scarred arena of war.

Return of the Native

Patriotism is a mixed blessing, like parental love. It can result in intense pleasure and intense pain, is unconditional, and lasts a lifetime. When I visited Atatürk's childhood home in Thessaloniki, it struck me that he wields some kind of supernatural charisma from beyond the grave, capable of affecting even the most sceptical anti-nationalists like me. He was ruthless, and capable of cruelty, but he is perhaps unparalleled in the history of modern nation building. His cult of personality imbues every corner of Turkey, so that anyone who has ever lived there indirectly absorbs the magic of his legacy. His face and form is so ubiquitous that it is part of the landscape – literally, in the case of the enormous artificial rock bust in the hillside of Buca, Izmir (where else?), a one-man Turkish Mount Rushmore, where Kemalist devotees make regular pilgrimages.

It was only after I was barred from Turkey that I really felt the emotional connection between geography and a sense of home. I miss the place itself – I wish I had taken more photos of the view from my apartment, more photos in general. In 1923, when the Greek Orthodox residents of Sinasos (modern-day Mustafapaşa) in rocky Cappadocia realized that they would be forced to leave their hometown in the population exchange, they set about planning their departure meticulously, budgeting for the transportation of as many of their possessions as possible. One man, Seraphaim Rizos, persuaded the other residents to raise extra funds to hire photographers to capture their beloved houses and churches before they left. His account of this process is recorded in the archives of the Centre for Asia Minor Studies in Athens:

'We were so weighed down by everyday concerns and our money was so tight that any proposal of mine for such a luxury was bound to be rejected . . .' Eventually, however, 'the sum of twenty Turkish sovereigns was made available.' The resulting 'gem' of a photo album arrived in his new home in Athens several months later.

Rizos's drive to preserve as many memories as possible is common among those who are forced into exile. In cases of war, the act of returning to destroyed homes lays bare the trauma of loss, stripped from the cosy nostalgia of memory, and yet people still cherish the physical relics of their former homes. Marwa al-Sabouni was among the residents of Homs allowed to return to her architect studio in the city centre during a rare ceasefire after four years of bombing.

'Streams of people flooded into the old city centre, remembering the last time they had set foot on their doorstep years before, everyone anticipating the results of destruction and looting [. . .]

what I didn't expect was the madness that filled the scorched air along with the dust and smoke. People were behaving like tourists, taking photos of themselves in the wreckage; some were even posing next to charred remains. Many were wandering around as if at some historic site, some crying, some laughing, I was amazed and troubled [. . .].[55]

'Then, as they left again, families filled up the long main street, carrying the most inconsequential belongings. It didn't matter what they were taking; as long as they had found something between the empty shell casings and the wreckage of their walls. Whether a broken picture frame or a gas cylinder, people were carrying little things back, saving the last bits of memory as a small torch of hope that they might one day return for good to the place that was theirs.'

Even people who have been born and brought up away from their ancestral homeland feel a need to 'return', a bit like I did – although in going to Turkey, and not to Cyprus, I was drawn to the bigger cultural magnet of Turkishness which I had experienced as a child via my mother and grandmother. In the last twenty to thirty years (although less so after the 2016 coup attempt), people with Turkish roots born in ex-Ottoman territories have been returning to Turkey. Some have been fleeing discrimination, like the Bulgarian or Thracian Turks. Some, like the German- or British-born Turks, were attracted by the economic growth of the first decade of Erdoğan's term in power, and others feel that Turkey is where they truly belong. The last group is the one that intrigues me – the strength of this feeling of 'belonging' to Turkey when generations of a family have never lived there. Sometimes, this mysterious sense of heritage, passed down to children through language and stories and indeed passports, are enough for someone to feel like a native of a country they have never set foot in before.

Returning 'home' does not always have the Hollywood ending people imagine it will. Emre the Thracian, for example, now living unmolested but alone in Turkey, has never got over his homesickness for Xanthi, despite feeling 'much more Turkish than Greek'. In her book *Border*, the Bulgarian writer Kapka Kassabova writes about a Bulgarian-born Turkish couple, Ayşe and Ahmet, who as children were part of the great exodus of Turks in 1989. Despite their horrible memories of the forced move, and the poverty that proceeded it, they return periodically to visit their old home, irresistibly drawn back. She relates how Ahmet's family was forced to leave their money in Bulgarian state banks, and to sell their house for a song.

'Years later, Ahmet's family went back and bought their house again – at double the price. But it was worth it, Ahmet said, it's where our memories are. Everything is still there, somehow.'[56]

But what happens when the native cannot return to the source of those memories? This question has acquired a personal urgency for me; although I am not a native of Turkey, I had made it my adult home. I wrote much of this book in a cottage on the island of Lesbos, where I masochistically moved a few months after finding out about the entry ban – perhaps this was equivalent to the denial stage of bereavement. I could see Turkey from my desk, and on clear days I could even make out the olive groves near Ayvalık. I was at the shortest point between the two coastlines, and could have crossed the Aegean in a small boat within half an hour, but I would have had to avoid the coastguards and leave as surreptitiously as I came.

Exile

On 15 July 2016, the night of the attempted coup against President Erdoğan, I ran past soldiers in Taksim Square and listened to F-16s zooming over my apartment. Like everyone else, I was thankful when dawn broke and we did not find ourselves under martial law. But the vengeful paranoia that followed was a warning of the purge to come. When I voiced these fears in writing, I received more death threats than usual, and a veiled warning from a presidential official in my Twitter inbox about my journalism. I left the country – temporarily, I thought – only to realize, in Thessaloniki, that I had been indefinitely barred from returning.

Exiles of politically repressive countries have a choice: they can fight to enact change from abroad, they can bemoan their fate, or they can simply resign themselves. One night in Lesbos, just over a year after I left Istanbul, I met a man in a taverna who had smoked a joint with the famous intellectual Sevan Nişanyan, shortly after the latter had escaped to the island from Turkey in July 2017. Nişanyan had served three and a half years of a twelve-year sentence; he has a long history of 'hate crimes', including making fun of the Prophet Muhammad. On 14 July – Bastille Day – he simply 'walked away' from the relatively lax Foça Prison on Turkey's Aegean coast, and got on a boat. He announced the news on Twitter with characteristic aplomb: 'The bird has flown. Wishing the same for the other 80 million left behind.'

When I got in touch with Nişanyan via the joint-smoking friend, he told me he was 'exhilarated' by his new life in Samos, another Greek island near Lesbos, running philosophical symposia and getting involved with local real estate. 'I am grateful to providence that the goatfuckers who run Turkey gave me, unintentionally, this splendid opportunity.' I wish I was as upbeat. Knowing that there are journalists far braver than me in jail gives me a kind of survivor's guilt; I wonder whether I have a moral obligation to lobby for political change in Turkey from the safety of exile. I also wonder how much that could realistically achieve. The current government seems immune to what little criticism comes its way. What should the role of a writer be, cut off from the pulse of their country?

The journalist Can Dündar thinks it is to keep shouting to whoever will listen. I first met Dündar in 2016, just before he was sentenced to nearly six years in jail for reporting on the Turkish government's arming of Syrian rebels in *Cumhuriyet*, the popular leftist paper he edited at the time. Just before he was sentenced, he narrowly escaped an assassination attempt outside the courthouse when his wife, Dilek, tackled the gunman. Dündar was abroad at the time of last year's coup attempt, awaiting his appeal, and was advised by his lawyer not to return to Turkey. He has been in Berlin ever since.

When I called him via Skype from Lesbos he immediately asked to be shown the view of Turkey. I dangled my laptop precariously out of the window, tilting the screen to the horizon.

'Ah, beautiful! Lucky you!'

'It's bittersweet,' I answered, grudgingly. 'To see it, and not be able to go.'

'Better than Berlin!' Dündar was still beaming when I faced the camera again, and I was reminded of the cheerfulness he displayed even when he'd just found out he could not return to Turkey. He seems to regard a positive attitude almost as an act of national service. 'Staying optimistic is part of the struggle,' he says. 'Of course, we should be realistic, but at the same time we have to wave the flag of optimism.'

Dündar sees himself as part of a legacy of Turkish dissidents in exile, one which stretches back to the empire. Atatürk's proud new Republic also had no time for dissidents; one of the most famous of these was the iconic leftist poet Nazim Hikmet, who wrote most of his avant-garde free verse behind bars, while Pablo Picasso and Jean-Paul Sartre campaigned for his release. Born in Thessaloniki in 1902, while it was still part of the empire, Hikmet's leftist politics were not tolerable in the young Republic. He was imprisoned for his poetry before going into exile in Russia; stripped of his citizenship in absentia in 1951, he died in Moscow twelve years later. The extract I quoted at the start of this chapter is from an ode to his *memleket* written in exile. In 2009, forty-six years after he died, his citizenship was posthumously restored.

Dündar's wife remains in Turkey under a travel ban. As I spoke to him, I wondered what a marriage in exile feels like, and asked him whether he ever worries that what he writes from Berlin may endanger her. 'I do worry about that, yes, but I have a brave wife,' he replied. 'We talked about it and she gave me the go-ahead. To be honest, I was much freer in jail because there was no danger of being put in jail. But now in Germany, in a free country, what I write puts my loved ones in danger. It is much more effective than a literal imprisonment. That is the logic of taking hostages. Under present circumstances, Turkey is not a paradise for me. I was in jail, I was shot at – Turkey means not having the freedom to live. We want our Turkey back. When it comes back, we'll go back all together.'

Those in exile can achieve what those at home cannot, and

Dündar has spent his exile campaigning against the arrests of journalists in Turkey from abroad.

'To be honest, Alev, I have become something different from a journalist. I have become an activist, which is not particularly good for my career. It's really a strange thing but it was not my choice . . . We are fighting for our right to express ourselves.'

It takes a special kind of resilience to keep fighting when there seems no hope, as Dündar does. I'm not sure I have it – perhaps you need to have children to feel such a strong investment in the future of your country. Recently I spoke to a Lebanese friend in London about Turkey's descent into chaos. 'Welcome to the club,' he said cheerfully. 'I have some advice for you: don't think about home. Stop reading the news. It's better for your mental health.'

Turkey was a hard-won second home for me. It is where I became an adult, where I immersed myself in my mother tongue, signed my first lease, learned to haggle and dodge tear-gas canisters. It is where I cut my teeth as a journalist and wrote my first book; it is where many of my dearest friends live. Building a home there was like reconnecting with an absent parent; it feels central to my identity. Now, it's gone – except that it's not gone. Some writers have observed that exile is like an amputation; you feel the ghost limb, ever-present, wherever you are. For me, observing the political nightmare unfolding every day on Twitter and worrying about my friends, that neural connection is painfully strong.

I've started to feel guilty about contacting my friends in Turkey – any links to a blacklisted person are toxic. The result is a much more intense form of isolation than the physical distance from Turkey, especially when that distance is minimized. Yet what I found in Lesbos was that the view of Ayvalık was a constant reminder that Turkey is more than the sum of its depressing headlines. It was a reminder of the country's natural beauty and its potential for normality and peace – I could see the same sleepy fishing villages and olive groves as in Lesbos, just across the water.

'The past is a foreign country,' writes L. P. Hartley in the *Go-Between*.[57] Looking across at the Turkish coastline from Lesbos is like being physically confronted by a memory – it is the recent past, the cruellest distance of all. In Lesbos, I began to consider from a personal perspective the questions I'd started thinking about during my travels: where or what is your homeland? Is it where you were born, where you grew up or where you choose to live? Is it where your ancestors were born? Is it a promised land or a forsaken one? Do you claim it or does it claim you?

Some question whether it exists at all. In *Inhale and Exhale* in 1936, the writer William Saroyan, born in California to Ottoman-born Armenians, claims that diasporic identification is more real than geographic identification: 'There is a small area of land in Asia Minor that is called Armenia, but it is not so. It is not Armenia. It is a place. There are only Armenians, and they inhabit the earth, not Armenia, since there is no Armenia. There is no America and there is no England, and no France, and no Italy. There is only the earth.'[58]

If we believe this, it makes a mockery of those who decide to return to what they imagine to be their 'homeland', but I'm not sure I do believe it. There is an interdependence between geography and culture which is strong enough to last millennia, as the Jewish people and their relationship to Israel will testify – whether real or imagined, that relationship shapes people's identity. Homeland is where the collective heart is, and all the turmoil contained therein – and sometimes, that is a place, not just a concept. In the absence of Turkey, my adult home, I returned to Cyprus, where my earliest memories were formed. Why? I cannot define exactly the emotional connection between geography and identity, but it is there, like a sharp-edged object in the dark. The physical existence of a homeland, the touch and smell of it, has an unexpectedly strong resonance for those whose cannot access it – as Nazim Hikmet found, puffing away on his dwindling stores of Turkish tobacco in exile. Reminders of the physicality of a place bring our past experiences back to life.

'Some Christians took a leaf or a flower or even an insect or a feather or a handful of earth because they wanted something from their native land,' wrote Louis de Bernières in *Birds Without Wings*.[59]

My grandmother kept a relic of the olive groves she had owned in Cyprus before the war: a large glass jar filled with dried leaves she had collected from the trees just before she left. Occasionally she would take one out and burn it to ward off evil spirits, a superstitious practice repeated frequently enough that, over the course of my childhood, my mother had to collect new leaves on our trips back to the island, to replenish the slowly emptying jar. The brittle feel of the thin, slightly curled leaves was a necessary luxury for my homesick grandmother. The jar also became a kind of totem for me as a child – there was something shamanistic about its contents, little shards of a distant place that my grandmother would destroy, one by one, with great ceremony. As the tip of each leaf smouldered and glowed, a curl of smoke would release its smell, the most evocative sense of all. Over time I realized that, in destroying the leaves, she was in fact keeping her memories of home alive. After my grandmother's death, my mother has taken to burning them, and I am the one who must replenish the jar.

Timeline of Countries

TURKEY

1299	Ottoman Empire established in Söğüt, north western Anatolia, by the Oghuz tribal leader Osman
1453	Mehmet II captures Constantinople, defeating Emperor Constantine XI and ending the Byzantine Empire
1839 – 1876	Tanzimat reforms, leading to the short-lived 1876 constitution
1908	Young Turk Revolution restores constitutional monarchy
1914 – 1918	Young Turks side with Germany in WWI
1919 – 1922	War of Independence led by Mustafa Kemal Pasha against Greek troops supported by the Allies
1922	Victory of Turkish forces and Abolition of the Sultanate; Mehmet VI is exiled to Malta
1923	Republic of Turkey established by Mustafa Kemal Pasha
1928	Modernisation of the Turkish language and introduction of the Latin script
1934	Mustafa Kemal Pasha is named 'Atatürk' – Father of the Turks – by the Turkish Parliament, which also passes the Surname Law and introduces women's suffrage

1955	Istanbul pogrom against religious minorities, leading to a significant exodus, especially of Greeks and Armenians
1960, 1971, 1980	Coups d'état, various
1989	Application made to join the predecessor of the European Union, the European Economic Community
2002	Recep Tayyip Erdogan comes to power in general elections

GREECE

1458	Capture of Athens by Ottoman forces
1579	Cyclades islands officially annexed by the Ottoman Empire having been under vassal status since the 1530s
1669	Crete ceded to Ottoman control from the Venetians at the end of the Cretan war
1821	Simultaneous national uprisings in Macedonia, Crete, Cyprus, and the Peloponnese
1821 – 1832	Greek War of Independence; Ibrahim Pasha of Egypt fights on behalf of the Ottomans against Greek uprising but is unsuccessful after Russia, Britain and France intervene on the Greek side
1834	Athens chosen as the capital of the newly independent Greek state
1920	King Alexander bitten by a pet monkey and dies
1923	Exchange of minorities between Turkey and Greece
1939 – 1945	Greece fights Italy and is partly occupied by Nazi forces
1946 – 1949	Greek civil war, fought between the Western-backed government and the Greek Communist Party, won by the government
1981	Greece becomes tenth member of the European Union

DODECANESE ISLANDS

| 1522 | Rhodes falls to Suleiman the Magnificent |
| 1830 | Excluded from the new kingdom of Greece |

1912	Occupied by Italy after the outbreak of the Italian-Turkish war over Libya
1923	Turkey renounces territorial claims
1943	Italy surrenders to the Allies
1943 – 1945	Germany occupies the islands after defeating the Allies in the Dodecanese campaign, before eventually surrendering to the British in May 1945
1947	Formally united with Greece as part of the peace treaty with Italy

CYPRUS

1570	Passed from Venetian to Ottoman control
1878	Sultan Abdul Hamid II leases Cyprus to Great Britain in exchange for British support for the Empire
1914 – 1925	British protectorate
1925 – 1960	British crown colony, growth of Greek and Turkish nationalist movements
1960	Cyprus achieves independence. Archbishop Makarios III becomes the first president, leading a mixed parliament of Greek and Turkish Cypriots
1974	Greece-backed coup followed by Turkish invasion of the north, civil war and internal displacement
1974 – present day	Island divided between the Turkish Republic of Northern Cyprus, and the Republic of Cyprus
2003	Border opens, island remains divided despite calls for unification
2004	Republic of Cyprus joins the European Union

BOSNIA AND HERCEGOVINA

1463	The kingdom of Bosnia falls to Ottoman control
1482	The region of Herzegovina falls to Ottoman control
1566	Mehmet Pasha Sokolovic orders construction of the bridge on the Drina, Visegrad

1878	Treaty of Berlin hands occupation and administration of Bosnia and Herzegovina to the Austro-Hungarian empire
1914	Archduke Franz Ferdinand assassinated by Yugoslav nationalist Gavrilo Prinkip in Sarajevo, leading to the outbreak of WWI
1918 – 1941	Following the defeat and collapse of the Austro-Hungarian Empire, the Kingdom of Serbs, Croat and Slovenes emerges (from 1929 renamed the Kingdom of Yugoslavia)
1941 – 1945	Invasion and occupation of Yugoslavia by Nazi Germany and its allies. Josip Broz Tito leads Communist resistance against the Nazis
1945 – 1992	The Socialist Federative Republic of Yugoslavia
1990	Yugoslav wars break out leading to disintegration of Yugoslavia
1992 – 1995	The Bosnian War, fought between Serb, Croat and Bosniak forces
1980	Tito dies
1995	War ends with the Dayton Agreement, enforced by NATO, and Bosnia and Herzegovina continues as independent state

SERBIA

1346	The Serbian Empire established by King Stecan Dušan "The Mighty"; territory included most of the Balkans
1355	King Stefan Dušan captures Adrianople (modern Edirne)
1369	Sultan Murad I captures Adrianople and makes it the capital of the Ottoman Empire
1389-1459	The Ottoman Empire expands into Serbian territory
1521	Belgrade captured by Suleiman the Magnificent, Christian subjects exported to Constantinople

1801	Renegade janissaries declare the Sanjak of Smederevo (central Serbia) independent of the Ottomans, and after two Serbian uprisings the semi-independent Principality of Serbia is established in 1817
1882	Kingdom of Serbia established
1912	First Balkan War – Ottoman forces defeated by the Balkan League (an alliance of the Kingdoms of Greece, Bulgaria, Serbia and Montenegro)
1941 – 45	Serbia occupied by Axis forces
1989	Serbian nationalist Slobodan Milošević becomes President of Serbia

KOSOVO

1389	Ottoman and Serbian armies both annihilated at the Battle of Kosovo. Murad I stabbed to death by a Serbian knight who had pretended to defect
1455 – 1912	Kosovo under Ottoman control, until the First Balkan War
1876 – 1878	Serbian-Ottoman war; tens of thousands of mainly Albanian Muslims flee from the Serbian province of Niš to Kosovo
1878	League of Prizren unites Albanians across the Empire in struggle for autonomy
1912	First Balkan War leads to greater Serbian control; many Albanians leave
1915 – 1916	Occupied by Bulgarian and Austro-Hungarian forces
1918	Allied victory grants control back to Serbia
1941 – 1945	Occupied by Axis powers (mainly Italian-controlled Albania)
1945 – 1989	Tensions between Kosovan Albanians and Yugoslav authorities
1990	Kosovan Albanians proclaim the Republic of Kosovo
1990 – 1999	Kosovan War

| 1999 | UN Security Council places Kosovo under NATO control |
| 2008 | Kosovo declares independence from Serbia |

BULGARIA

1393	Second Bulgarian Empire falls to Ottomans after Battle of Nicopolis
1878	Northern Thrace incorporated into the Ottoman province of Eastern Rumelia under the Treaty of San Stefano
1885	The semi-autonomous Ottoman province of Eastern Rumelia unites with Bulgaria
1908	Bulgaria declares itself an independent state
1912	Defeat in Second Balkan War
1914 – 1918	Fights with Central powers against the Allies
1922	Thrace divided between Bulgaria, Greece and Turkey at the end of the Greco-Turkish war.
1941	Bulgaria sides with Axis powers
1944	Monarchy abolished
1946 – 1989	One party people's republic
1989	Collapse of Eastern Blok, exodus of ethnic Turks to Turkey
2007	Joins European Union

MACEDONIA

1395	Ottoman victory at Battle of Rovine establishes the Sanjak of Ohrid
1392	Ottomans capture Skopje, the capital, and occupy Macedonian territory
1903	Following a nationalist movement, Macedonian-Bulgarians revolt unsuccessfully against Ottoman rule
1913	Following Ottoman defeat in the Balkan Wars, territory of Macedonia annexed by Serbia and named South Serbia

1915	Bulgaria gains control of Macedonia until end of WWI, when it reverts to Serbian control; Bulgarian books banned, clergy and teachers expelled
1929	Macedonia forms part of the new Kingdom of Yugoslavia
1941 – 1945	Occupied by Axis powers
1963	Renamed the Socialist Republic of Macedonia following renaming of Socialist Federal Republic of Yugoslavia
1991	Declares independence and does not participate in the Yugoslavian wars of following decade
2018	Agreement signed with Greece to change name from the 'FYRM' (Former Yugoslav Republic of Macedonia) to 'Republic of North Macedonia'

ARMENIA

1639	Western Armenia becomes part of the Ottoman empire after the Ottoman-Persian war
1829	Russia gains sovereignty of Eastern Armenia in the Treaty of Adrianople following the Russo-Turkish war of 1828-1829
1917	Russian advance into Western Armenia as part of the Caucasus campaign halted following the Russian revolution
1918	Caucasus campaign fought between the Ottoman Empire and Russia terminated by the Treaty of Brest-Litovsk.
1918	Caucasus campaign between the Ottoman Empire and Armenia, Azerbaijan and Georgia terminated by the Treaty of Batum, which declares the independence of the First Republic of Armenia
1920	First Republic invaded by both Turkish and Soviet forces
1922 – 1990	Armenia under Soviet control
1991	Armenia declares independence

LEBANON

1516	Selim I defeats the Mamukes of Egypt and gains control of Lebanon and Syria (later considered part of Greater Syria)
1516 – 1917	Lebanon allowed to operate fiefdoms under feudal system; the Druze and Maronites emerge as most powerful rival sects
1635	Overambitious local ruler Fakhr-al-Din II executed on the orders of Sultan Murad IV
1839 – 1841	Egyptian-Ottoman War; Muhammed Ali Pasha sends his son Ibrahim to occupy Lebanon
1840	Britain helps Sultan Abdulmejid I regain control of the region; Abdulmejid I appoints the Maronite leader Bashir III as Emir of Mount Lebanon, ushering in a period of sectarian conflict
1914 – 1918	Arab nationalist movement crushed by Young Turks
1916	Execution of twenty-one Arab nationalists in "Martyr Square" in Beirut, ordered by Cemal Pasha
1918	Ottoman Empire loses Greater Syria along with other territories in WWI defeat. Unofficial French control until mandate established in 1923
1923 – 1943	French Mandate of Lebanon
1926	Lebanese Constitution outlines equal rights for Christians and Muslims
1943	Independence and establishment of ruling troika
1948 – present day	Conflict with Israel, including Israeli occupation 1982-1985, and 2006 war
1975 – 1990	Lebanese Civil War; Syrian occupation

PALESTINE and ISRAEL

1516	Selim I gains control of the Greater Syria region
1880	Jewish immigration from Europe begins as part of the Zionist movement

1917	Balfour Declaration promises British support for the establishment of a Jewish state in Palestine; soon after, British take Jerusalem
1922	British mandate of Palestine
1947	After the Holocaust and end of WWII, UN pass resolution to partition Palestine and award Jewish state; civil war follows
1948	Arab-Israeli War fought between Jordan and newly formed state of Israel
1967	Six Day War, during which Israel establishes settlements on Palestinian land
1987 – 1993	First Palestinian Intifada
1988	Declaration of State of Palestine
2000	Second Intifada; Israel builds wall
Present day	Israeli occupation of Palestinian land illegal under international law

Notes

Introduction: *Sultans Old and New*

1. www.turkiye.gov.tr.
2. 'E Devlet soyağacı sorgulama hizmeti ufuk açtı!' *Hurriyet*, 19 February 2018.
3. Anderson, Benedict (1983). *Imagined Communities: Reflections of the Origin and Spread of Nationalism*. London: Verso. p.86.

A Historical Note: *Classified Infidels*

4. Mansel, Philip (1995). *Constantinople: City of the World's Desire*. New York: St Martin's Press.
5. 'The Seleucid, Parthian and Sasanian periods' (1996). *The Cambridge History of Iran* Vol. 3(2), ed. Ehsan Yarshater. Cambridge: Cambridge University Press.

6. Lewis, Bernard (2014). *The Jews of Islam*. Princeton: Princeton University Press. p.28.

7. Zubaida, Sami (2015). 'Sectarianism in Middle East Politics'. *Routledge International Handbook of Diversity Studies*, ed. Steven Vertovec. Oxford: Routledge. p.195.

8. 'Alevi Dedesinden, Cumhurbaşkanı Gül'e 3. Köprü Ricası' *Haberler*, 24 July 2013.

9. Zachs, Fruma and Bawardi, Basilius (2005). 'Ottomanism and Syrian Patriotism in Salim al-Bustani's Thought'. *Ottoman Reform and Muslim Regeneration*, ed. Itzchak Weismann and Fruma Zachs. New York: St Martin's Press. p.114.

10. 'Nation and tribe the winners' *Economist*, 22 April 1999.

Turkey: Heart of the empire

11. 'Gezi Parkı'nın yanı başındaki Ermeni mezarlığı' *Agos*, 26 August 2011.

12. *The Cambridge History of Turkey Vol.* 2, 'The Ottoman Empire as a World Power 1453–1603'. ed. Suraiya N. Faroqhi and Kate Fleet (2013). Cambridge: Cambridge University Press. p.379.

13. *Seyahatname* extract (VI 48a34) in Dankoff, Robert (2004). *An Ottoman Mentality: The World of Evliya Celebi*. Boston: Brill.

14. *Seyahatname* extract (I23) in Dankoff. *An Ottoman Mentality*.

15. 'Lady Montagu and the introduction of inoculation' *Wellcome Library blog*, 25 May 2016

16. Taken from a letter from Lady Mary Montagu, Pera, 16 March 1717, to Lady Rich. *The Works of Lady Mary Wortley Montagu*, (1825) London: J. F. Dove.

17. Mazower, Mark (2005). *Salonica: City of Ghosts*. London: Harper Collins. p.11.
18. Al-Sabouni, Marwa (2016). *The Battle for Home: The Memoir of a Syrian Architect*. London: Thames and Hudson. p.31.
19. Ibid. p. 67
20. 'Mardin'de kilise Diyanet'e devredildi' *Sözcü*, 24 June 2017.
21. Maalouf, Amin (2000). *Balthasar's Odyssey*. New York: Arcade Publishing. p.226.

Scattered Pomegranates

22. Sebag Montefiore, Simon (2011). *Jerusalem: The Biography*. London: Weidenfeld and Nicolson. p.295.
23. 'MİT'in Kosova'da operasyonla Türkiye'ye getirdiği 6 'FETÖ' şüphelisi tutuklandı', *T24*, 12 April 2018.
24. Lewis. *The Jews of Islam*, p.136.
25. Dankoff, Robert (2004). *An Ottoman Mentality: The World of Evliya Celebi*. Boston: Brill. p. 68.
26. Pentzopoulos, Dimitri (2002). *The Balkan Exchange of Minorities and its Impact On Greece*. London: Hurst & Company.
27. Sebag Montefiore. *Jerusalem*.
28. From a letter dated 17 June 1717 from Belgrade Village, Istanbul. *The Letters and Works of Lady Mary Wortley Montagu Vol. 2* (1861) London: Henry G. Bohn. p.36.
29. Balakian, Nona (1998). *The World of William Saroyan*. London: Associated University Presses.
30. Saroyan, William (1936). *Inhale and Exhale*. London: Random House.
31. Ibid.

Ghosts of Troy

32. De Bernières, Louis (2005). *Birds Without Wings*. London: Vintage. p.123.
33. Ibid.
34. From a conference on the refugee crisis at Birkbeck University, 20 June 2016.
35. Mazower. *Salonica*, p.356.
36. Clark, Bruce (2007). *Twice a Stranger*. London: Granta Books. p.27.

Minarets in the West

37. Andric, Ivo (1977). *The Bridge on the Drina*. Chicago: The University of Chicago Press. p.26.
38. 'MİT'in Kosova'da operasyonla Türkiye'ye getirdiği 6 'FETÖ' şüphelisi tutuklandı', T24, 12 April 2018.
39. 'The authentic fantasies of suffering that fuel Trump's nationalism' *Washington Post*, 6 December 2017
40. Ibid.
41. 'Conversations: Emir Kusturica; A Bosnian Movie Maker Laments the Death of the Yugoslav Nation' *New York Times*, 25 October 1992.
42. Kassabova, Kapka (2017). *Border: A Journey to the Edge of Europe*. London: Granta.
43. Ibid.

Spires in the East

44. Klein, Menachem (2014). *Lives in Common: Arabs and Jews in Jerusalem, Jaffa and Hebron.* Oxford: Oxford University Press. p.45.

45. Ibid. p.46.

46. Ibid. p.53.

47. Fortna, Ben, Katsikas, Stefanos, Kamouzis, Dimitris, Konortas, Paraskevas (2013). *State-Nationalisms in the Ottoman Empire: Greece and Turkey.* London: Routledge. p.5.

48. Mazower. *Salonica*, p.67.

49. Rogan, Eugene (2015). *The Fall of the Ottomans.* London: Penguin.

50. Taken from a letter from Lady Mary Montagu, 1717, to a friend. *The Turkish Embassy Letters*, ed. Teresa Heffernan and Daniel O'Quinn (2013). London: Broadview. p.109.

51. Lewis. *The Jews of Islam*, p.ix.

52. Ibid.

Memleket: Homeland

53. 'Germany's "homeland" propaganda is making an inglorious return' *Washington Post*, 10 February 2018.

54. Maalouf, Amin (2000). *On Identity.* London: Random House. p.108.

55. Al-Sabouni, Marwa (2016). *The Battle for Home: The Memoir of a Syrian Architect.* London: Thames and Hudson. p.50.

56. Kassabova, Kapka (2017). *Border: A Journey to the Edge of Europe.* London: Granta.

57. Hartley, L. P. (1997). *The Go-Between*. London: Penguin Modern Classics. p.1.

58. Saroyan. *Inhale and Exhale,* p.437.

59. De Bernières. *Birds Without Wings,* p.559.

Index